KATE GREENAWAY

THE LIFE AND WORK OF
KATE GREENAWAY

BY

M. H. SPIELMANN

AND

G. S. LAYARD

FROM LADY VICTORIA HERBERT'S BOOK-PLATE

BRACKEN BOOKS
LONDON

Previously Published by Adam Charles Black
London in 1905

This edition published 1986 by Bracken Books,
a division of Bestseller Publications Ltd,
Brent House, 24 Friern Park, North Finchley, London

Copyright © Bracken Books 1986

ISBN 0 946495 79 3

Printed and bound in
Yugoslavia by Grafoimpex

THIS BOOK

A TRIBUTE TO THE MEMORY OF

KATE GREENAWAY

IS DEDICATED

TO

JOHN GREENAWAY

HER ONLY BROTHER AND LIFE-LONG COMPANION

Preface

APART from her work, full record of which is made in the following pages, there was in the life of Kate Greenaway one outstanding feature—her friendship with John Ruskin. To this, without the permission of the great critic's legal representatives, no sort of justice could have been done. It is therefore our first duty and pleasure to put on record our great indebtedness to Mrs. Arthur Severn, Mr. Alexander Wedderburn, K.C., and Mr. George Allen, for their liberality in allowing us to make copious extracts from Ruskin's side of the vigorous correspondence which was carried on between him and Kate Greenaway for so many years ; this generous permission is only accompanied by the proviso that, in accordance with the undertaking announced by the editors and publisher of the Library Edition of Ruskin's complete work, all of his published letters shall ultimately be included in that noble issue. These letters have here been printed with the strictest adherence to Ruskin's peculiar method of punctuation—long and short dashes in place of commas, semicolons, and the like. From Kate Greenaway's side of the correspondence abundant drafts have also been made, for they reveal the writer's character and method of thought better than any independent estimate could do. That no violence has been done to her native modesty is proved by the following letter

Kate Greenaway

kindly communicated to us by Mrs. Severn. It was written at the time when the preparation of the ultimate *Life of Ruskin* was under discussion :—

8*th June* 1900.
39, FROGNAL, HAMPSTEAD, N.W.

My dearest Joanie—. . . . . . I feel it is very kind of you to consider my wishes about the letters, as I know of course you could do as you wished about them. In the later letters, I think, there is nothing I should object to any one reading—in the early ones nothing I should mind you reading ; but there might be things in some one would feel perhaps better not published. . . .

I have a great many letters of his—one for nearly every day for three years, but they are all of the time of my early letters, before his great illness. Since—he has never written—as you will remember. I should like to have any letters in the Life, if one is written, that were thought desirable.

I am not sure the later ones of mine are much in a literary way ; but he did say some of the earlier ones 'ought to exist as long as the most beautiful of my drawings should—because they were also beautiful.' I tell you this because you know how great was the affection between us that you will not think it conceit. I feel so honoured by it, that I can only feel honoured for my name ever to appear near his. My dearest love to you.   KATIE.

From the facsimile letter given in the following pages, it will be observed that Kate Greenaway later on developed a habit of frequently employing capital letters in unusual places. These, as a mere eccentricity, have been corrected in transcription.

Our gratitude—may we say the gratitude of our readers also ? —is due to the several ladies and gentlemen who have supplied us with reminiscences, correspondence, and other information duly acknowledged in the text ; indeed, with but one or two exceptions, we have been favoured with the most obliging responses. Mrs. Arthur Severn, Lady Maria and the Hon. Gerald Ponsonby, Mrs. Frederick Locker-Lampson, Mr. Austin Dobson, Miss

Preface

Violet Dickinson, Mr. William Marcus Ward, the Rev. W. J. Loftie, Mr. Edwards Jones, Mr. Ernest G. Brown, and the late Mr. Edmund Evans, whose death at the age of seventy-nine occurred as this book was passing through the press, all have shown an interest and have extended a friendly help which cannot be too highly appreciated or too cordially recognised.

A word must be said concerning the illustrations. The published works of Kate Greenaway are known, and ought to be found, in every house where children live and are loved. We have therefore confined ourselves, with a few rare and intentional exceptions, to work quite unknown to the public, such as early drawings of the cottage at Rolleston where her career, undreamed of as yet, was being determined, thumb-nail sketches with which she embellished her letters, and more important drawings done for sale to picture-buyers or for presentation to friends. About half a hundred have been reproduced with particular care by the 'three-colour process,' for the most part with extraordinary success, the rest by other methods suited to the exigencies of the case. For the use of the originals we are indebted to the kindness of many owners—to Her Grace the Duchess of Bedford, to Mr. Ernest G. Brown, Miss Violet Dickinson, Mr. Alfred Emmott, M.P., Mr. W. Finch, Mr. Campbell S. Holberton, Mr. Charles P. Johnson, Mrs. W. Levy, the Hon. Gerald Ponsonby, Mr. John Riley, Mr. Stuart M. Samuel, M.P., Mrs. Arthur Severn, Mr. Henry Silver, the Hon. Mrs. W. Le Poer Trench, Mr. Harry J. Veitch, Mr. Wm. Marcus Ward, and Mr. Creeser, as well as to Mr. John Greenaway. Other illustrations come from the collections of Miss Evans, Lady Victoria Herbert, Mrs. F. Locker-Lampson, Rev. W. J. Loftie, F.S.A., Lady Pontifex, and Mr. B. Elkin Mocatta. To all of them we express our hearty thanks, and to Messrs. Cassell & Co. our indebtedness for having permitted the publication of the border illustration with Mr. Austin Dobson's 'Home Beauty,' the

Kate Greenaway

copyright of which they hold ; and to Messrs. M'Caw, Stevenson & Orr, Ltd., of Belfast, similar acknowledgments must be made for according their consent in respect of the three famous Christmas cards which appear in colour. Our thanks are also due to Messrs. Frederick Warne & Co. for their courtesy in allowing us to reproduce the illustrations of 'Bubbles' and 'The Bubble.' Messrs. Warne are the present holders of the bulk of Kate Greenaway's published copyright work as well as of the stock of books which were originally issued by Messrs. G. Routledge & Sons, and from them nearly all the books dealt with in the following pages are still to be obtained.

Contents

Kate Greenaway

Contents

CHAPTER XII

1891–1895

CHAPTER XIII

1896–1897

CHAPTER XIV

1898–1901

CHAPTER XV

Kate Greenaway

CHAPTER XVI

Kate Greenaway

List of illustrations

IN COLOUR

Kate Greenaway

IN BLACK AND WHITE

Kate Greenaway

Kate Greenaway

KATE GREENAWAY

CHAPTER I

INTRODUCTORY

On a Letter to Ruskin.

ABOUT the name of Kate Greenaway there floats a perfume so sweet and fragrant that even at the moment of her death we thought more of the artist we admired than of the friend we had lost. Grateful for the work she had produced, with all its charm and tender cheerfulness, the world has recognised that that work was above all things sincere. And, indeed, as her art was, so were her character and her mind : never was an artist's self more truly reflected in that which her hand produced. All the sincerity and genuine effort seen in her drawings, all the modesty, humour, and love, all the sense of beauty and of charm, all the daintiness of conception and realisation, the keen intelligence, the understanding of children, the feeling for landscape, with all the purity, simplicity, and grace of mind—all those qualities, in short, which sing to us out of her bright and happy pages—were to be found in the personality of the artist herself. All childhood, all babyhood, held her love : a love that was a little wistful perhaps. Retiring, and even shy, to only a few she gave her friendship—a precious possession. For how many are there who, gifted as she was, have achieved a triumph, have conquered the applause and admiration of two hemispheres, and yet have chosen to withdraw into the shade, caring for no praise but such as she might thankfully accept as a mark of what she was trying to accomplish, never realising (such was her innate modesty) the extent and significance of her success?

Kate Greenaway

Here was a fine character, transparently beautiful and simple as her own art, original and graceful as her own genius. Large-hearted and right-minded, Kate Greenaway was gentle in her kindness, lofty and firm in principle, forgiving to the malevolent, and loyal to her friends—a combination of qualities happily not unrivalled among women, but rare indeed when united to attributes of genius.

It is true that what Kate Greenaway mainly did was to draw Christmas cards, illustrate a score or two of toy-books, and produce a number of dainty water-colour drawings ; and that is the sum of her work. Why, then, is her name a household word in Great and Greater Britain, and even abroad where the mention of some of the greatest artists of England of to-day scarcely calls forth so much as an intelligent glance of recognition ? It is because of the universal appeal she made, almost unconsciously, to the universal heart.

All who love childhood, even though they may not be blessed with the full measure of her insight and sympathy, all who love the fields and flowers and the brightness of healthy and sunny natures, must feel that Kate Greenaway had a claim on her country's regard and upon the love of a whole generation. She was the Baby's Friend, the Children's Champion, who stood absolutely alone in her relations to the public. Randolph Caldecott laboured to amuse the little ones ; Mr. Walter Crane, to entertain them. They aimed at interesting children in their drawings ; but Kate Greenaway interested us in the children themselves. She taught us more of the charm of their ways than we had seen before ; she showed us their graces, their little foibles, their thousand little prettinesses, the sweet little characteristics and psychology of their tender age, as no one else had done it before. What are Edouard Frère's little children to hers ? What are Fröhlich's, what are Richter's ? She felt, with Douglas Jerrold, that ' babes are earthly angels to keep us from the stars,' and has peopled for us a fairy-world which we recognise nevertheless for our own. She had a hundred imitators (from whom she suffered enough), but which of them is a rival on her own ground ? M. Boutet de Monvel was inspired by her ; but with all his draughtsman's talent and astonishing invention and resource, he has not what she has : he has given us the *insouciance* of childhood, but at what sacrifice of touch ; he has given us some of the beauty, but at what surrender of nearly all the lovableness and charm. And not babies

2

Introductory

and school-girls only, but maidens who are past the ignorance though not the innocence of childhood ; not roses only, but all the flowers of the garden ; not the fields only, but the fair landscape of the English country-side,—all these things Kate Greenaway has shown us, with winning and delightful quaintness, and has made us all the happier for her own happiness in them ; and, showing us all these things, she has made us love them and her drawings the more for the teaching and the loveliness in them, and herself as well for having made them.

The children who welcomed her work when it first appeared are grown up now and are looking rather old, and those who bought the picture-books 'for the little ones' (as they said) but enjoyed them so much themselves, are mostly wearing spectacles. And all the while Kate Greenaway worked hard, making hundreds, and thousands, of her little pictures, and doing more for the pleasure and happiness of the little folks than most little folks know. So that now when her pencil and her brush are laid aside for ever, and herself has been called away, her life-task being done, it is surely well that we should remember her in affection, and wrap up the memory of her name in a little of the lavender of her love that filled her heart and welled over into her work.

One of the charms, as has been said, most striking in the character of 'K. G.' (as she was called by her most intimate friends and relatives) was her modesty. A quiet, bright little lady, whose fame had spread all over the world, and whose books were making her rich, and her publisher prosperous and content—there she was, whom everybody wanted to know, yet who preferred to remain quite retired, living with her relatives in the delightful house Mr. Norman Shaw had designed for her—happy when she was told how children loved her work, but unhappy when people who were not her intimate friends wanted to talk to her about it. She was, therefore, so little seen in the world that M. Arsène Alexandre declared his suspicion that Kate Greenaway must really have been an angel who would now and then visit this green earth only to leave a new picture-book for the children, and then fly away again. She has flown away for ever now ; but the gift she left behind is more than the gift of a book or of a row of books. She left a pure love of childhood in many hearts that never felt it before, and the lesson of a greater kindness to be done, and a delight in simple and tender joys. And to children her gift was not only this ; but she put before them pictures more beautiful in their way and quaint

3

Kate Greenaway

than had ever been seen, and she taught them, too, to look more kindly on their playmates, more wisely on their own little lives, and with better understanding on the beauties of garden and meadow and sky with which Heaven has embellished the world. It was a great deal to do, and she did it well—so well that there is no sadness in her friends' memory of her; and their gratitude is tinged with pride that her name will be remembered with honour in her country for generations to come.

What Kate Greenaway did with her modest pencil was by her example to revolutionise one form of book-illustration—helped by Mr. Edmund Evans, the colour-printer, and his wood-blocks, as will be shown later on. And for a time she dressed the children of two continents. The smart dress with which society decks out its offspring, so little consonant with the idea of a natural and happy childhood, was repellent to Kate Greenaway. So she set about devising frocks and aprons, hats and breeches, funnily neat and prim, in the style of 1800, adding beauty and comfort to natural grace. In the first instance her Christmas cards spread abroad her dainty fancy; then her books, and finally her almanacks over a period of fifteen years, carried her designs into many countries and made converts wherever they were seen. An Englishman visiting Jules Breton, in the painter's country-house in Normandy, found all the children in Greenaway costumes; for they alone, declared Breton, fitted children and sunshine, and they only were worthy of beautifying the *chef-d'œuvres du bon Dieu*.

Indeed, Kate Greenaway is known on the Continent of Europe along with the very few English artists whose names are familiar to the foreign public — with those of Millais, Leighton, Burne-Jones, Watts, and Walter Crane—being recognised as the great domestic artist who, though her subjects were infantile, her treatment often elementary, and her little faults clear to the first glance, merited respect for originality of invention and for rare creative quality. It was realised that she was a *tête d'école*, the head and founder of a school—even though that school was but a Kindergarten—the inventor of a new way of seeing and doing, quite apart from the exquisite qualities of what she did and what she expressed. It is true that her personal identity may have been somewhat vague. An English customer was once in the shop of the chief bookseller of Lyons, who was showing a considerable collection of English picture-books for children. 'How charming they are!' he cried; 'we have

Introductory

nothing like them in France. Ah, say what you like—Walter Crane and Kate Greenaway are true artists—they are two of your greatest men ! ' It was explained that Kate Greenaway was a lady. The bookseller looked up curiously. ' I can affirm it,' said the visitor ; 'Miss Greenaway is a friend of mine.' ' Ah, truly ? ' replied the other, politely yet incredulous. Later on the story was duly recounted to Miss Greenaway. ' That does not surprise me,' she replied, with a gay little laugh. ' Only the other day a correspondent who called himself " a foreign admirer " sent me a photograph of myself which he said he had procured, and he asked me to put my autograph to it. It was the portrait of a good-looking young man with a black moustache. And when I explained, he wrote back that he feared I was laughing at him, as Kate is a man's name—in Holland.'

But if her personality was a ' mystification ' to the foreigner, there was no doubt about her art. In France, where she was a great favourite, and where her extensive contribution of drawings to the Paris Exhibition of 1889 had raised her vastly in the opinion of those who knew her only by her picture-books, she was cordially appreciated. But she had been appreciated long before that. Nearly twenty years earlier the tribute of M. Ernest Chesneau was so keen and sympathetic in its insight, and so graceful in its recognition, that Mr. Ruskin declared to the Oxford undergraduates that no expressions of his own could vie with the tactful delicacy of the French critic. But in his lecture on ' The Art of England ' (*Fairyland*) Ruskin found words to declare for himself that in her drawings ' you have the radiance and innocence of reinstated infant divinity showered again among the flowers of English meadows.' And privately he wrote to her : ' Holbein lives for all time with his grim and ugly " Dance of Death " ; a not dissimilar and more beautiful immortality may be in store for you if you worthily apply yourself to produce a " Dance of Life." '

The touchstone of all art in which there is an element of greatness is the appeal which it makes to the foreigner, to the high and the low alike. Kate Greenaway's appeal was unerring. Dr. Muther has paid his tribute, on behalf of Germany, to the

Kate Greenaway

exquisite fusion of truth and grace in her picture-books, which he declared to be the most beautiful in the world ; and, moreover, he does justice to her exquisite feeling for landscape seen in the utmost simplicity—for she was not always drawing children. But when she did, she loved the landscape setting almost, if not quite, as much as the little people whom she sent to play in it.

In speaking of Kate Greenaway as a 'great' artist, we do not, of

From a Pencil Sketch in the possession of Lady Pontifex.

course, mean that she was technically accomplished in the sense or degree that a great picture-painter or a sculptor may be. Her figure-drawing was by no means always impeccable ; and the fact of the design and composition being generally 'right' arose, we imagine, as much from intuition as from the result of scholarly training. And that is the chief thing. As he grows older, even the artist who is primarily technician and purist is apt to ask, 'What does technical excellence matter so long as the gist of the thing is there ? Is not that a finer thing which convinces us from the

6

Introductory

instinct of the painter than that which satisfies us from his knowledge of it ?' Yet Kate could draw an eye or the outline of a
face with unsurpassable skill : firmness and a sense of beauty were
among her leading virtues. The painter with whom she had
most affinity was perhaps Mr. G. D. Leslie, for her period and
treatment are not unlike. Her sense of humour is allied to that
of Stacy Marks ; and her sentiment to that of Fred Walker.
Yet she was wholly personal (as will be shown later on when the
details of her art come to be discussed), and full of independence,
courage, and fixity of purpose. And just as G. F. Watts
in his portraits of men and women invariably sought out the
finest and most noble quality in his constant search for beauty in
the sitter, not only in features but in character, so did Kate
Greenaway in her quiet little drawings show us all that was sweet
and pleasant and charming in children's lives of days gone by
in country-side and village, and left out all that was ugly, wrong,
or bad.

The life and progress of the fascinating artist lie here before
the reader, with their quaint beginning and logical development.

Book-plate designed for Lady Victoria Herbert.

7

CHAPTER II

On a Letter to Ruskin.

KATE GREENAWAY was born at 1, Cavendish Street, Hoxton, on the 17th day of March 1846. She was the daughter of John Greenaway and of his wife, Elizabeth Jones. John Greenaway was a prominent wood-engraver and draughtsman, whose work is to be found in the early volumes of the *Illustrated London News* and *Punch*, and in the leading magazines and books of the day. His paternal grandfather was also the forebear of the artist, Mr. Frank Dadd, R.I., whose brother married Kate's sister.

The family consisted of (1) Elizabeth Mary ('Lizzie'), afterwards Mrs. Frank Coxall, born in 1841 ; (2) Catherine ('Kate'), born in 1846 ; (3) Frances Rebecca ('Fanny'), afterwards Mrs. Edward Martin Dadd, born in 1850 ; and (4) Alfred John, born in 1852. It was the intention of the parents that the second child should bear the name of Kate, but by a blunder Catherine was substituted. Kate she called herself all her life, and so entirely was Catherine dropped that she always had to be reminded of her real name before she put her signature to any document in which strict accuracy was required.

Kate's early life was, in the general acceptance of the term, uneventful. Unimportant, childhood never is ; but what is important in it is generally hard to come at. The reason is that we are

Early Years

rarely able to recall the trivial yet very material events which make up the sum of child-experience; and the biographer is commonly left to ferret out the more salient points of the little one's surroundings, and dress out his own conjectures of the effect they may have exercised upon the subject of his memoir. In the case of Kate Greenaway we are in a better position, for there are in existence certain records from the pen of the artist herself, candid and direct, and as particular in detail as if they had been studied, as it were, with her eye at the microscope of memory. These records, however, are not the best that could be desired, either in kind or in form, so that their proper presentation is not without some difficulty.

A few years before her death Miss Greenaway conceived the idea of writing the autobiography of her childhood. This she did not live to accomplish, nor did she succeed in producing what can properly be called a complete rough draft of her nursery days. What she left behind is the long detailed record of undigested recollections and sensations as she recalled them, marked by discursiveness and lacking in literary form. In the desire to render acceptable such of them as are here reproduced, we have deemed it wise to substitute, in the main, the third for the first person singular.

No apology need be offered for dwelling upon the trifling personal details with which character is built up, more particularly when they are revealed by a searching observation reinforced by an unusually retentive memory. These things come to be of peculiar interest and, combining to form a study of child-life, may be said to possess real value and importance. A certain lack of sequence and cohesion may be apparent in the record of these early days; but the events happened and the impressions were created, and from them there arose the Kate Greenaway who was destined to be beloved of two continents. The reader is therefore prepared, so far as the early years are concerned, for a cumulative effect rather than for a rigidly consecutive narrative.

Kate's own ideas on the relative merits of biography and autobiography may be gathered from the following quotations from letters written to her friend, Miss Violet Dickinson, in 1897 :—

What an interesting thing nearly every one's life would be if they could put it all down; but it is only the horrid ones who will, like Marie Bashkirtseff or Rousseau—but if nice people could tell all their mind it would be charming. Did you ever read Goethe's *Life*—the

2

Kate Greenaway

autobiography? All the early part is so charming,—only there you feel he also was very heartless. And he was, but it is so charmingly told. Sometimes frankness is curious. I once met a young man who told me he was a coward and a liar—and it turned out *he was*, to my great surprise. It isn't often people know themselves so truthfully, or, if they know, they don't say.

And again :

I am longing to read the Tennyson *Life*—shall send for it next week. I don't know, I'm sure, who is best to write a Life—outsiders don't know half what any one is like, and relations often get a wrong idea of you because they are cross at little points in your character that annoy them. I feel an autobiography or diary is best. A person must reveal himself most in that.

Kate was a precocious child. We have it on her authority that when she was eight months old she could walk alone, and while still an infant criticised the pronunciation of her sister Lizzie, who was five years her senior. She was not a year old when she was taken by her mother to visit her great-aunt, Mrs. Wise, the wife of a farmer at Rolleston, a village some five miles from Newark and fourteen from Nottingham. And Aunt Aldridge, her mother's sister, lived in the neighbourhood, at a lonely farm, weirdly called the 'Odd House.'

At Aunt Wise's house Mrs. Greenaway was taken seriously ill, and it was found necessary to put little Kate out to nurse. Living on a small cottage farm in Rolleston [1] was an old servant of Mrs. Wise's, Mary Barnsdale, at this time married to Thomas Chappell. With the Chappells lived Mary's sister, Ann. It was of this household that Kate became an important member, and forthwith to the child Mary became 'Mamam,' her husband 'Dadad,' and her sister Ann 'Nanan.' This was as soon as she found her tongue. Among her earliest recollections came a hay-field named the 'Greet Close,' where Ann carried Kate on one arm, and on the other a basket of bread and butter and cups, and, somehow, on a third, a can of steaming tea for the thirsty haymakers —which tells us the season of the year. Kate was sure that she had now arrived at the age of two, and for the rest of her life she vividly remembered the beauty of the afternoon, the look of the sun, the smell of the tea, the perfume of the hay, and the great feeling of

[1] The drawings of the cheese-press, the pump, and the fireplace in the kitchen of the cottage, as well as of the croft at Rolleston, here reproduced, were executed by Kate Greenaway while she was still a girl.

Early Years

Happiness—the joy and the love of it—from her royal perch on Ann's strong arm.

Another remembrance is of picking up tiny pebbles and putting them into a little round purple-and-white basket with another little girl named Dollie, who was engaged in the same serious business with another purple-and-white basket. Kate was

SKETCH OF THE KITCHEN AT ROLLESTON.
Showing the disposition of the apartment pictured in the three coloured illustrations.

dressed in a pink cotton frock and a white sun-bonnet—she would have sworn, she tells us, to the colours half a century later, under cross-examination if necessary. Indeed, she seems never to have forgotten the colour of anything her whole life long.

But great as was the joy of tiny pebbles and of playmate Dollie, far greater was the happiness inspired by the flowers, with which she struck up friendships that were to last to her life's end. There was the snapdragon, which opened and shut its mouth as she chose to pinch it. This she 'loved'; but the pink moss rose,

11

Kate Greenaway

which grew by the dairy window, she 'revered.' It grew with
the gooseberry bushes, the plum tree, and the laburnum in the
little three-cornered garden near the road. Then there was a
purple phlox on one side of the gate and a Michaelmas daisy on
the other side ; and outside the gate (she put this into a picture
years afterwards, and to her indignation was laughed at for it)
grew a wallflower. But though she loved and revered the garden
flowers, they were never to her what those were which grew of
their own free will in the fields and hedgerows. There were the
large blue crane's-bill, the purple vetch, and the toad-flax, and, above
all others, the willow-herb, which to her sisters and brother was
'Kitty's flower.' These were the prime favourites, and, in the
absence of the most elementary botanical knowledge, had to be
christened 'my little blue flower,' 'yellow dragon's-mouth,' or
what not, for private use.

Farther away were the more rarely visited fairylands of the
Cornfield and the Flower-bank, only to be reached under Ann's
grown-up escort when she was free of a Sunday. In the first,
where the corn-stalks grew far above Kate's head, the enchanted
vistas reached, so it seemed, away for ever and ever, and the
yellow avenues were brilliant with pimpernels, pansies, blue and
white veronica, tiny purple geraniums, the great crimson poppies,
and the persistent bindweed, which twined up the stems of the
wheat. But the Flower-bank was better still—a high raised path-
way which sloped down to a field on the one side and what was
to her a dark, deep stream on the other, with here and there
stiles to be climbed and delightfully terrifying foot-planks to be
crossed ; then through a deep, shady plantation until a mill was
reached, and right on, if one went far enough, to the river Trent
itself. Then, in the plantation grew the large blue crane's-bill,
the purple vetch, and the large white convolvulus, which with
the vetch trailed over the sloe and blackberry bushes. And up
in the trees cooed wood-pigeons ; and, in the autumn, all sorts
of birds were gathered in view of flights to warmer lands.
Round the mill wound the little river Greet, with forget-me-nots
on the banks and overhanging apple trees, from which apples,
falling off in the autumn, would float away and carry with them
Kate's baby thoughts on and on to the sea, and so to the new and
wonderful world of the imagination which was to be her heritage,
and which she was to share with children yet unborn.

One thing only marred her pleasure, one note of melancholy

Early Years

discord on these Sunday morning walks—the church bells, which from earliest childhood spoke to her of an undefined mournfulness lying somewhere in the background of the world of life and beauty. She had heard them tolled for the passing of some poor soul, and ever after that they took the joy out of her day for all their assumption of a gayer mood.

As Kate grew a year or two older, another prime entertainment was to rise at five o'clock in the morning and go off with Ann to the 'Plot' to fetch the cows. The 'Plot' was a great meadow to which all the Rolleston cottagers had the right to send their cows, the number of beasts being proportioned to the size of the cottage. The Chappells sent three, Sally, Strawberry, and Sarah Midgeley, and the sight was to see Ann running after them—Ann, tall and angular, running with great strides and flourishing a large stick which she brought down with sounding thwacks on to tough hides and protruding blade-bones. The cows were evil-minded and they resented uncalled-for interference with their morning meal. They were as determined to stay in the plot as Ann was to get them out of it ; sometimes, indeed, so determined were they on defiance that they would wander into the 'High Plot,' and then their disgrace and punishment were terrible to behold. 'Get along in, ye bad 'uns,' she would cry in her shrill voice, and down the stick would come ; until at last, hustling each other from where the blows fell thickest, and running their horns into each other's skin, while little Kate grew sick with terror, they were at last marshalled to the milking-place, and peace would reign once more.

After a year or two at Rolleston, Kate was taken back to London, to Napier Street, Hoxton, whither the Greenaways had now moved.

Up to this time the family had been in easy circumstances, but trouble was now to come. Mr. Greenaway had been engaged to engrave the illustrations for a large and costly book. The publishers failed and he never received a penny of his money. There was nothing for it but to make the best of a bad job, and Mrs. Greenaway was not one to be daunted. The family was removed to Upper Street, Islington, opposite the church, and while her husband sought further work, Mrs. Greenaway courageously set up shop and sold lace, children's dresses, and all kinds of fancy goods. The venture was successful, and the children found nothing to complain of in their new surroundings.

13

Kate Greenaway

Fashioned out of the middle portion of an old Elizabethan country house, the wings being likewise converted into two other small shops and the rooms apportioned accordingly, the new home was a very castle of romance. To the Greenaways fell the grand staircase and the first floor, with rambling passages, several unused rooms, too dilapidated for habitation, and weird, mysterious passages which led dreadfully to nowhere. At the back was a large garden, the use of which was held in common by the three families.

It was in Islington that Kate had her first taste of systematic education, from Mrs. Allaman, who kept an infants' school—an old lady with a large frilly cap, a frilly muslin dress, a scarf over her shoulders, and a long apron. Here she learned her letters and how to use needle and cotton. On the whole, she liked the old lady, but all her life long she could feel the sounding tap of her admonitory thimble on her infant head in acknowledgment of a needle negligently and painfully presented point first to the mistress's finger.

Of all her relations Kate loved best her mother's mother, 'Grandma Jones,' who lived in Britannia Street, Hoxton, in a house of her own. She was a bright, clever old lady, with a sharp tongue, fond of shrewd sayings and full of interesting information. Not her least charm was that she always had Coburg loaves for tea, beautiful toast, raspberry jam, and honey. Of Grandfather Jones, Kate writes :

My mother's father was a Welshman. She used to tell us he belonged to people who were called Bulldicks because they were big men and great fighters, and that they used as children to slide down the mountains on three-legged milking-stools. He was very bad-tempered and made them often very unhappy, but he was evidently intellectual and fond of reading. My mother has often told me how he read *Sir Charles Grandison*, and she used to stand behind his chair unknown to him and read it also over his shoulder.

On her twentieth birthday he insisted upon giving a party, because he said he should die before she was twenty-one, and he did.

Other relations of whom the little Greenaways saw a great deal were their aunts Rebecca, a bookbinder, and Mary, a wood-engraver. Aunt Mary was a great favourite because she always had bread and treacle or bread and butter and sugar for tea. But on Sundays there were oranges and apples, cakes and sweets, with *The Pilgrim's Progress, John Gilpin*, or *Why the Sea became Salt*

14

OFF TO THE VILLAGE.

SISTERS.

IN THE CHAPPELLS' COTTAGE AT ROLLESTON—THE KITCHEN.

THE KITCHEN PUMP AND OLD CHEESE PRESS, ROLLESTON.

WINTER, 1892.

THE OPEN DOOR.

THE CHAPPELLS' COTTAGE, FARM, AND CROFT AT ROLLESTON.

THOMAS CHAPPELL ('DADAD').

Early Years

to follow.   Especially from Aunt Mary, later on, did Kate derive her deep love of poetry.

It was in Aunt Mary's company that a certain disastrous walk was taken up the City Road one enchanted night, dimly lighted by the stars overhead and by the red and blue chemist's-bottles in the windows below.   Sister Fanny was of the company, and both the little girls, overcome by the splendours of the scene, tumbled off the curb into the road, and arrived home muddy and disgraced. And the whole was the more terrible because Fanny was resplendent —(for there seems no limit to Kate's sartorial recollection)—Fanny was resplendent in 'a dark-red pelerine, with three rows of narrow velvet round the cape, and a drab plush bonnet, trimmed with chenille and red strings ; and Kate in a dark-red frock, a bonnet like her sister's, and a little grey cloth jacket scalloped at the edge, also bound and trimmed with red velvet.   And each had a grey squirrel muff.'   From which particularity we see how the artist *in posse* was already storing her mind with matters which were to be of use to her in garment-designing in time to come.   As we proceed, we shall more and more realise how important a factor in her artistic development was this early capacity for accurate observation, ravenously seizing upon and making her own the infinitely little details of her childish experiences.   It was the vividness of these playtime impressions that made their recall possible at such period as her life-work had need of them.

There was another aunt, Mrs. Thorne, Mrs. Greenaway's youngest sister, who lived at Water Lane, near the River Lee, of whom Kate by no means approved, for hers was an extremely ill-ordered household.   But though visits there left a very disagreeable impression, they were big with something of delightful import which had its development many years later.   It illustrates well how impressions absorbed in early years coloured the artist's performances in far-off days to come.

Aunt Thorne's garden was overrun with a glory of innumerable nasturtiums.   They were, in Kate's own words, the 'gaudiest of the gaudy,' and she 'loved and admired them beyond words.' She was possessed by their splendour, and finally got them visualised in a quite wonderful way in a dream with a background of bright blue palings.   For many a long year she bore the entrancing vision about with her, and then gave it permanent expression for the delight of thousands in her picture of Cinderella fetching her

Kate Greenaway

pumpkin. The visits, therefore, which were so distasteful at the time were neither without result nor unimportant. Moreover, the nasturtium dream brought to Kate, who as a child was a great dreamer, a new experience. Two or three years before she had dreamed that she had come to a cottage in a wood and knocked at the door. It was opened by an old woman whose face suddenly assumed an expression so awful that she awoke frightened and trembling. In the nasturtium dream there was just such another cottage with just such another door, at which, after she had passed through the garden and had absorbed its beauties, she also knocked. Then in a moment she knew that the door would be opened by the old woman with the horrible face of three years before. A deadly faintness seized upon her and she again woke in horror. This was her first experience of a dream within a dream.

Many of her dreams were recurrent and are common enough to childhood. One constantly repeated vision, she tells us, brought to her her dearly loved father. She would dream that, gazing into his face, the countenance would change and be, not his face, but another's. With this change would come an agony of misery, and she would desperately tear off the false face, only to be confronted by another and yet another, but never his own, until in mercy she awoke and knew that the terrible mutations were as unreal as they were terrifying. Again, an often-repeated dream was of falling through water, down, down past the green weeds, slowly, slowly, sink, sink, with a sort of rhythmic pause and start until the bottom was reached, and she gently awoke. Or something would be in pursuit, and just as capture was imminent, she would feel that she could fly. Up, up she would soar, then float down over a steep staircase, out at one window and in at another, until she found herself lying in an ecstasy awake and wanting the delightful experience all over again.

Kate's childhood seems, on the whole, to have been happy enough, not so much in consequence of her surroundings as of her temperament. Writing to Miss Violet Dickinson forty years later, she says :

Did you ever know Mr. Augustus Hare ? I find his book so very interesting. I once was at the Locker-Lampsons' when he was there. I did not feel very sympathetic then, but now I read his Life, I feel so very sorry for the poor unhappy little child he was. And the horrid stern people he lived with—it makes me feel I don't know what, as I read. . . .

16

Early Years

I can't think *how* people can be hard and cruel to children. They appeal to you so deeply. I had such a very happy time when I was a child, and, curiously, was so very much happier then than my brother and sister, with exactly the same surroundings. I suppose my imaginary life made me one long continuous joy—filled everything with a strange wonder and beauty. Living in that childish wonder is a most beautiful feeling—I can so well remember it. There was always something more—behind and beyond everything—to me ; the golden spectacles were very very big.

Late on in life, too, she used to compare the ' don't-much-care ' attitude of the modern child with the wildness of her own enjoyments and the bitterness of her own disappointments. It was a complaint with her that the little girl in Jane Taylor's poems who cried because it rained and she couldn't go for a drive was a child of the past, whereas her modern representative, surfeited with treats, takes her disappointments stoically, or at least apathetically, and never sheds a tear. There may have been some grounds for the comparison, but probably what she missed in the modern child was the latent artistic emotion with which she had been endowed at birth. For this power of joyful realisation had its necessary converse : the very intensity of anticipation which made it necessary for treats to be concealed from her until the morning of their occurrence, and her wild abandonment to pleasure when it came, found its counterpart in fits of depression and gloom, such as do not come to the humdrum and unimaginative child. At such times she would make up her mind not only to be not happy, but to be aggressively gloomy. One day, indeed, she went so far as to announce at breakfast that she did not intend to smile the whole day long, nor indeed to utter a single word. The announcement was received with derisive laughter, for the others knew it was only Kate's way, and that at the afternoon party which was imminent she would be the gayest of the gay. And the worst of it was that Kate knew in her heart of heart that they were right, and that when the time came she would laugh and be happy with the rest.

One of these well-remembered gatherings was the B.'s party, an annual affair, held in a long rambling furniture shop, full of dark corners, weird shadows, and general mystery. Here it was, year in, year out, that they met the little Miss C.'s, who, full of their own importance, seeing that they were much better dressed than the other children, annually sat silent, sulky, and superior.

Kate Greenaway

Here too disported himself the debonnaire Johnny B., a very wild boy, who generally managed to break some furniture, and had such dexterity in the lancers that he could shed his shoes as he went round and get into them again without stopping. Fate claimed him for the Navy, and he passed out of their lives in a midshipman's uniform.

Another was Mr. D.'s annual Twelfth Night party, notable for its very big Twelfth cake, its drawing for king and queen, and its magic-lantern. Kate never became queen, but at Miss W.'s party, quite the most important of the year, she once had her triumph. According to her own account—

It was some way off; even now I remember the shivery feeling of the drive in the cab, and the fear that always beset me that we might have gone on the wrong day. There was Miss W., Miss W.'s brother, Miss W.'s aunt, and Miss W.'s mother. Miss W. taught my eldest sister Lizzie music, and all her pupils were invited once a year to this party, their sisters also, but no brothers—at least, two brothers only I ever remember seeing there.

There was one big tomboy sort of girl, with beautiful blue eyes and tangled fair hair, who used to have a grown-up brother come to fetch her; this girl I loved and admired intensely, and never spoke to her in my life. She had merry ways and laughing looks, and I adored her. The other brother was the cause of my one triumph. One party night there was just this little boy—among all the girls—and tea over and dancing about to begin, the boy was led to the middle of the room by Miss W., and told out of all the girls to choose his partner for the first dance. He took his time—looked slowly round the room, weighing this and that, and, to my utter discomfiture and dire consternation, he chose me—moment of unwished triumph—short-lived also, for he didn't remain faithful, but fell a victim later on to the wiles of some of the young ladies nearly twice his age. I remember I was much relieved, became fast and devoted friends with a nice little girl, passed an agreeable evening, and remember at supper-time surreptitiously dropping an apple-tart I loathed behind a fender. I daresay it was good really, but it was tart with the tartness of lemonade and raspberryade, two things I disliked at that time.

On a Letter to Ruskin.

But delightful as were these private parties, they were as

18

Early Years

nothing compared with the rarer visits to the theatres or other places of entertainment. On these never-to-be-forgotten occasions Mr. Greenaway, whose work was chiefly done away from home, would turn up quite unexpectedly at tea-time, would pretend that he had come home for nothing in particular, and would playfully keep the eager children on the tenterhooks of expectation. But it was only part of a playful fraud, for they knew well that nothing would tempt him early from his work but some thrilling treat in store for them. What delight there was, when finally the secret of their destination leaked out, to scramble over tea, hurry on best clothes, thread dark streets, and finally blink their way into the magic circle of the blazing theatre itself, with its fascinating smell of oranges and gas, the scraping of violins, and all the mysterious titillations of the expectant senses.

Kate's first taste of the theatre was *Henry the Fifth* at Sadler's Wells. Then came the *Midsummer Night's Dream, Henry the Fourth, The Lady of Lyons,* and (at Astley's) *Richard the Third.* It was at Astley's, too, when she must have been several years older, that she saw a piece called *The Relief of Lucknow,* in which General Havelock rode on to the stage on a beautiful white horse. This made so great an impression upon her that she burst into tears, whereupon her sister said she was 'a silly' and her father said she wasn't ; for the awful tragedy of the Indian Mutiny was at that time filling everybody's thoughts, and with the details of it she had grown terribly familiar by poring over the pictures in the *Illustrated London News.* Moreover, her imagination had stimulated her pencil at this time to make many dramatic drawings of ladies, nurses, and children being pursued by bloodthirsty sepoys ; but the pencil was of slate, and consequently these earliest known drawings were wiped out almost as soon as executed.

Hardly less enchanting than these theatrical experiences were the days which brought them tickets for the Polytechnic or took them to the Crystal Palace. The former was not yet the haunt of Pepper's Ghost, or of Liotard (in wax) on his trapeze, but it was quite enchanting enough with its Diving Bell and the goggle-eyed Diver, who tapped the pennies, retrieved from the green depths of his tank, on the sounding brass of his helmet. The Palace, with its Alhambra Courts, its great fountains, its tall water towers, and other innumerable delights, was an Abode of Bliss. Those were days in which, to her memory, the sun

19

seemed always to be shining, the sky always to be blue, and the hours never long enough for all their joyous possibilities. And, though the time had to come when the sun sometimes forgot to shine, and, when it did, threw longer shadows before her, Kate Greenaway never wholly forgot, but kept these joys alive in her heart for the enchantment of others.

Book-plate designed for
Miss Hannah Jane Locker-Lampson,
1898.

CHAPTER III

On a Letter to Ruskin.

WHEN Kate was midway between five and six years of age, the family moved into a larger house and shop nearer to Highbury. Here they fairly established themselves, and here was the home of her recollection when she looked back on her childhood.

Then a new world opened to her, a new, boundless world, unfenced about with material walls, illimitable, inexhaustible—the world of books and measureless imagination. Of a sudden, to her mother's and her own great happiness and surprise, she found that she could read ! First came the two-a-penny Fairy Tales in coloured paper covers. There were larger ones for a penny, but the half-penny ones were better. *Pepper and Salt* was one of the most enjoyably and delightfully afflictive. Who that has read it in tender years can ever forget how the Cruel Stepmother kills Salt and buries her, or the mysterious voice that chanted—

'She drank my blood and picked my bones,
And buried me under the marble stones.'

Kate never forgot them, as, indeed, she never forgot *Bluebeard*, or *Toads and Diamonds*, or *Beauty and the Beast*. But, although she never forgot them, she never remembered them too well. The delicious excitement could always be renewed. A hundred times she had heard Bluebeard call in his awful voice to Fatima to come down. A hundred times Sister Ann had cried her shrill reply : 'I see the sky that looks blue and the grass that looks green.' A hundred times the little cloud of dust had risen, and

21

Kate Greenaway

the brothers had come in the nick of time to save her. But, at the hundredth reading, Kate's fear was as acute and her relief as great as at the first.

Other favourites were *Frank, Harry, and Lucy, The Purple Jar, The Cherry Orchard, Julianna Oakley, The Child's Companion,* and *Line upon Line.*

Then there were the verses of Jane and Ann Taylor, rendered especially delightful by Mrs. Greenaway's dramatic rendering at bedtime—'Down in a green and shady bed,' 'Down in a ditch, poor donkey,' and 'Miss Fanny was fond of a little canary.' The last harrowed Kate with an intense sorrow, as indeed it did to the day when she set to work to illustrate it for the joy and delight of a later generation in a volume dedicated to Godfrey, Dorothy, Oliver, and Maud Locker.[1] Others which she could never hear too often were 'Greedy Richard,' 'Careless Matilda,' 'George and the Chimney-Sweep,' 'Dirty Jim,' 'Little Ann and her Mother,' and 'The Cow and the Ass.'

> 'Take a seat,' said the Cow, gently waving her hand.
> 'By no means, dear Madam,' said he, 'while you stand.'
> Then showing politeness, as Gentlemen must,
> The Ass held his tongue that the Cow might speak first.

But one book there was which, whilst it delighted the rest, depressed little Kate horribly and miserably, though she would never confess it, partly out of loyalty to her father and partly from shame at what she felt might be regarded as a foolish weakness. This was a book of rhymes for which Mr. Greenaway had engraved the wood-blocks. It contained the 'Courtship, Life, and Death of Cock Robin and Jenny Wren'; 'The Three Bears'; 'The Little Man and the Little Maid'; 'The Wonderful History of Cocky Locky, Henny Penney, and Goosey Poosey'; and a story of a Goose and her three daughters, Gobble, Goosey, and Ganderee, which began

> A Goose who was once at the point of death
> She called her three daughters near.

These seemed to her tender heart cruel and terrible tales, and their funny names and affectation of gaiety in no way palliated their brutality or comforted their little reader.

Other books over which she would pore were the Plays of Shakespeare, illustrated by Kenny Meadows, all of which she

[1] *Little Ann and other Poems,* by Jane and Ann Taylor, illustrated by Kate Greenaway, printed in colours by Edmund Evans. London : George Routledge & Sons, etc. (n.d.)

22

Childhood in Rolleston

managed to read before she was many years older, two large volumes of the *Illuminated Magazine*, an odd volume of the *Illustrated Family Journal*, and a monster scrap-book of coloured and uncoloured prints, collected probably by her father in the course of his occupation. One dreadful print there was among the last which had for her a horrible fascination. It was the etched plate by George Cruikshank from Ainsworth's *Tower of London*—'The Burning of Edward Underhill on Tower Green,' where, according to Reid's rather lurid description, we see 'the victim losing self-command in his horrible sufferings, and in agony plunging his hands into his flesh.' It is easy to realise the effect of such a scene upon a child so sensitive that she could not bear to dwell even upon the sufferings of Gobble, Goosey, and Ganderee. And yet, terrible as it was, she would not, if she could, escape from its dreadful attractiveness. Into the victim's stricken face she would gaze and gaze until she trembled with horror. Then seizing it and shutting her eyes, she would frantically hide it away in a cupboard filled with copies of the *Illustrated London News*, slipping it blindly in amongst the reams of printed paper, half hoping never to see it again. Then would pass an interval of relief, only to be followed as certainly as night follows day by an irresistible craving to look upon the awful thing again, a frantic search, another horrified glance, and again a hasty but not a final occultation.

On a Letter to Ruskin.

But such experiences were few and detached. The prevailing notes of her life, she insists, were wonder and delight. How limitless, for example, were the pleasures to be got out of the streets, where, with her younger sister Fanny, she was allowed to roam, so long as she kept away from the forbidden land

Kate Greenaway

which lay beyond Wellington Street on the one hand and Barnsbury Street on the other. All else was out of bounds. Of course, like all imaginative children, they played at the fascinating game of 'Pretence,' merging their individualities in those of grand and mysterious children whom, nurse-guarded, as the little Greenaways were not, they met on their daily walks. Two there were in particular who, they made believe, had their home in the sky, descending to earth daily for their morning's exercise. And surely there was nothing incongruous or surprising in the fact that these celestial visitors should choose Islington as the most eligible part of this best of all possible worlds for the purpose. Where else could they see such fascinating shops and such rustling, perfumed ladies? 'Where else such a Fancy Emporium into which you could gaze and gaze for ever (until driven away by the owner) at the picture-books and puzzle-maps in the glass case at the side of the door-way?' And when chased away from there, where such another print-shop with its coloured engravings after John Martin—'Belshazzar's Feast,' 'The Great Day of Wrath,' and 'The Plains of Heaven'?—pictures which Kate never wearied of, and which from their wealth of detail could never be wholly mastered.

If variety of entertainment were wanted, was there ever such a diversity of side-shows as the corner of Wellington Street, by great good fortune just within bounds?—by good fortune, because Kate and her sister, being out on parole, never dreamed of straying beyond the permissible limit. Here one day would be found a sailor with one leg real and the other of wood, appealing to the sympathetic passer-by by means of a large and lurid picture of a ship overturned by a whale. Another day the pitch would be taken by an impostor of the same feather who set forth an equally lurid representation of a battle on ship-board, with a cannon-ball exploding in the midst of a crowded deck and dealing around all manner of grisly and impossible hurts. Impostor he must have been, for no brave man ever hit out so viciously as he did with his crutch at well-behaved children, directly he found that no grown-up people were looking, just because he knew that there were no coppers coming to him from that quarter. Again, there was the Punch and Judy show. Hither at the first sound of the drum and Punch's weird screech the little Greenaways' feet would be set incontinently running. Arrived, with breathless interest they would follow the familiar tragedy, thrill at the ghost, pity the poor trembling protagonist, and follow the drama

24

responsively to its close. But there were times when their eagerness was cruelly balked. As the drama drew to its most thrilling moment, there would fall a great despair upon the little onlookers. Of a sudden the play would stop, and the stage manager, stepping forward, would declare that the audience was not a paying one, and that unless a certain amount of hard cash were forthcoming, he couldn't afford to go on. Now the little Greenaways never had any money, so they were helpless in the matter, and, if the rest of the audience happened to be in the same plight, as was not rarely the case, there was an abrupt termination to the play for that day, and Punch struck his camp for some less impecunious sphere.

But the corner was full of possibilities. As likely as not the faithless Punch would be replaced in almost no time by the hardly less fascinating Fantoccini—of which Mother Goose with her milk-pails from which jumped little children, the skeleton that came to bits and joined itself together again, and the four little figures dancing a quadrille dwelt longest in the memory. Indeed, rarely was this wonderful corner unoccupied, for, lacking the more regular entertainers, there was always the chance of tumblers, or tight-rope dancers, or a Happy Family. The last-named, by the way, not infrequently belied its description, and had to be hastily curtained for the saving of its impresario's reputation. Such *contretemps*, it need hardly be said, met with hearty appreciation from the audience, for children, like their elders, bear with more than equanimity the misfortunes of others. Again, there were dancing dolls which knocked each other about in very lively fashion, a variety of peep-shows, and a delightful organ with a scene of great ingenuity on the top, in which an executioner cut off the head of a queen about once every minute, to the tune of the 'Marseillaise.'

There was one dreadful day when there came something more than little Kate had bargained for. In place of the looked-for entertainment, there marched along a man dressed in skins, a modern edition of Solomon Eagle, who blew blasts out of a great brass trumpet and announced in a loud voice that the End of the World was at hand. The shock was a terrible one. For months Kate went about haunted by the gloomiest forebodings. Those gruesome pictures of Martin's in the print-seller's window assumed a new significance. She began to guess at what we call inexorable fate, to catch a glimpse of destiny. Nor was this all. From

Kate Greenaway

pondering, fearsomely, the world's imminent destruction so convincingly announced, she came to trying, in a hopeless, childish fashion to hark back to the beginning of things. Driving herself almost frantic with terror at the thought of burning worlds afloat in space as dark as night, she would rack her brains as to what was behind it all, until she faced the blank black wall of nothingness, against which she was not the first to knock her poor little head. Then baffled and despairing she would run away, she says, seeking relief and forgetfulness wherever it might be found.

Fortunately she had not a few distractions. There were her dolls, which ranged from the little giant 'Gauraca' (given to Kate for learning a piece of pianoforte music so entitled, then in vogue), so huge—more than a yard and a quarter long—that she could only be carried with legs trailing on the ground, to the little group of Dutch mannikins of which half-a-dozen could be grasped in one hand. By right of bulk Gauraca claimed precedence. She wore the discarded clothes of brother John, the tucks in which had to be let down to make them big enough, and took full-sized babies' shoes. She was a wonder, not indeed altogether lovable; rather was she of value as a stimulator of covetous feelings in others. Below Gauraca came dolls of all sorts and sizes, too many for enumeration, but all of importance, seeing that on their persons were performed those tentative experiments which were to colour the work of twenty years later.

On these dolls Kate dilates at some length, and the gist of her record is this. Least in size though first in rank came the Royal group, with Queen Victoria (who had cost a halfpenny) as its centre, supported by Prince Albert (also a halfpenny) appropriately

Prince albert the Queen the Princess Royal.

Childhood in Rolleston

habited in a white gauze skirt trimmed with three rows of cerise satin, and, for further distinction and identification, a red ribbon tied across his shoulder and under his left arm. These garments could only be removed by an actual disintegration. The Royal circle was completed by the princes and princesses at a farthing apiece. Their dresses were made from the gauze bonnet linings just then going out of fashion, and such scraps of net and ribbon as had proved unsaleable.

The little Greenaways were profoundly interested in the doings of the august personages who were their prototypes. They knew their names, ages, and birthdays as well as they knew each other's, and eagerly studied their likenesses in the *Illustrated London News*. On great occasions the children would be taken by Mr. Greenaway to peep in at the gates of Buckingham Palace itself, and Kate wished and wished with all her might that she might be driven through them, as an invited guest, in a Royal coach. Little did she dream that thirty years later would indeed find her an honoured visitor within the sacred precincts, entertained by the Princess Royal (then Crown Princess of Germany), and chatting on easy terms with the future ruler of the German Empire. It was only when she was actually driving between those gates, not exactly in a 'Royal coach,' that the memory of her ardent wish suddenly recurred to her, for she had never thought of it since ; and it filled her mind as she entered the Royal presence. Then it was she learned that, whilst she as a child had envied the lot of those within, the Princess as a child had envied the freedom of those without, and that a prison is none the less a prison because the bars are of gold. Here also she had the privilege of meeting the Princess Helena (by that time Princess Christian), who doubtless would have been highly amused had she known how often the artless-looking little lady before her had boldly represented her in bygone days when 'pretending' in the wilds of Islington. How heartily, too, would she have laughed (nay, perhaps she may laugh still) at the picture of the farthing wooden effigy which an enthusiastic little loyalist had invested with her exalted personality in those fast-receding days.

After the wooden dolls, with their crude and irremovable garments, came the far more human-looking effigies in china, which populated the cupboard in the little girls' bedroom. Their clothes were all exquisitely made by Kate, and were all removable. They took their walks abroad on the mantelpiece. Their hats

27

Kate Greenaway

were made of tiny straw-plaits trimmed with china ribbons and the fluffy down culled from feathers which had escaped from the pillows. They revelled in luxurious gardens made of fig boxes filled with sand collected on Sunday walks to Hampstead Heath, and planted with the tiniest of flowering plants, which often had to be replaced, as they would not thrive in the uncongenial soil. Furniture was hard to come by at a farthing a week, which was Kate's income at this time, but twenty-four weeks' saving got a sixpenny piano, for the sake of which the sacrifice of other expensive pleasures during that period was considered not unreasonable. Once indeed Aunt Aldridge came to town and presented the dolls with a work-table, but so great a piece of good fortune never again befell.

Later there were Lowther Arcadian dolls at fourpence halfpenny apiece, but these like the royal group were short-lived and ephemeral. They passed away so rapidly that memory lost their identity, whereas ' Doll Lizzie,' made of brown oak, legless, armless, and devoid of paint, and ' One-eye,' equally devoid of paint, half-blind, and retaining but one rag arm, were seemingly immortal, and were more tenderly loved than all, notwithstanding the fact that their only clothing consisted of old rags tied round them with string. These remnants went to bed with the little girls, and enjoyed other privileges not accorded to the *parvenues*.

London, as we see, was now the home of Kate Greenaway, but fortunately there was Rolleston and the country always in the background as a beautiful and fascinating possibility ; and it was rarely that a year passed without a visit, though now and again not enough money had been saved to make the thing feasible.

In Kate's own simple words :

In these early days all the farm things were of endless interest to me. I used to go about in the cart with Dadad, and Nancy to draw us. He thought wonderful things of Nancy—no pony was like her. I shared his feeling, and when my Uncle Aldridge used to inquire how the high-mettled racer was, I felt deep indignation. There was no weight Nancy couldn't draw—no speed she could not go at (if she liked), but there was no need on ordinary occasions—there was plenty of time. The cart had no springs—it bumped you about ; that didn't matter to me. Sometimes we used to go to Southwell to get malt. This was a small quiet town two and a half miles off, and the way to drive was through green lane-like roads. It took a good while. Nancy went at a slow jog-trot ; I didn't mind how long it took, it was all a pleasure.

Childhood in Rolleston

There was an old cathedral called Southwell Minster, with quaint old carvings in stone and old stained-glass windows which they said were broken and buried in Cromwell's time so as to save them. Southwell now possesses a Bishop, but it did not then. Then we used to go to the 'Plot,' where all the cottage people had land, to get potatoes or turnips. At hay-time and harvest the cart had one of those framework things fitted on, and Nancy fetched corn or hay.

I had a tiny hayfork, a little kit to carry milk in, and a little washing-tub, all exactly like big real ones, only small. I washed dolls' things in the tub, and made hay with the fork, and carried milk in the kit.

Then, besides Nancy, there were the three cows, numerous calves, two pigs, two tortoiseshell cats, and a variable number of hens. Variable, for barring 'Sarah Aldridge,' the tyrant of the yard, their lives were sadly precarious, and the cooking-pot insatiable. 'Sarah Aldridge,' so named after the giver, was a light-coloured, speckled, plump hen with a white neck—a thoroughly bad character, a chartered Jezebel of a fowl, bearing a charmed and wholly undeserved existence. She took, says Kate Greenaway, the biggest share of everything, chased all the other hens, and—*crowed*.

Stowed somewhere in Mary Chappell's memory was the old proverb—

A whistling woman and a crowing hen
Are neither good for God nor men.

'Sarah Aldridge' crowed. And when she crowed Mary became strangely moved with mingled rage and fear. She would fling down whatever she was doing. She would fly after 'Sarah' breathing dreadful threats. She would run her well-nigh out of her life, nor desist until she was compelled for want of breath. Then she would fall into an awe-stricken state, which she called a 'dither,' convinced that because of this monstrous breach of nature some terrible thing would be sure to happen.

But, notwithstanding her superstitions, Mrs. Chappell was a truly worthy woman,—one of the noblest. Indeed, Kate Greenaway always insisted that she was the kindest, most generous, most charitable, the cheerfullest, and most careful woman she had ever known. To quote her words, 'in all things she was highest and best.' She meant nothing derogatory to her husband when she told every one before his face that he was a 'poor creature.' He entirely agreed. There was no hint at his being 'wanting' in any particular, but rather that Providence was at fault in not vouchsafing him a full measure of health and

29

Kate Greenaway

strength. Indeed, he felt rather distinguished than otherwise when his wife drew attention to his infirmities. He was one of those who thoroughly enjoyed his bad health.

It was a rule of life with Mrs. Chappell never to speak ill of her neighbours. 'Ask me no questions and I will tell you no stories,' was the letter always on her lips, and the spirit of charity was always in her heart. She combined the utmost generosity with a maximum of carefulness. She did not know how to be wasteful. She had a merry heart, and Kate always maintained that it was through her that she learnt to be in love with cheerfulness. So that more than one unmindful generation has since had cause to bless the memory of Mary Chappell. Her real name was Phyllis, Phyllis Barnsdale, previous to her marriage. Before going to Rolleston she had been in service with a Colonel, a

friend of Lord Byron's and a neighbour of his at Newstead Abbey. Of her reminiscences Kate retained just two things. Of Byron, that his body was brought home in spirits of wine. Of the Colonel, that he was so short-sighted that the groom only rubbed down his horse on the near side, secure that the half-heartedness of his service would never be discovered.

Coming to Rolleston, Phyllis Barnsdale entered the service of the Fryers, farmers and butchers. Mrs. Fryer, to whom she was devoted, was very severe, a violent-tempered woman but very kind-hearted. Here Phyllis stayed until she married, doing unheard-of quantities of work, up at half-past two in the mornings, or three at the latest, doing all the

MRS. CHAPPELL, DRESSED FOR SUNDAY, TAKING HER USUAL NAP AGAINST THE COPPER.

domestic work of the farm-house, and washing the clothes of her master, her mistress, two girls, and ever so many boys.

Work was her business in life and she didn't care how much she did. One condition only and there was nothing she was too proud to put her hand to. In one thing was she unyielding. She must have the highest wages in the village. These she *would* have, not because she loved money but just because her pride lay that way.

Childhood in Rolleston

When Kate first went to Rolleston the Fryers' farm had passed into the hands of a married daughter, Mrs. Neale, whose husband, an idle, good-natured, foolish man, smoked and drank whilst the butcher-business slipped through his fingers. In Kate's earliest days they were seemingly prosperous enough, and one of the first things the little Greenaways had to do on arrival at Rolleston was to make an odd little morning call at 'The House,' where they were regaled with cowslip wine and sponge-cakes. This was the etiquette of the place : it was the respect due from Cottage to Farm.

The Fryers' garden was, in Kate's own words years afterwards, 'my loved one of all gardens I have ever known,' and that was saying a good deal, for it would be hard to find anywhere a greater lover of gardens than she was. It was her real Paradise. Round the windows of ' The House ' grew the biggest and brightest convolvuluses in the world (at least in the world she knew)—deep blue blossoms with ' pinky ' stripes and deep pink blossoms with white stripes. Her intimacy with them told her every day where the newest blooms were to be found. Across the gravel path on the left as you emerged from 'The House' was a large oval bed, with roses, pinks, stocks, sweet Sultans, the brown scabious, white lilies, red lilies, red fuchsias, and in early summer, monster tulips, double white narcissus, peonies, crown imperials, and wallflowers. Indeed, all lovely flowers seemed to grow there. And the scent of them was a haunting memory through life. Then there were the biggest, thickest, and bushiest of box borders, nearly a yard high, so thick and solid that you could sit on them and they never gave way. These bounded the long gravel walk which led straight down to the bottom of the garden, and along which grew flowers of every lovely shape and hue. Beyond them on the left was the orchard—apples, pears, plums, and bushy filberts ; on the right the kitchen garden—currant bushes with their shining transparent bunches, red and white, gooseberries, strawberries, feathery asparagus, and scented herbs such as good cooks and housewives love. It was an enchanted fairyland to the little Londoner and had a far-reaching influence on her life and work. Later on her letters teemed with just such catalogues of flowers. So great was her love for them that, next to seeing them, the mere writing down of their names yielded the most pleasurable emotions.

Another thing which greatly appealed to her was the spaciousness of everything—the great house seemingly illimitable in itself, yet stretching out farther into vast store-houses and monster barns. For those were days when threshing machines were unknown and corn had to wait long and patiently to fulfil its destiny. Indeed, people took pride in *keeping* their corn, un-threshed, just to show that they were in no need of money. Then large bands of Irishmen wandered over the country at harvest-time, leisurely cutting the corn with sickles, for the machine mower was at that time undreamed of.

At the Neales', too, there were birds innumerable—peacocks strutting and spreading their tails, guinea-fowls, turkeys with alarming voices and not less alarming ways, geese, pigeons, ducks, and fowls. All these things were in the early Rolleston days, but they did not last.

By degrees, through neglect and carelessness, the business drifted away from the Neales into more practical and frugal hands, and in the end they were ruined—wronged and defrauded by the lawyers, the Chappells believed, but in reality abolished by the natural process of cause and effect. Anyhow, the Chappells acted up to their belief, and with unreasoning loyalty gave them money, cows, indeed everything they had, until they were themselves literally reduced to existing on dry bread and were involved in the general downfall. In this Mary Chappell was, of course, the moving spirit, but her husband agreed with all she did, and took his poor fare without complaint.

But before the crash came there were many happy days and lively experiences. There was Newark market on Wednesdays, to which Mary Chappell always went with Mrs. Neale, sometimes, but rarely, accompanied by the latter's husband. On special occasions Kate went too. Fanny, the brown pony, drew them in a lovely green cart. When Mr. Neale went, Mrs. Chappell and Kate sat behind. When he didn't, Kate sat behind alone and listened to the two ladies talking about Fanny as if she were a human being, discussing her health, her likes and dislikes of things she passed on the road, in full enjoyment of the never-failing topic of 'the old girl.'

There was a good deal of preliminary interest about these expeditions. There was the walk up to 'The House' with Mary Chappell heavily laden with baskets of butter on each arm. Mary was no ordinary butter-seller. She would no more have dreamed of standing in the butter-market to sell her butter than she would

Childhood in Rolleston

have dreamed of selling it to the shops to be vended over the counter like ordinary goods. Only people who did not keep their pans properly clean would stoop to that. No, she ''livered' her own butter. She had her own regular customers who had had her butter for years, and they always wanted more than she could supply. The making of good butter and cheese was part of her religion. She would drop her voice and speak only in whispers of people—half criminals she thought them—whose puncheons were not properly cleansed, whose butter might 'turn' and whose cheese might 'run.'

Arrived at 'The House,' they would find the green cart waiting before the door. Then a farm hand would stroll leisurely round with Fanny and put her into the shafts. Everything was done slowly at Rolleston, and bustle was unknown. Next would come Sarah Smith, the maid, with a basket after her kind. Then a help or out of-door servant, with another after his kind. A minute later some one bearing ducks or fowls with their legs tied. These went ignominiously under the seat, and took the cream, as it were, off Kate's day. Their very obvious fate made her miserable, but she cajoled herself into something like happiness by imagining that some one might buy them 'who didn't want to eat them and would put them to live in a nice place where they could be happy.'

MRS. NEALE.

As the prospect of starting became more imminent, Mrs. Neale would arrive with the whip and a small basket. Then Mr. Neale, and the two young Fryer nephews who lived with them, would stroll round to see them off. At the last moment would arrive baskets of plums, apples, pears, and, perhaps, sage cheeses, and a start would then be made.

The five miles into Newark, through Staythorpe, Haverham, and Kelham, where the Suttons, to whom nearly all Rolleston belonged, lived at 'The Hall,' was a progress of great enjoyment and variety, for they knew not only all the people they met on the road, but all the animals and all the crops, and these had all to be discussed.

Kate Greenaway

Arrived at Newark, Mrs. Neale was left at the inn, whilst Mary and Kate went their rounds with the butter. All the customers got to know Kate, and the little girl received a warm welcome year after year in the pretty red-brick, green-vine-clad courtyards with which Newark abounded. When the butter was sold the shopping came, and when all the necessary groceries and supplies had been laid in, a stroll through the market-place, where peppermints striped and coloured like shells were to be got. Why people bought groceries when they could afford peppermints Kate didn't know.

In the market of course everything was on sale that could be imagined, from butter to boots, from pears to pigs, from crockery to calves. But it was the crockery that had a peculiar fascination for Mary, and many an unheard-of bargain made a hole in her thinly-lined pocket. These pots were from Staffordshire and became Kate's cherished possessions in after years.

At last there was the weary return to the inn-yard to find Mrs. Neale, who might or might not be ready to go home. Anyhow Fanny and the cart were always welcome enough when the time came to exchange the confusion and hubbub of the town for the quiet country roads again.

It didn't matter what time they arrived home, Chappell would always be found watching for them at the gate. Tea was ready and they were hungry for it; Chappell, too, for he spent the whole afternoon on market days leaning over the gate. It was his one chance in the week of seeing his acquaintances as they passed to Newark, and it was his one chance of buying pigs. He had a weakness for pigs, and he would stop every cart that had a likely one on board. Sometimes he would have out a whole load, would bargain for half-an-hour, and then refuse to have one. Time was of no consequence to him, but the owner's wrath would be great, for all the pigs that were wanted in Newark might be bought before he could arrive there. Then the cart would be driven away to a blasphemous accompaniment, leaving Chappell blandly smiling, placid and undisturbed. This would be repeated many times until the pigs arrived which took his fancy.

On great and rare occasions, Kate would go to market with Aunt Aldridge in a high dog-cart behind a spanking horse named Jack. Then she would have a taste of really polite society, and would be taken to dine in a big room at the chief inn with the leading farmers and their wives. For in the Nottinghamshire of

Childhood in Rolleston

those days the farmers were in a large way, prosperous and with plenty of money to spend. It was quite a shock and surprise to her in after life to see farmers in other parts of the country little better than labourers. For this reason she never cared for Thomas Hardy's books ; she never could get on terms with his characters. But with George Eliot's it was quite another matter. Mrs. Glegg, Mrs. Tulliver, Mrs. Poyser, and the rest, she had

'DADAD' AND ANN GOING TO CHURCH.

known all her life. They were old friends and she felt at home with them at once.

Kate was present at two great events at Rolleston—a fire and a flood. Here is her own account of them :—

The fire happened in a cottage joining Mrs. Neale's farm. It joined the kitchen. It was a blazing hot day in August, in the morning, about 11 o'clock, when suddenly there were loud shrieks of 'Fire !' and I saw Ann rushing to the gate shouting out 'Fire !' at the top of her voice, quite unconscious of what she was doing. It was far off us. But the danger was to Mrs. Neale's. They all started off except Ann and me. Then groups of people went rushing by to help ;

35

Kate Greenaway

by and by came my Aunt Aldridge and my sister Lizzie and all the work-women and servants that could possibly be spared. The small fire-engine was miles away at Southwell, so the men and women were formed into a long line from the house to the nearest point of the stream, and passed buckets of water from hand to hand (they could hardly use their hands for days afterwards). But the cottage was burnt down and a bit of the roof of Mrs. Neale's kitchen. Fortunately it stopped there, but they moved all the things out of the house for fear it should not be saved. The best bedroom floor of polished oak was so slippery the men could hardly walk about to move the things. Some of the men behaved disgracefully, tapping the casks of wine and beer that had to be brought out into the yard. I shall never forget my terror and fright of this day, and to 'Mamam' it was as the end of all things.

One summer when we went down—the day was pouring wet, it had been very rainy—I went to the Chappells', Lizzie to Aunt Aldridge's. When I got up the next morning I found a great event had taken place in the night—the floods were out—rose in the night. They (the Chappells) were called up about 11 o'clock and had to get up and go off to save their animals, which all had to be brought home. Fortunately they were in time to save them all—others were not so lucky. The house and the next house and the croft were high and dry. The croft was filled with animals—sheep and calves. When you looked out at the front gate, each way you looked you saw a stream of muddy water rushing across the road. There was a tendency to floods at Rolleston, only not bad like this. Both Trent and Greet overflowed and met and then flooded all over the country. No houses at Rolleston were washed away, but the lower parts of the houses were flooded, cellars and drains were filled up with water, the contents floating on the top. The people used to wait at the end of the street where the water rushed over, and people who were passing in carts would drive them through the water, and boys crossed over in washing-tubs. A great many animals were drowned. The Neales lost a great many sheep. After some days the floods began to subside and you could begin to get about, and then my sister could get down to see me, for we were quite separated for days. After the water had all gone the country was horrible, covered with mud and dead worms, and it smelt dreadfully. I stayed some weeks, and before I left it had returned pretty much to its old look again. This was the only time I was ever there in what they called 'the waters being out.'

Next we have a glimpse of Kate making triumphant progresses in the corn-waggons and hay-carts as they rattled back empty to the fields. The corn-waggons, it must be admitted, had

Childhood in Rolleston

a drawback in the little dark beetles—'clocks' as the waggoners called them—which ran about and threatened her legs. But these were soon forgotten in the near prospect of a ride back perched high on the Harvest Home load, decked with green branches, while the men chanted—

'Mr. —— is a good man,
He gets his harvest as well as he can,
Neither turned over nor yet stuck fast,
He's got his harvest home at last.
Hip, hip, hip, hurrah!'

And she loved to sit on the stile watching for the postman. In earliest days 'he was an imposing person who rode on a donkey and blew a brass trumpet. If you wished to despatch a letter and lived alongside his beat you displayed it in your window to attract his attention. When he saw a letter thus paraded, he drew rein, blew a blast, and out you ran with your letter. If you lived off his route you had to put your letter in somebody else's window. So with the delivery. Aunt Aldridge's letters, for example, were left at the Chappells' and an old woman got a halfpenny a letter for taking them up to the Odd House.' In those days the postman was clearly not made for man, but man for the postman.

Once and once only Kate went fishing at the flour mill, which had its water-wheel on the Greet. She sketches the scene vividly in a few words. How lovely it all was, she tells us—the lapping of the water against the banks of the reedy river, the great heaps of corn, the husks, the floury sacks and carts, the white-coated millers, the clean white scent, and, above all, the excitement of looking out for the fish! What could be better than that? It was about as good as good could be, when of a sudden all was changed. There was a jerk of the rod, a brief struggle and a plunge, and there lay a gasping fish with the hook in its silly mouth, bleeding on the bank. What could be worse than that? It was about as bad as bad could be. The sun had gone in. The sky was no longer blue, and misery had come into the world. She loathed the task of carrying the poor dead things home to be cooked, and she refused to partake of the dreadful dish. It was all too sad. The pleasant river and the bright glorious days were all over for them and she was not to be comforted. And that was the end of Kate's single fishing experience. Surely fate was in a singularly ironical mood when, in later years, it brought her

37

Kate Greenaway

a letter of hypercritical remonstrance because of her supposed advocacy of what the writer considered a cruel and demoralising sport !

Indeed, we have only to read her rhyme of 'Miss Molly and the little fishes' in *Marigold Garden* to realise that her sentiments as a child remained those of the woman :

> Oh, sweet Miss Molly,
> You're so fond
> Of fishes in a little pond.
> And perhaps they're glad
> To see you stare
> With such bright eyes
> Upon them there.
> And when your fingers and your thumbs
> Drop slowly in the small white crumbs,
> I hope they're happy. Only this—
> When you've looked long enough, sweet miss,
> Then, most beneficent young giver,
> Restore them to their native river.

In this fashion the little 'Lunnoner,' as she was always called, got her fill of the country, and her intimacy with more or less unsophisticated nature—a love which was her prevailing passion throughout her life.

Her early education was alike unsatisfactory and varied, for at that time it was extremely difficult to find girls' schools at once convenient of access and reasonable in price, where the teaching was of any value. After leaving Mrs. Allaman's, of whom mention has been made, Kate was handed over to a Miss Jackson, where she remained only a few days. Thence she went to a Miss Varley, but here also her career was a short one. She soon fell ill, 'under the strain,' said Mrs. Greenaway, 'of impossible lessons,' and was promptly removed.

Then a trial was made of some ladies named Fiveash. Here again Kate's health flagged. She herself was inclined to put it down to the fact that Miss Anne Fiveash, of whom she was otherwise fond enough, had a cross eye, which filled her with terror. At any rate, the new scheme succeeded no better than the old ones, and this for the time being was an end of school. Henceforward the child's education was continued, if it could properly be said yet to have begun, by a lady who came two or three afternoons a-week to give lessons (very bad ones they were) in French and music. This arrangement lasted

Childhood in Rolleston

for several years; at the end of which time Kate went back to Miss Fiveash's, where she remained until she left school altogether. During all this time she was drawing as much as she could in private.

When Kate was six years old her brother John was born; and of course she remembered to her dying day all the clothes he ever had, and all those which she and her sisters had at the same time; and she notes the details of three of his earliest costumes which she remembered to good purpose. First, a scarlet pelisse, and a white felt hat with feathers; next, a drab pelisse and a drab felt hat with a green velvet rosette; and thirdly, he was resplendent in a pale blue frock, a little white jacket, and a white Leghorn hat and feather—all of which afterwards found resurrection in the Greenaway picture-books.

There was always a deep bond of sympathy between Mr. Greenaway and his little daughter, whom, by the way, he nicknamed 'Knocker,' to which it amused him to compare her face when she cried. Her devotion to her father doubtless had far-reaching results, for not only was Mr. Greenaway an accomplished engraver, but an artist of no mean ability. And there was a fascination and mystery about his calling which made a strong appeal to her imagination. On special occasions he would be commissioned to make drawings for the *Illustrated London News*, and then Kate's delight would be unbounded. The subject might be of Queen Victoria at some such ceremony as the opening of Parliament; or sometimes of some more stirring occurrence— such, for example, as that which necessitated the long journey into Staffordshire to make sketches of the house and surroundings of the villainous doctor, William Palmer, the Rugeley murderer, an event which stood out in her memory as of supreme interest and importance.

Mr Greenaway's office, as long as Kate could remember, was 4, Wine Office Court, Fleet Street. There most of his work was done; but when, as frequently happened, there was a scramble to get the wood blocks engraved in time for the press, he would have to work the greater part of two consecutive nights. Then he would bring portions of his blocks home, distributing the less important sections among his assistants, so that the whole might be ready in the morning.

These were times of superlative pleasure to Kate. She would wake up about midnight and see the gas still burning outside in

Kate Greenaway

the passage. This meant that her father was hard at work downstairs. About one o'clock he would go to bed, snatch an hour or two's sleep, and be at it again until it was time to be off to the City. This was his routine, and Kate quickly planned how to take advantage of it.

Waiting till sister Fanny was asleep, she would slip out of bed, hurry into her clothes, all except her frock and shoes, and, covering them with her little nightgown, creep back into bed again. Thus prepared for eventualities, she would fall asleep. But not for long. Somehow she would manage to wake again in the small hours of the morning and see if the light of the gas jet in the passage still shone through the chink of the door. If it did, she would climb with all quietness out of bed, doff her nightdress, slip into her frock, take her shoes in her hand and creep softly down to the drawing-room, where her father was at work. Then he would fasten her dress and she would set to work to make his toast. And so the two would breakfast together alone in the early hours with supreme satisfaction.

Here Miss Greenaway's autobiographical notes come to an abrupt termination, save for a sheet of memoranda which stimulate but do not satisfy curiosity. How, we may ask, did the 'Fear of Water-taps' take her?—a fear which lasted all her life. What confessions did she contemplate under the heading 'My Religious Fit,' and 'My Fight,' and what episodes would have grouped themselves under 'Pincushions'?

EXPLANATORY SKETCH OF ROLLESTON COTTAGE FARM.
Gate to Croft. Cart Shed. Gate to Garden. Our Bedroom. Mamam's Bedroom.
Kitchen. House. Parlour.
Road.

CHAPTER IV

STUDENT DAYS AND EARLY SUCCESS: EARLY PROMISE AND
ART CLASSES—SOUTH KENSINGTON PRIZES—LADY BUTLER
—DUDLEY GALLERY—REV. W. J. LOFTIE AND MESSRS.
MARCUS WARD—'AMATEUR THEATRICALS'—TOY-BOOKS
AND FAIRY-TALES—PROGRESS.

IN 1857 the whole of Great Britain, as has been said, was stirred to
its depths by the terrible events which were taking place in India.
People talked and thought of little else besides the Mutiny, and
the papers, prominent among them the *Illustrated London News*,
properly played up to the public's dreadful hunger for literary and
pictorial details. Many of the latter passed through the hands of
Mr. Greenaway, and nothing was more natural than that Kate,
with her inborn artistic capacity, should try her hand at expressing the sensations so aroused, pictorially. Here is her own
memorandum on the subject, written on an isolated leaf of the
autobiographic notes :—

At the time of the Indian Mutiny I was always drawing people
escaping. I wish I had some of the old drawings, but they were
nearly always done on a slate and rubbed off again. We knew all
about it from the *Illustrated London News*, and the incident of the
Highland woman who heard the bagpipes made a great impression on
me. I could sit and think of the sepoys till I could be wild with
terror, and I used sometimes to dream of them. But I was always
drawing the ladies, nurses, and children escaping. Mine always
escaped and were never taken.

Fortunately, Kate's father and mother were not blind to the
promise of these tentative efforts. The root of the matter they
felt was in her, and the first opportunity must be taken of giving
it a chance of growth and development. This opportunity was
not long in coming, and by the time she was twelve years old her
artistic education had already begun.

The first art class to which she went was that held at William
Street, Clerkenwell, close to Claremont Square. A girl-cousin

Kate Greenaway

(one of the Thornes) was at that time being educated as a wood-engraver by Mr. John Greenaway, who sent his pupil to this evening class—a school in connection with the Science and Art Department (now the Board of Education). So that she should not go alone, his daughter was sent to bear her company; and Kate soon showed such undoubted signs of ability that it was decided her attendance should continue. She was soon promoted to the day class carried on by Miss Doidge, which was held at Miss Springet's school at Canonbury House, also under the Science and Art Department, and Kate remained a member of it during its successive removals to St. George's Hall, Barnsbury Street, and Myddleton Hall, close to the Greenaways' dwelling. To Kate, Canonbury House was an ancient palace. It was an interesting old place, with beautiful moulded ceilings and a wonderful Jacobean fireplace, which is figured and described in Nelson's *History of Islington*. It stood immediately behind Canonbury Tower, which was said to have been one of Queen Elizabeth's innumerable hunting-boxes, and was popularly believed to have subterranean passages leading to Smithfield.

So satisfactory and encouraging was Kate's progress—her first prize was gained when she was twelve years old—that in due time it was determined that she should make Art her profession, and she forthwith joined the chief school of the Art Department, then under Mr. R. Burchett, who soon formed a very high opinion of her talents and prospects. In 1861 she was awarded the bronze medal (local), Stage 10 A; in 1864 the 'National,' Stage 22; and in 1869 the silver (South Kensington), Stage 17 B.[1] The set of six tiles, here reproduced, display charming harmonies of colour. One is composed of olive-green and two different yellows on a slate-blue ground, while the flowers are outlined with white edges. In another, crimson-purple, russet-yellow, and blue are on a slate-grey ground; and in a third the grey-blue flowers are outlined with white, and grey-green, violet, purple, and yellow tell richly on a brown ground. The other schemes of colour are equally well combined, and the pattern designs are all good, and display a sense of grace and ability in line and arrangement.[2] In addition to the awards mentioned,

[1] The head in water-colours, which won her the silver medal, was bought by the late Sir Julian Goldsmid.
[2] Official inscription on the drawing: 'National Medallion Award. Finsbury, 1864. Stage 22. Aged 17 years. Time in School, 9 sessions, 4 hours a week. Medals already obtained in Stages 4ᵇ, 10ᵃ, 10ᵇ, 22ᶜ. Teachers: S. A. Doidge, S. Hipwood.'

Student Days and Early Success

Kate received many book prizes in lieu of medals to which she was later entitled. Here she worked for several years with great diligence and thoroughness, undaunted by difficulties and hardships such as fall to the lot of few students. Indeed, so eagerly industrious was she that at the same time she attended the Life Classes at Heatherley's, and later on the newly opened London Slade School, then in charge of Professor Legros and his assistants.

It has often been said of Kate Greenaway that she did not sufficiently draw from the nude, and, as will be seen later on, Professor Ruskin implored her to undertake this severer form of study, in order to correct and improve her figure drawing ; and it has been too readily assumed that her training was lacking in this essential element of an artist's academic education. As a matter of fact, Kate executed a vast number of careful studies from the figure, both at Heatherley's and at a studio which she occupied with Miss Elizabeth Thompson (afterwards Lady Butler) —who, like Miss Helen Paterson (Mrs. William Allingham), was her fellow-student at South Kensington—and at her death between fifty and a hundred were still in existence. Many of them were in 'the old South Kensington manner'—in pencil or chalk, plenty of stump-work, and heightening of the lights with white chalk : dull, uninspired things, excellent in proportion and construction, and not without use for the acquisition of knowledge of the human frame. There were also short-time sketches, but only a few of the chalk drawings have been preserved.

Of these student days Lady Butler kindly sends the following note :—

She and I were keen competitors in the Sketching Club competitions at South Kensington. She was a very quiet student, so that it is difficult to find anything striking to say of her. I have no letters of hers and no sketches. We were very good friends, she and I, in spite of our rivalry in the sketching club ; and indeed so quiet and peaceable a student was necessarily liked, and she never, to my knowledge, gave trouble or offence to any one in the schools. I wish I could give you more material, but the character of the girl was such as to supply very little wherewith to make up a biographical sketch. I only knew her at the schools, not in her home life.

It may be added that Miss Thompson and Kate Greenaway were both such enthusiastic workers that they would bribe the custodian to lock them in when the other students were gone, so that they might put in overtime.

Kate Greenaway

Such was the regularity and steady application of Kate's eager student days. By the time she was twenty-two she was exhibiting at the old Dudley Gallery a water-colour drawing entitled 'Kilmeny,' illustrating a versified legend, and 'six little drawings on wood': the latter, as we shall see, fortunate enough to attract the attention of an excellent judge and discriminating editor. This was in the year 1868, and here, in the old Egyptian Hall, her work made its first public appearance. Then there came a series of small pictures in water-colour at the same gallery, in which she already gave evidence of the bent which her brush was to follow with such remarkable success.[1] Even then her fancy was leading her back to the quaintly picturesque costume which was in vogue at the close of the eighteenth century. Not that her enthusiasm for our grandmothers' gowns at once tickled the fancy of the public. That was to come. Indeed, she herself was as yet only feeling her way, though with remarkable deliberation and thoroughness. No doubt it was in her first remunerative but anonymous work of designing valentines and Christmas cards that the possibilities which lay in childhood archaically, or at least quaintly, attired first presented themselves to her, but the goal was not to be reached without unstinted labour and active forethought. Her subsequent success rested upon the thoroughness with which she laid her foundations.[2] She did not merely pick up an old book of costumes and copy and adapt them second-hand to her own uses. She began from the very beginning, fashioning the dresses with her own hands and dressing up her models and lay-figures in order to realise the effects anew. She would not allow herself any satisfaction until her models lived and moved in her presence as their parents or grandparents had lived and moved in the previous century. Only then was she sure of her ground and could go forward with confidence.

[1] The following is a complete list of her exhibits at the Dudley Gallery :—

1868—Kilmeny.	(3) Birthday Tea.
1869—The Fairies of the 'Caldon Low.'	(4) A Procession of Children with
1870—Apple Blossom—A Spring Idyll.	Flowers.
1872—(1) A Study.	1878—(1) A Procession of Children.
(2) A Reverie.	(2) Darby and Joan.
1875—Little Miss Prim.	(3) Miss Patty.
1876—Little Girls at Play.	1879—(1) Prissy.
1877—(1) In Spring Time.	(2) A Morning Call.
(2) Dorothy.	

[2] See Mr. Lionel Robinson's introduction to the Exhibition of Kate Greenaway's Works in 1891.

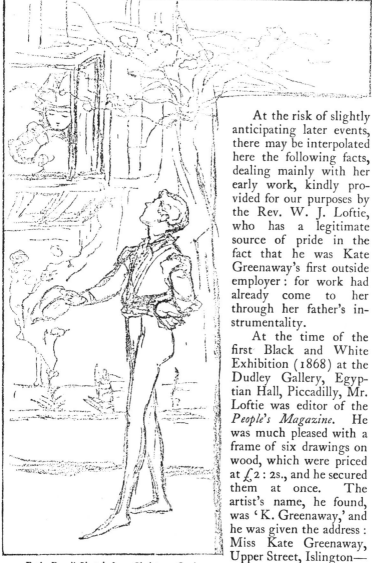

Early Pencil Sketch for a Christmas Card.

At the risk of slightly anticipating later events, there may be interpolated here the following facts, dealing mainly with her early work, kindly provided for our purposes by the Rev. W. J. Loftie, who has a legitimate source of pride in the fact that he was Kate Greenaway's first outside employer: for work had already come to her through her father's instrumentality.

At the time of the first Black and White Exhibition (1868) at the Dudley Gallery, Egyptian Hall, Piccadilly, Mr. Loftie was editor of the *People's Magazine.* He was much pleased with a frame of six drawings on wood, which were priced at £2 : 2s., and he secured them at once. The artist's name, he found, was 'K. Greenaway,' and he was given the address: Miss Kate Greenaway, Upper Street, Islington—

Kate Greenaway

a student at South Kensington. The drawings were equally divided between fairy scenes in outline and pictures of child life. He used them in the magazine as occasion allowed, and some of his leading contributors, Charles Eden, Robert Bateman, John Richard Green, who were charmed with their beauty, wrote little tales or verses to suit one or other, until three or four were disposed of. But he was puzzled about the rest, and eventually wrote to ask Miss Greenaway to tell him the subjects.[1] She called immediately at the office. She was very small, very dark, and seemed clever and sensible, with a certain impressive expression in her dark eyes that struck every one. Her visit led to further acquaintance, in which Mrs. Loftie shared, and she became a frequent visitor at 57, Upper Berkeley Street, where they then lived. The magazine soon came to an end, but Miss Greenaway was an artist who never disappointed her employers, and before long many opportunities occurred for recommending her. She had some work to do for Kronheim & Co. about that time, but —forgetting, apparently, her excellent achievement at South Kensington—she found a difficulty with colours. Like many beginners, she imagined that a sufficient number of bright colours made a bright-coloured picture, and being disappointed with the result, complained to Mr. Loftie. So he got the little manual of Colour-Harmony which was prepared by Redgrave for the South Kensington authorities and gave it to her. In the meanwhile Messrs. Marcus Ward of Belfast had consulted Mr. Loftie as to extending their business, and proposed to carry out a scheme he had laid before them some time before for issuing artistic Christmas cards and valentines in gold and colours. Miss Greenaway entered into the idea with great zest, but at first her designs were, as she said herself, gaudy. A little study of colour-harmony soon showed her where the fault lay, and she used to ask her friend to set her exercises in it—in primaries, or secondaries, or tertiaries, as the case might be. She derived extraordinary pleasure from studying the colour scale of such a picture as Van Eyck's ' Jean Arnolfini and his Wife ' in the National Gallery, or Gainsborough's so-called ' Blue

[1] These were the first things she ever sold publicly. Mr. Loftie forgets the apparent fact that the two remaining designs were also published, though at a later date, for on looking through the volume of the *People's Magazine* for 1873 we find on pp. 24 and 97 two of her drawings (unsigned) written up to respectively by ' M. E. ' and ' E. J. Ellis.' The first accompanies a set of verses entitled ' Nonsense about Cat's Cradle ' ; the second a sort of Alice-in-Wonderland story entitled ' Bebel,' an ingenious rendering of a somewhat cryptic design.

JOHN GREENAWAY (FATHER OF KATE GREENAWAY), WOOD-ENGRAVER,
AT WORK.

Pencil Drawing by Birket Foster, R.W.S. In the possession of John Greenaway, Esq.

KATE GREENAWAY'S STUDENT WORK.

Set of Tile Drawings in Colours, executed at the age of 17. Bronze Medal awarded and Drawing purchased by the Science and Art Department.

At the age of 16.

KATE GREENAWAY.

At the age of 21.

RAPID ALTERNATIVE PENCIL SKETCHES FOR TRAGEDY AS TITLE-PAGE TO 'AMATEUR THEATRICALS,' BY WALTER HERRIES POLLOCK AND MRS. POLLOCK.

In the possession of Revv. W. J. Loftie, F.S.A.

JOHN GREENAWAY, ESQ.

Pencil Sketch by Kate Greenaway of her brother at study (about 1870).

PENCIL SKETCHES.

In the possession of Rev. W. J. Loftie, F.S.A.

KATE GREENAWAY, 1880.

From a photograph by Elliott & Fry.

FREDERICK LOCKER-LAMPSON.

From the Water-Colour Drawing by Kate Greenaway. In the possession of Mrs. Locker-Lampson.

Student Days and Early Success

Boy.' It was only by incessant study of this kind earnestly pursued that she acquired the delicate and exquisite facility for figures and flowers in colour by which she soon became known. Meanwhile she drew constantly in black and white, and illustrated a child's book, *Topo*, by Miss Blood, afterwards Lady Colin Campbell, which was published by Messrs. Ward and speedily went out of print. A volume of valentines, *The Quiver of Love*, was published about the same time, and contained specimens of colour-printing by the same firm after her drawings and those of Mr. Walter Crane.[1]

Miss Greenaway worked very hard at the production of the designs for birthday cards and valentines. They constantly improved in harmony of colour and delicacy of effect. A curious chance revealed to her the wonders of medieval illumination. Mr. Loftie was engaged at the time on a volume of topographical studies for the Society for the Promotion of Christian Knowledge, and wanted a copy from the pages of the book of Benefactors of St. Albans Abbey—*Nero*, D. 7, in the MS. room at the British Museum. Mr. Thompson, better known as Sir E. Maunde Thompson, Principal Librarian, was head of the department, and showed her many of the treasures in his charge, and he arranged her seat and gave her every possible assistance. She undertook to make a coloured drawing of Abbot John of Berkhampstead wringing his hands, for Mr. Loftie's book. Being still in want of work, this particular job, with its collateral advantages in learning, pleased her very much. Another lady who was copying an illuminated border was her next neighbour at the same table, and they seem to have made one another's acquaintance on the occasion. In after years Miss Greenaway quaintly said 'this was the first duchess she had ever met'—the late Duchess of Cleveland, Lord Rosebery's mother, who was a notable artist, and who died only a few months before Miss Greenaway herself. As for the Abbot, the committee of the S.P.C.K. rejected him, and the picture passed into and remained in Mr. Loftie's possession. It figured later in his *London Afternoons* (p. 110), as Miss Greenaway only a few days before her death gave him leave to make what use of it he pleased.

Her first great success was a valentine. It was designed for Messrs. Marcus Ward, whose London manager hardly recognised, her introducer thought, what a prize they had found. The rough

[1] This was also published by Messrs. Marcus Ward & Co.

47

Kate Greenaway

proof of the drawing, in gold and colour, is both crude and inharmonious, but it has merits of delicacy and composition which account for the fact that the firm is said to have sold upwards of 25,000 copies of it in a few weeks. Her share of the profits was probably no more than £3. She painted many more on the same terms that year and the next, and was constantly improving in every way as she became better acquainted with her own powers and with the capabilities, at that time very slight, of printing in colour. 'I have a beautiful design,' says Mr. Loftie, 'in the most delicate tints, for another valentine, which she brought me herself to show how much better she now understood harmony. It was unfinished, and in fact was never used by the firm. I need not go into the circumstances under which she severed her connection with them, but I well remember her remarkable good-temper and moderation. In the end it was for her benefit. Mr. Edmund Evans seized the chance, and eventually formed the partnership which subsisted for many years, till near the end of her life.'

About the year 1879 Mr. Loftie met her one day at a private view in Bond Street. She was always very humble about herself. She was the very last person to recognise her own eminence, and was always, to the very end, keen to find out if any one could teach her anything or give her a hint or a valuable criticism. She was also very shy in general society, and inclined to be silent and to keep in the background. On this occasion, however, she received him laughing heartily. 'The lady who has just left me,' she said, 'has been staying in the country and has been to see her cousins. I asked if they were growing up as pretty as they promised. "Yes," she replied, "but they spoil their good looks, you know, by dressing in that absurd Kate Greenaway style"— quite forgetting that she was talking to me!' Kate would often repeat the story with much zest.

On two subsequent occasions did she execute work for books in which Mr. Loftie was concerned. In 1879 he asked her for some suggestions for illustrations of Mr. and Lady Pollock's *Amateur Theatricals* in his 'Art at Home' Series (Macmillan & Co.). She sent him half-a-dozen lovely sketches, of which only three were accepted by the publishers. The frontispiece, 'Comedy,' a charming drawing, was not well engraved. A tailpiece on p. 17 shows a slight but most graceful figure of a young girl in the most characteristic 'Kate Greenaway' costume. The third, less characteristic, is even more charming—'Going on.' Among the sketches was a 'Tragedy,' represented by a youthful Hamlet in black velvet holding a large turnip apparently to represent the skull of Yorick. This was never completed.

Once again, in 1891, she made a drawing at Mr. Loftie's instance. He was editing the fourth edition of the *Orient Guide* for Mr. J. G. S. Anderson, the Chairman of the Orient Line, who had lately, through his wife, Mrs. Garrett Anderson, M.D., made Miss Greenaway's acquaintance. It was suggested that she might design a title-page for the guide, which she did with alacrity, refusing remuneration, and only stipulating for the return of her drawing. It was a charming border, consisting of twelve delightful little girls and two little boys, all 'Kate Greenaway' children, very dainty, but extraordinarily inappropriate for the title-page of a steamship company's guide-book.

As soon as the introduction to Messrs. Marcus Ward was brought about, Kate Greenaway made a practice of consulting Mr. William Marcus Ward on the subject of her artistic and literary ambitions. In the matter of her drawing and painting she bowed to his expert opinion, unhesitatingly destroying her work when he told her that it was bad, and for years profited by his kindly advice ; but when in the matter of her verses he told her that her efforts were 'rubbish and without any poetic feeling,' though she listened meekly enough, she reserved her opinion —as we shall see in the event, not without some measure of justification.

After working for the firm for six or seven years, during which time her designs were trump cards in their annual pack, she was advised by friends that the drawings ought to be returned to her after reproduction. This new departure, however, did not meet with her employers' approval, and the connection ceased.

Amongst the early and unsigned work done for Messrs. Kronheim, who had a great colour-printing establishment in Shoe Lane, may be mentioned *Diamonds and Toads*, in 'Aunt Louisa's London Toy Books' Series (published by Frederick Warne & Co.), containing six full-page unsigned drawings of no striking promise and crude in colour, the harshness mainly due, no doubt, to the rude methods of engraving and colour-printing for children then in vogue. Far better was the work done in the same style and for the same firm in 1871 for a series of 'Nursery Toy Books' (published by Gall & Inglis), amongst which

Kate Greenaway

may be mentioned, for the sake of the collector, *The Fair One with Golden Locks*, *The Babes in the Wood*, *Blue Beard*, *Tom Thumb*, *Hop o' my Thumb*, *Red Riding Hood*, *The Blue Bird*, *The White Cat*, and *Puss in Boots*. In these the illustrations, remarkably well composed and drawn, rise somewhat above the level of children's coloured books of the period. The figures were mainly studied from members of her own family. The letterpress consisted for the most part of translations from the *Fairy Tales* of Madame la Comtesse d'Aulnoy, the well-known author of the *Memoirs and Voyages in Spain*, who flourished at the end of the seventeenth and the beginning of the eighteenth century. Her fairy tales had been originally published in Amsterdam in eight little volumes, with thirty-three plates signed 'S. F. inv. et sc.'—a set very different from the fanciful illustrations of Kate Greenaway.

Up to the year 1871 it is not possible to be very precise as to Kate's progress towards the overwhelming popularity which she was so soon to win. But from that time onwards her systematic keeping of accounts enables us to be definite. Besides the work done for Messrs. Kronheim, for which she was paid £36, we have the entry, 'Happy Wretched Family,' 10s.; 'Tracts' (apparently for the Religious Tract Society), £2 : 5s.; and commissions for a Mr. Sheers and Mr. Griffith,[1] £24 : 10s.; the year's takings amounting to something over £70.

The preceding year she had been represented at the Dudley Gallery by a water-colour drawing entitled 'Apple-Blossom—A Spring Idyll'; and in Suffolk Street, for the first time, by another entitled 'A Peeper,' representing children at play. In 1871 too, as we have seen from Mr. Loftie's note, she was designing Christmas cards for Messrs. Marcus Ward of Belfast. In these drawings she adopted the style of dress which she had seen as a child about the farm at Rolleston, where there was a survival of costumes which had long since disappeared from the towns and more 'progressive' villages and country districts, adapting them to her purpose and filling her wardrobes with frocks, bonnets, and jackets and other garments, partly conjured up from memory and partly invented. She soon began to discover that she was creating a vogue. She felt their quaintness and charm herself, and was hardly surprised that others found them equally attractive. And notwithstanding some doubts thrown by her father, artist

---

[1] Of Messrs. Griffith, Farran, & Co., for whom she worked later.

Student Days and Early Success

though he was, upon her wisdom in proceeding upon these lines, she determined to persist, and events proved her instinct to be right. Fortunately, her friend Mr. Stacy Marks, R.A., at the moment of crisis gave her strong support, and in the face of universal opposition urged her to continue in the path on which she had entered.

In 1872 she was designing yellow-back covers for Mr. Edmund Evans, of whom much will be heard later.[1] At the same time she was doing more work for Kronheim, she found her way into the *Illustrated London News*, and she sold her pictures at the Dudley Gallery for something like £20.

By 1873, doubtless through the influence of her father, who at that time was doing much work for Messrs. Cassell, Petter, & Galpin, Kate made her first appearance in *Little Folks*, for which, as well as for other publications of the firm, she executed innumerable dainty and characteristic drawings. This, of course, was mostly journeyman's work, and she was hampered by having to express other people's ideas pictorially. She never excelled as an illustrator, and it was not till she had a free hand that she did herself full justice. It was, however, an excellent school wherein to test her powers and to gain the experience which led her eventually to 'find herself.' In many of these wood-engravings it is interesting to notice the joint signature 'K. Greenaway, del.,' and 'J. Greenaway, sc.' She disliked being bound by another person's imagination, and her aversion to 'mere illustration' remained with her to the end. As late as February 1900, when she was asked if she would make a drawing to a story by Mrs. M. H. Spielmann, she wrote : 'It would rather depend if I saw my way to making a good illustration. I'm a very tiresome person and do things sometimes very badly. I should, if I could, like to do it very much, especially as it is Mrs. Spielmann's. I've not made any drawings for illustration for so long, and now I've just taken a book to do ! '[2]

In this same year (1873) her pictures at the Dudley and Suffolk Street Galleries found a market, and 'A Fern Gatherer,' at the Royal Manchester Institution, was bought by Mr. John Lomax for fifteen guineas. The following year (1874) her gross earnings

---

[1] An excellent account of Mr. Evans's work is to be found in *The British and Colonial Printer and Stationer* for March 31, 1904.

[2] *The April Baby's Book of Tunes*, by the author of *Elizabeth and her German Garden*.

Kate Greenaway

were £120, and she realised that she was progressing steadily in public favour.

Kate was now a person of some importance in the Greenaway establishment. Not only had she adopted a profession, but she was making that profession pay, and the time was coming when she felt that there should be some tangible sign, at least so far as she was concerned, of the improvement in their fortunes. It was a cause of profound gratification to her mother, who, by dint of thrift and self-sacrifice and devotion amounting almost to heroism, had been enabled to realise her ambition to educate each of her children to the greatest advantage. Her eldest daughter was sent to the Royal Academy of Music; her son to the Royal College of Chemistry; and Kate to South Kensington and Heatherley's. All of them were on the high-road to success, and a sense of satisfaction and good-humour permeated the household.

Good-humour, indeed, was characteristic of Kate, and to this sweetness of disposition and thoughtfulness for others she owed not a little of her success. Artists' grown-up models are often difficult enough to manage, but child-models are apt to prove exasperating; and it was due only to her infinite tact and un-wearying resourcefulness in inventing amusements and distractions for her little sitters that she coaxed them into good temper and into displaying the charm which she was so successful in reproducing.

During the last year or two spent in Islington, Kate rented near by a room which she fitted up as a studio, but about 1873 or 1874 she and her father between them bought the lease of a house in Pemberton Gardens, where the family lived till 1885.

Her friend Mrs. Miller writes of her at this period : 'She was then as ever gentle, patient, industrious, exquisitely sensitive, ex-traordinarily humorous, while under and over it all was an indomit-able will. I always remember one little remark she made to me once when we were walking from her home in Islington to a little room she had taken as a studio (her first) in a side street. It was wet and miserable, the streets vulgar and sordid. "Never mind," she said, " I shall soon be in the spring." The first primrose she drew upon the sheet before her would place her in another world. She loved all sorts of street music, and once said to me, " The moment I hear a band, I am in fairyland." '

In 1874 Kate Greenaway illustrated a little volume of fairy sotries, issued in coloured boards by Griffith & Farran, entitled

Student Days and Early Success

Fairy Gifts; or A Wallet of Wonders. It was written by Kathleen Knox, the author of *Father Time's Story-Book*, and contained four full-page and seven small woodcuts, engraved by John Greenaway. The more important illustrations are prettily composed, while revealing a fine taste in witches and apparitions ; and the small sketches are daintily touched in. It was Kate's first appearance on any title-page. There was nothing remarkable in the little volume, yet it met with considerable popular favour. The first edition consisted of 2,000 copies ; in 1880 it was reprinted to the extent of half as many. In 1882 a cheap edition of 5,000 copies was issued, and later in the year this large number was repeated. To what extent the artist shared in the success does not appear.

The year 1875, so far as earnings were concerned, was a lean year, and introduced the names of no new clients. This does not indicate that her activity was any the less than the year before. Indeed, we must remember that in the life of the artist results, so far as monetary reward is concerned, represent previous rather than contemporaneous activity, for payment is made certainly after the work is sold, and in the case of work for the press as often as not after publication. In the following year (1876) her earnings again ran into £200, her water-colour drawing at the Dudley being sold for twenty guineas, and her two black-and-white drawings for ten guineas the pair. But the crowning event of this year was the publication by Mr. Marcus Ward of the volume mentioned by Mr. Loftie, entitled ' *The Quiver of Love, a Collection of Valentines, Ancient and Modern,* with Illustrations in Colours from Drawings by Walter Crane and K. Greenaway.' All the designs had already been published separately. The verses were mainly from the pen of Mr. Loftie himself, although he is modest enough not to claim them in his notes.

None of the illustrations in this volume is signed, but the following are the productions of Kate Greenaway : (1) The Frontispiece ; (2) the illustration to 'Do I love you ?' by Julia Goddard ; (3) that to 'The Surprise,' anonymous ; and (4) that to 'Disdain,' by F. R. It would have been difficult to arrive at their authorship without the direct evidence of Mr. Walter Crane, who has identified his part in the publication. Probably, had not Kate Greenaway's name appeared on the title-page, it would scarcely have occurred to any one, even to those best acquainted with her work, that she had had any hand in the

53

production at all. The volume is merely interesting as a curiosity. It is not surprising to learn that the re-publication in permanent form, with his name attached, of ephemeral and unsigned work executed for the butterfly existence of a valentine, did not commend itself to Mr. Crane ; and to neither artist did any profit accrue.

Book-plate designed for
Miss Maud Locker-Lampson.

CHAPTER V

1877–1878

So far Kate had been going through the usual experiences of the free-lance who with pen or pencil in hand sets forth to win recognition from the public. Public taste is the hardest thing in the world to gauge by those who would be original according to their talents, and harder still is it to arrest attention, save by gasconades of which she certainly was wholly incapable. Hitherto she had been the servant eager to please the whim of her master, but the time was coming when she would call the tune and the public would delight to dance to it.

Kate Greenaway was now in her thirty-third year, and, though fairly prosperous, could scarcely consider herself successful. Commissions were certainly coming in faster and faster, and in 1877, when she took her studio to College Place, Liverpool Road, Islington, her earnings had nearly reached £300; but she had not yet made any great individual mark. She appeared in the Royal Academy Exhibition and sold her picture 'Musing' for twenty guineas. She was a recognised contributor to the Dudley Gallery, and was pretty sure of buyers there. She was getting more or less regular employment on the *Illustrated London News*. She had been asked by Mr. W. L. Thomas of the newly established *Graphic* to provide him with a running pictorial full-page story after the manner of Caldecott, and had succeeded in satisfying his fastidious taste,

55

Kate Greenaway

though the first sketch-plan which she sent seemed to him lacking in humour. 'They strike me,' he wrote, 'as being a little solemn in tone.' But this defect was soon rectified, and the result was so greatly admired that it led to many further commissions from the artist-editor.

These were gratifying and encouraging results, but in Kate's opinion they were but the prizes of the successful artist-hack. Her name had not yet passed into the mouth of the town. Though she had drawn many charming pictures, she had not yet drawn the public.

What was true of the public was true of the publishers. Though Messrs. Marcus Ward of Belfast had seen the possibilities that lay in her designs for valentines, Christmas cards, and the like, and had achieved a real success by their publication, Kate was but yet only the power behind the throne. She was the hidden mainspring of a clock with the maker's name upon the dial. Now all this was to be changed by a business arrangement, almost amounting to a partnership, in which she was to take her full share of the credit as well as of the spoil.

The story will be best told in the words of the man who so boldly backed his opinion as to print a first edition of 20,000 copies of a six-shilling book written and illustrated by a young lady who could hardly yet be said to have commanded anything like wide public approval. This was Mr. Edmund Evans.

Mr. Edmund Evans was primarily a colour-printer ; his wood-engraving department was subsidiary. For the purposes of his business he owned a good many machines ; he had three houses full of them in the City, and he was sometimes puzzled to find work to keep them going, to do which is at the root of commercial economy and success in his business. He printed most of the 'yellow-backs' of the time, covers for books as well as for small magazines of a semi-religious character, working-men's magazines, and so forth, all with much colour-work in them. Mr. Evans also executed much high-class work of the kind, such as Doyle's *Chronicles of England*, which had done much to make his reputation. Therefore, to fill up the spare time during which his machines would otherwise be idle, he began publishing the toy-books of Mr. Walter Crane, then those of Randolph Caldecott, and finally he turned his attention to Miss Kate Greenaway.

It should be recorded to the credit of Mr. Evans that he

The Triumph of 'Under the Window'

excelled all others in the skill with which he produced his colour-effects with a small number of printings. Mr. John Greenaway, himself an expert in the preparation of blocks for colour-printing, as well as an artist of much intelligence, used to declare that no other firm in London could come near the result that Edmund Evans would get with as few, say, as three colour-blocks, so wonderful was his ingenuity, so great his artistic taste, and so accurate his eye.

Mr. Evans informs us :

I had known John Greenaway, father of K. G.,[1] since I was fourteen years of age. He was an assistant engraver to Ebenezer Landells,[2] to whom I was apprenticed. I knew he was having one of his daughters educated for the musical profession and another for drawing. I had only seen engravings made from drawings on wood by 'K. G.' for Cassell & Co., as well as some Christmas cards by Marcus Ward & Co. from water-colour drawings of very quaint little figures of children. Very beautiful they were, for they were beautifully lithographed.

About 1877-78 K. G. came to see us at Witley, bringing a collection of about fifty drawings she had made, with quaint verses written to them. I was fascinated with the originality of the drawings and the ideas of the verse, so I at once purchased them and determined to reproduce them in a little volume. The title *Under the Window* was selected afterwards from one of the first lines. At the suggestion of George Routledge & Sons I took the drawings and verses to Frederick Locker, the author of *London Lyrics*, to 'look over' the verses, not to rewrite them, but only to correct a few oddities which George Routledge & Sons did not quite like or understand. Locker was very much taken with the drawings and the verses, and showed them to Mrs. Locker with quite a gusto ; he asked me many questions about her, and was evidently interested in what I told him of her. I do not think that he did anything to improve the verses, nor did K. G. herself.

Locker soon made her acquaintance and introduced her into some very good society. She often stayed with them at Rowfant, Sussex, and also at Cromer.

George Eliot was at the time staying at Witley. She called on us one day and saw the drawings and was much charmed with them. A little time afterwards I wrote to George Eliot to ask if she would write me a short story of, or about, children suitable for K. G. to illustrate. Her reason for refusing was interesting :—

---

[1] As 'K. G.,' the reader should be reminded, Miss Greenaway was known to most of her friends, and even to many of her relations as well.

[2] The originator of *Punch*.

Kate Greenaway

'The Heights, Witley,
October 22, 1879.

'Dear Mr. Evans—It is not my way to write anything except from my own inward prompting. Your proposal does me honour, and I should feel much trust in the charming pencil of Miss Greenaway, but I could never say "I will write this or that" until I had myself felt the need to do it. . . .—Believe me, dear Mr. Evans, yours most sincerely,   M. E. Lewes.'

After I had engraved the blocks and colour-blocks, I printed the first edition of 20,000 copies, and was ridiculed by the publishers for risking such a large edition of a six-shilling book ; but the edition sold before I could reprint another edition ; in the meantime copies were sold at a premium. Reprinting kept on till 70,000 was reached.[1]

I volunteered to give K. G. one-third of the profit of this book. It was published in the autumn of 1879. We decided to publish *The Birthday Book for Children* in 1880. Miss Greenaway considered that she should have half the profits of all books we might do together in future, and that I should return to her the original drawings after I had paid her for them and reproduced them. To both these terms I willingly agreed.[2] . . . Then came the *Birthday Book, Mother Goose*, and part of *A Day in a Child's Life*, in 1881 ; *Little Ann*, 1883 ; the *Language of Flowers, Kate Greenaway's Painting - Book*, and *Mavor's Spelling-Book*, 1884-85 ; *Marigold Garden* and *A Apple Pie*, 1886 ; *The Queen of The Pirate Isle* and *The Pied Piper of Hamelin*, 1887 ; *The Book of Games*, 1888 ; *King Pepito*, 1889. Besides the above and a certain number of smaller issues, minor works, and detached designs, the artist was responsible for an Almanack from 1883 to 1897, with the sole exception of the year 1896.

The books named above are those which we did together.

There is a little story my daughter Lily tells of her tenderness towards animals. She was walking one day and came upon a stream with a rat sitting on a stone. Lily wished to startle it, and was about to throw a stone in the water, but K. G. exclaimed—'Oh, don't, Lily, perhaps it's ill !' We all loved her.

---

[1] In addition there were French and German editions, which probably brought up the number to 100,000 copies.

[2] It should be understood, however—lest the strict facts of the arrangement mislead the reader—that the half-share royalty only became payable after the expenses of publication had been cleared off—that is to say, after the sale had passed a given number of copies. Consequently, as certain of the books never reached the limit, K. G. only received payment for the use of the drawings, which were returned to her. Such failures, commercially speaking, were *A Day in a Child's Life*, the Calendars, and one or two more. It was found in practice that, except in rare cases, books with music were not successful.

58

The Triumph of ' Under the Window '

This interesting account of what is one of the most important events in Kate's life may be supplemented by the following charming sketch taken from an article written by Mrs. Edmund Evans at the request of the editor of the *Girl's Own Paper*, shortly after her death. It was published on December 26, 1901, together with a photograph of the artist taken by Miss Lily Evans and four pen-and-ink drawings done by Kate Greenaway for the Evans children. Miss Lily Evans was Mr. Evans's second daughter and a special favourite with Kate Greenaway, who dedicated *Mother Goose* to ' Lily and Eddie ' (Kate Greenaway's nephew), ' the two children she loved most in the world.'

Kate Greenaway (wrote Mrs. Evans) had a very interesting personality, and was extremely fond of the country and of flowers, and could draw them beautifully, and always liked those best of a more simple form—not orchids nor begonias ; she loved daffodils and roses, and few things gave her more pleasure than a copse yellow with primroses. Her favourite time of year was when apple trees were in blossom ; she especially liked them when they were in the garden of a picturesque farm or cottage. One such cottage at Hambledon, Surrey, she particularly admired, where a green door had faded to a peacock blue. She liked only blue and white skies ; stormy effects gave her no pleasure. . . . ' The sincerest form of flattery ' (imitation) annoyed her, and did her reputation harm, as her many imitators went beyond, in fact out-Kate-Greenawayed Kate Greenaway in their caricatures, and many people did not know one from the other. She herself was waiting in a bookseller's shop at Hastings, and a lady came in and asked for Kate Greenaway's books. The shopman spread a handful out before her. The lady asked, ' Are those all by Kate Greenaway ? ' The man assured her they were. Kate Greenaway was near enough to see that not one was her work.

She had a very affectionate nature, very tender-hearted—seeing even an insect in pain wounded her. She could not tolerate flies caught in traps, or see a beetle or a spider killed. Seeing a mouse in a trap tempted her to set it free ; in fact, the ' cruelty of nature ' in the animal world quite troubled her. (She could not understand it or reconcile it with the goodness of God.[1]) Dogs and cats recognised this quality by showing their devotion and imposing on her good-nature. She would never even scold them. This was simply kindness—not indicating a weak nature. She was a decidedly strong-minded woman.

---

[1] These words have been added in MS. by Mr. Evans.

Kate Greenaway

Of Kate Greenaway's letters Mrs. Evans writes :—

I am sorry now I did not keep her letters. They were often very interesting and unlike ordinary people's, but when I had a great many it did not seem worth while, and I never do keep letters. As you know, she was so unassuming and homely, and liked our unostentatious way of living so much, it was difficult to realise she was a celebrated person.

Here, however, is one which has escaped destruction :—

KATE GREENAWAY TO MRS. EVANS

[Undated.]

Dear Mrs. Evans—The flowers came quite safely. I am always so pleased when the postman brings the little box. How strange and beautiful the daffodil is—I never saw one like it before. Also thank W. for the snowdrops.

The party was not very lively, only a few children. The songs sounded so well. The 12 Miss Pelicoes very funny, and the procession song pretty. Also there was an æsthetic artist there—real genuine sort—who drank in the Elgin marbles for recreation. No wonder du Maurier hates them.

The other day I heard I was sixty !—to-day I hear I am making £2000 a year !

I don't think you'd find it worth while to come up for the Dudley. I like to meet the people, of course ; they are very funny. I saw Mrs. —— the other day at the Old Masters' in a crimson velvet pelisse ; everybody stared and smiled. She is very pretty, but so much commoner than Mrs. ——.— With love,   K. GREENAWAY.

Of *Under the Window*, which was published at the end of 1878, it is no exaggeration to say that it was epoch-making ; its popularity was such that Kate tasted the bitter-sweet experience— shared in our own time by Frederick Sandys in respect of his great skit on Millais's 'Sir Isumbras at the Ford,' and by Mr. Brandon Thomas in respect of *Charley's Aunt* — of finding her work coolly appropriated by others. One—a lady of Twickenham— calmly gave herself out as the artist-author, explaining that she had preferred to issue her work under an assumed name. To enter into an elaborate description of the book would be super-fluous, for it still holds its place in every properly constituted children's library, and should be constantly taken out for renewed inspection. So, too, would it be superfluous to make extensive quotations from the eulogiums of the reviewers. We may content

The Triumph of ' Under the Window '

ourselves with the following prophecy from the *Saturday Review*, which seems now to be within measure of its fulfilment. ' In time,' the writer says, 'the hands of children will wear away, and their pencils and paint-brushes deface Miss Kate Greenaway's beautiful, fantastic, and dainty work *Under the Window*. Probably some wise collector will lay up a little stock for future use while the impressions are in their first freshness. His treasure will come to be as valuable as that parcel of unbound and uncut Elzevirs which Mottley found in Hungary, and which, after filling the hearts of bibliophiles with joy for years, was burned by the Commune.'

There are, however, one or two facts connected with the book which demand attention. In the first place, it must be borne in mind that from this moment Kate Greenaway's name became a household word, not only in Great Britain, but in a vast number of homes on the continents of Europe and America. In the second place, that now for the first time she was not hampered in her published work by adapting her fancy to the literary ideas of other people, but was inspired by subjects which came red-hot from the furnace of her own imagination.

This is a matter of no little importance. It is clear that the ideal illustrator of a literary idea, if only the technical skill is not wanting, is the person to whose mind that idea first presents itself. In the mind of any other the conception is but a second-hand affair, and but the reflection, more or less accurate, of the original, conveyed on to the mental retina of the artist through the somewhat opaque medium of language. The writer alone knows exactly what he means and what he wants. His pencil may be unskilled, but it is nerved by the original thought. ' I wish to goodness I could put it upon paper myself,' said Barham to Bentley, writing about an illustration for the *Mousquetaire*, even while Cruikshank and Leech were at his service. It is because Thackeray had the double gift that his drawings, although so weak in execution, yet so evidently imbued with the living literary inspiration, so greatly commend themselves to those who look for genuine sincerity of inspiration, and not only for beauty of composition and execution. That is why the world revelled in du Maurier's *Peter Ibbetson* and *Trilby*, and why Blake's *Songs of Innocence and Experience* is one of the completest and most harmonious books in existence.

What Blake did, Kate Greenaway was now enabled to do, in her own fashion, in *Under the Window*. She was expressing her own literary thoughts and at the same time treating them pictorially.

Kate Greenaway

One word about her verses, of which more will be said later on. Alone they would probably not have attracted much serious attention, and doubtless would have met with criticism. For there are in them faults of scansion, rhythm, and rhyme which it is easy enough to reprobate. But their sincerity, gaiety, and feeling appealed to such unimpeachable judges as Frederick Locker and Mr. Austin Dobson, the latter of whom declares, 'She was very deficient in technique, but she had the root of the matter in her.' During the last months of her life she found much pleasure in composing many more of those charming little verses, of which examples will be found in a later portion of this book.

Here is an amusing sample from *Under the Window*, written for children :

> Five little sisters walking in a row ;
> Now, isn't that the best way for little girls to go ?
> Each had a round hat, each had a muff,
> And each had a new pelisse of soft green stuff.
>
> Five little marigolds standing in a row ;
> Now, isn't that the best way for marigolds to grow ?
> Each with a green stalk, and all the five had got
> A bright yellow flower, and a new red pot.

It must not be supposed that Kate had any illusions about her literary gifts, or that she placed her own productions on a par with those of others whose work she illustrated. But she preferred her liberty and found her pencil better inspired by her own pen than by the pens of others with whom she was called upon to collaborate. Other verses were obviously cleverer and daintier than hers, but her own simple thoughts were more in harmony with her delightful little pictures.

It was not only the critics but the public who acclaimed her, for she had got at the secret of the beauty and charm of childhood, and the appeal was universal. As Mr. Lionel Robinson wrote :—

The moment selected for striking this note was well chosen. Abroad and at home the claims of children were asserting themselves more loudly than ever. German and French artists had alike proved unequal to the task, notwithstanding the temporary popularity of L. Fröhlich, of Ludwig Richter, and, in a high degree, of Édouard Frère and others. Clever as many of these showed themselves, they failed to render the more transient graces of little children, whilst they were,

62

KATE GREENAWAY'S PRIZE STUDENT-WORK.

THE ELF RING.

THE LITTLE MODEL.

'MARY HAD A LITTLE LAMB.'

THE LITTLE GO-CART.

PINK RIBBONS.

The Triumph of 'Under the Window'

with the exception of Frère, apparently indifferent to the bright surroundings and beauties of nature with which Miss Greenaway heightened the charm of her work. It is this absolute harmony between the figures and the landscape which makes her work so complete. Mr. Ruskin devoted one of his lectures at Oxford to the place occupied by Miss Greenaway in modern art, and bestowed upon her praise without stint. 'Observe,' said he, 'that what this impressionable person *does* draw she draws as like as she can. It is true that the combination or composition of things is not what you see every day. You can't every day, for instance, see a baby thrown into a basket of roses ; but when she has once pleasantly invented that arrangement for you, baby is as like baby and rose as like rose as she can possibly draw them. And the beauty of them is in being like, they are blissful

On a Letter to Miss Violet Dickinson.

just in the degree that they are natural ; the fairy-land that she creates for you is not beyond the sky nor beneath the sea, but near you, even at your doors. She does but show you how to see it, and how to cherish.'

When the original drawings for *Under the Window* were exhibited at the Fine Art Society two years later, the critics vied with one another in their applause. Ruskin in particular exhausted the splendour of his vocabulary in his praise of their unaffected beauty, their sweetness and naïveté, their delicacy of sentiment, subtlety of humour, and the exquisiteness of technique, and what he added to the artist privately has already been quoted here. Furthermore Mr. Austin Dobson wrote that 'since Stothard, no one has given us such a clear-eyed, soft-faced, happy-hearted childhood ; or so poetically "apprehended" the coy reticences, the simplicities, and the small solemnities of little people. Added to this, the old-world costume in which she usually elects to

Kate Greenaway

clothe her characters lends an arch piquancy of contrast to their innocent rites and ceremonies. Her taste in tinting, too, is very sweet and springlike; and there is a fresh, pure fragrance about all her pictures as of new-gathered nosegays.'

Wherefore it is evident that the success was as deserved as it was instantaneous. Nor was it due only to the fortunate moment chosen for launching the book. There was at least one other felicitous circumstance: Miss Greenaway was exceptionally fortunate in her interpreter, who had brought colour-printing by means of wood blocks to a pitch of excellence never before attempted. A description, therefore, of the process is of exceptional interest. The following account of the method is taken from notes supplied by Mr. Edmund Evans himself.

In the first place, a photograph is taken and printed on the whitened surface of the wood from the original drawing in line. This is engraved as faithfully as possible, no notice being taken at this stage of colour. From the engraving thus made 'transfers,' 'sets off,' or 'proofs' are pulled in dark brown or black ink. These, laid face downwards on the blocks prepared for the colour printing, which equal in number the colours to be used, are passed through the press. By this means the wet ink is transferred and set-off on to the blocks, and a number of facsimiles of the original drawing are ready for the engraver, who prepares for his work by painting-in, on each, that part of the tinting which is to be printed from that particular block. On one he paints in all the red that is to be used and engraves so much on that block, on the next all the blue that is to be used and engraves so much on that block, and so on until all the colours are represented, some of them overlapping or superimposed where they have to cross and modify other colours. Then the engraver sets to work with his engraving until he has prepared a separate block for each colour. In theory of course a proof printed from each block should exactly reproduce the blue, red, and other colours used in the original picture, but, 'alas,' as Mr. Evans says, 'the eye, brain, and hand of the engraver are not up to the eye, brain, and hand of the painter,' so that the print suffers by comparison. No doubt the coloured inks can be ground and mixed as surely as by the painter on his palette, but the mechanical print must ever come short of the nerve-driven original. When all the proofs taken from the several blocks are pronounced satisfactory, a print is taken from the key block. Upon that is superimposed a print from the other blocks charged each with

The Triumph of 'Under the Window'

its properly coloured ink, the greatest care being taken to get the 'register' correct—that is to say, that each block is printed accurately in its place upon the paper with relation to those which have gone before. From this it will be seen how important it is that the colours used should be as few as possible so as to keep within bounds the cost of engraving and to simplify the difficulties of printing. Of course, had Kate Greenaway worked in the twentieth century, the conditions would have been altogether different. Now coloured wood-engravings have been almost wholly superseded by the 'Three-Colour Process,' which owes its rise to the possibilities which have been found to lie in the use of filtering screens, bichromate of potash, and metal plates—possibilities of which full advantage has been taken in this volume.

Even with these advantages, we cannot entirely reproduce the daintiness and incisiveness of her drawing, the transparency and brilliancy of her colouring, the microscopic touch of the stipple, the delicacy of the greys, and the inexpressible charm of the whole. The three-colour process at its best is, after all, mechanical, and just falls short of giving 'the spider's touch, so delicately fine,' which 'feels at each thread and lives along the line.' Near to perfection it has got, especially when dealing with full-coloured drawings, but it cannot be said that any one who has not seen the originals can estimate to the full the charm and daintiness of these pictures, which seem to have been blown rather than painted on to the paper. Bartolozzi with his clever graver doubtless improved the work of those for whom he acted as middleman, but it would have taken a greater than Bartolozzi to have bettered (except in the academic quality of the drawing) the work of Kate Greenaway. In his 'Lecture on Mrs. Allingham and Kate Greenaway' in *The Art of England* (published by Mr. George Allen) Ruskin said :

I may best indicate to you the grasp which the genius of Miss Kate Greenaway has taken upon the spirits of foreign lands, no less than her own, by translating the last paragraph of the entirely candid, and intimately observant, review of modern English art given by Monsieur Ernest Chesneau, in his small volume, *La Peinture Anglaise*. . . .

He gives first a lovely passage (too long to introduce now) upon the gentleness of the satire of John Leech, as opposed to the bitter malignity of former caricature. Then he goes on : 'The great softening of the English mind, so manifest already in John Leech, shows itself in a decisive manner by the enthusiasm with which the public have lately

65   9

Kate Greenaway

received the designs of Mr. Walter Crane, Mr. Caldecott, and Miss Kate Greenaway. The two first-named artists began by addressing to children the stories of Perrault and of the *Arabian Nights*, translated and adorned for them in a dazzling manner ; and, in the works of all these three artists, landscape plays an important part ;—familiar landscape, very English, interpreted with a " bonhomie savante " ' (no translating that), 'spiritual, decorative in the rarest sense—strange and precious adaptation of Etruscan art, Flemish and Japanese, reaching, together with the perfect interpretation of nature, to incomparable chords of colour harmony. These powers are found in the work of the three, but Miss Greenaway, with a profound sentiment of love for children, puts the child alone on the scene, companions him in all his solitudes, and shows the infantine nature in all its naïveté, its gaucherie, its touching grace, its shy alarm, its discoveries, ravishments, embarrassments, and victories ; the stumblings of it in wintry ways, the enchanted smiles of its spring-time, and all the history of its fond heart and guileless egoism.

'From the honest but fierce laugh of the coarse Saxon, William Hogarth, to the delicious smile of Kate Greenaway, there has past a century and a half. Is it the same people which applauds to-day the sweet genius and tender malices of the one, and which applauded the bitter genius and slaughterous satire of the other ? After all, that is possible—the hatred of vice is only another manifestation of the love of innocence.' . . .

I have brought with me to-day in the first place some examples of her pencil sketches in primary design. . . . You have here for consummate example, a dance of fairies under a mushroom, which she did under challenge to show me what fairies were like. ' They'll be very like children,' she said. I answered that I didn't mind, and should like to see them all the same ;—so here they are, with a dance, also, of two girlies, outside of a mushroom ; and I don't know whether the elfins or girls are the fairyfootedest : and one or two more subjects, which you may find out ;—but in all you will see that the line is ineffably tender and delicate, and can't in the least be represented by the lines of a woodcut.[1] . . .

So far of pure outline. Next, for the enrichment of it by colour. Monsieur Chesneau doubts if the charm of Miss Greenaway's work can be carried farther. I answer, with security,—yes, very much farther, and that in two directions : first, in her own method of design ; and secondly, the manner of its representation in printing.

First, her own design has been greatly restricted by being too

---

[1] From a letter written in 1879 it will be seen that the heaviness of her line had before been a matter of complaint with him.

The Triumph of ' Under the Window'

ornamental, or, in our modern phrase, decorative ;—contracted into any corner of a Christmas card, or stretched like an elastic band round the edges of an almanac. Now her art is much too good to be used merely for illumination ; it is essentially and perfectly that of true colour-picture, and that the most naïve and delightful manner of picture, because, on the simplest terms, it comes nearest reality. No end of mischief has been done to modern art by the habit of running semi-pictorial illustration round the margins of ornamental volumes, and Miss Greenaway has been wasting her strength too sorrowfully in making the edges of her little birthday-books, and the like, glitter with unregarded gold, whereas her power should be concentrated in the direct illustration of connected story, and her pictures should be made complete on the page, and far more realistic than decorative. There is no charm so enduring as that of the real representation of any given scene ; her present designs are like living flowers flattened to go into an herbarium, and sometimes too pretty to be believed. We must ask her for more descriptive reality, for more convincing simplicity, and we must get her to organise a school of colourists by hand, who can absolutely facsimile her own first drawing.

This is the second matter on which I have to insist. I bring with me to-day twelve of her original drawings, and have mounted beside them, good impressions of the published prints.

I may heartily congratulate both the publishers and possessors of the book on the excellence of these ; yet if you examine them closely, you will find that the colour blocks of the print sometimes slip a little aside, so as to lose the precision of the drawing in important places ; and in many other respects better can be done, in at least a certain number of chosen copies. I must not, however, detain you to-day by entering into particulars in this matter. I am content to ask your sympathy in the endeavour, if I can prevail on the artist to undertake it.

Only in respect to this and every other question of method in engraving, observe further that *all* the drawings I bring you to-day agree in one thing,—minuteness and delicacy of touch carried to its utmost limit, visible in its perfectness to the eyes of youth, but neither executed with a magnifying glass nor, except to aged eyes, needing one. Even I, at sixty-four, can see the essential qualities of the work without spectacles ; though only the youngest of my friends here can see, for example, Kate's fairy dance, perfectly, but *they* can with their own bright eyes.

The year 1878, which gave *Under the Window* to the world, also produced *Topo: A Tale about English Children in Italy*,

Kate Greenaway

written by Miss Gertrude Blood, afterwards Lady Colin Campbell, who adopted for the occasion the pen-name of 'G. E. Brunefille,' 'with 44 pen-and-ink Illustrations by Kate Greenaway.' It was published by Messrs. Marcus Ward & Co. For the sake of the collector, it may be said that the first issue was printed on thick and a subsequent issue on thin paper. The design in black and gold on the green cloth cover was also from a drawing by Kate Greenaway. The full-page frontispiece is printed in green and gold; the rest of the illustrations are wood-engravings incorporated in the text. Of these the little girl on p. 17, the singing boy and smallest singing girl on p. 24, the little boy in his nightshirt on p. 31, and the choir boys on p. 45 are admirable, notwithstanding the poor printing. Apart from these, the illustrations are of no great account. Indeed, some of the figures are very indifferent, more particularly the middle of the three children on p. 52, which not only is very poor in the legs and feet (a constant difficulty with Kate through life), but is curiously faulty in its relation to the leading figure.

Concerning the book Lady Colin Campbell has supplied the following information :—

The child's book, *Topo: or Summer Life in Italy*, which she illustrated, I wrote when I was only fifteen, so of course there was no need for her to write to a child-author. The chief point of interest is not only the beauty of the drawings, but also that it was the first book she had ever illustrated[1]—before that she had only done calendars and Christmas cards, etc., for Marcus Ward & Co. Marcus Ward & Co. agreed to pay me £5 for the book, and they were so pleased with it that they sent me £10, which I should think was the only case on record of a publisher doubling the price in an author's favour without being asked.

For the illustrations, Mr. William Marcus Ward tells us, Kate Greenaway made innumerable sketches—was indeed tireless in her determination to do the best for her text. These preliminary designs were thrown off with amazing rapidity, 'almost as quickly as they could be talked about.' Those rejected she would ruthlessly tear up or beg him to do so. For the donkey she made at least a dozen drawings, but with no success, and finally had to submit to the mortification of the animal being drawn by some one else.

[1] The reader will see that this is a misconception, as *Fairy Gifts* preceded it by four years.

The Triumph of ' Under the Window '

This year Kate was represented at the Academy by her
' Little Girl with Doll,' while two of her pictures at the Dudley
Gallery sold for fifteen guineas and fifteen pounds respectively,
her gross takings from this source being nearly fifty pounds. Now,
too, began her connection with the Scribners, for whom she
worked for several years. From this time forward her accounts,
to those who enjoy figures, make very cheerful reading. In
1878 she earned nearly £550, in 1879 over £800, in 1880
rather more, and in 1881 over £1500, the enormous rise being
due to the accumulating royalties on the books engraved and
printed by Mr. Evans and published by George Routledge &
Sons.

At this time Randolph Caldecott, born in the same year
as Kate Greenaway, was at once her rival in the affections of the
young people of the 'seventies and 'eighties, her competitor on the

SKIT IN THE KATE GREENAWAY MANNER BY RANDOLPH CALDECOTT.

publishers' prospectuses, and her admiring friend and helpful
comrade. A story is told of him that one morning, staying with
her in the same country-house (probably that of Mr. and Mrs.
Locker-Lampson), he came down declaring that he had lost all
power of working in his own style and everything came out Kate
Greenaways. He then produced a telling little skit on her
manner which so delighted Kate Greenaway that she preserved it
till her dying day.

Kate Greenaway

Randolph Caldecott to Kate Greenaway

46, Great Russell Street, Bloomsbury,
September 30, 1878.

Dear Miss Greenaway—The two children of whom I spoke were recommended to me by a Mr. Robertson of 6, Britten Street, Chelsea, himself a model. He seemed to say that he had the power of causing the children to sit. One is a 'Saxon boy' of six years old—called A. Frost; the other is a 'vivacious girl of an auburn colour' entitled Minnie Frost.

I do not know anything of Mr. Robertson either as a professional model or as a private gentleman. He has called on me twice for a few minutes at each time.

The brown ink of which I discoursed will not, when thickly used with a pen, keep itself entirely together under the overwhelming influence of a brush with water-colour. I have found this out to-day. But the liquid Indian ink used for lines will stand any number of damp assaults. This I know from much experience.—Believe me, yours very truly,   R. Caldecott.

P.S.—I hope the above information may be of use to you.—R. C.

On the death of Caldecott, Miss Greenaway wrote as follows to Mrs. Severn :—

50, Frognal, Hampstead, N.W.,
17th Feb. 1886.

Dearest Joanie—. . . Isn't it sad about Mr. Caldecott? The last I heard he was so much better—and now—dead. It looks quite horrid to see the black-bordered card with his books in the shop windows— it feels horrid to want to sell his books somehow, just yet. I'm very sorry. . . .—Good-bye, with dearest love,   Katie.

The good understanding between the two artists was probably known outside their own circle, and strange deductions were occasionally drawn. One day a gentleman said mysteriously to Mr. Rider, the head of the firm who built Miss Greenaway's house at Frognal :

'You know, I suppose, who Kate Greenaway really is?'

'Perfectly,' said Mr. Rider.

'She's not Kate Greenaway at all,' said his informant, confidentially, '*she's Mrs. Randolph Caldecott*. I chance to know that she married Randolph Caldecott'; and Mr. Rider utterly

The Triumph of ' Under the Window '

failed to establish the truth in the mind of his visitor, for it was a belief held by not a few.

On the other hand, with Mr. Walter Crane—with whose name her own was so often linked in the public mind, as well as in publishers' announcements—Kate Greenaway had but the slightest acquaintance, though for his work she entertained unbounded admiration. Mr. Crane informs us :

I only met her on one occasion, and that was at a play given in Argyll Street, wherein Tennyson's second son, Lionel Tennyson, appeared, and in which the Lockers were interested.

My impressions of Kate Greenaway were of a very quiet and unobtrusive personality, probably quietly observant, self-contained, reserved, with a certain shrewdness. She was small and plainly dressed.

In those days it was usual to bracket Kate Greenaway, Randolph Caldecott, and myself together as special children's-book providers, ignoring very great differences of style and aims (ignoring, too, the fact that I began my series of picture-books more than ten years before either Caldecott or Miss Greenaway were known to the public). Both those artists, however, were, I fancy, much more commercially successful than I was, as, when I began, children's-book designs were very poorly paid. I was glad to be of some service to Caldecott when he started his series through Messrs. Routledge in 1878. My *Baby's Opera* was published in 1877 by the same house, and proved so successful that the publishers wanted me to follow it up immediately with another. Being engaged in other work, I did not see my way to this ; but the publishers were equal to the emergency, for I was rather startled about Christmas to see Kate Greenaway's first book, *Under the Window*, announced by them as 'companion volume' to *The Baby's Opera*. To this I naturally objected as misleading, and the advertisement was withdrawn.

The grace and charm of her children and young girls were quickly recognised, and her treatment of quaint early nineteenth-century costume, prim gardens, and the child-like spirit of her designs in an old-world atmosphere, though touched with conscious modern ' æstheticism,' captivated the public in a remarkable way.

May I confess that (for me at least) I think she overdid the big bonnet rather, and at one time her little people were almost lost in their clothes ? However, one saw this in the actual life of the day.

I remember Miss Greenaway used to exhibit drawings at the old Dudley Gallery general exhibition, but her larger, more elaborated studies were not so happy as her book designs in simple outline taste-fully tinted.

71

Kate Greenaway

Mr. Walter Crane speaks here of their difference of aims.
Those who recall the public discussion between Mr. Crane and
Professor Ruskin on the subject of children's books will remember
that what the former had greatly in mind was a special appeal to
the eyes and artistic taste of the little ones : his purpose was in a
measure educative. Kate Greenaway, on the other hand, sought
for nothing but their unthinking delight ; and whether her aim
was higher or lower than that of her fellow-artist, there was no
doubt of the esteem and affection in which she was now held by
all little people as well as by their elders.

Book-plate designed for Godfrey Locker-Lampson.

CHAPTER VI

1879–1880

THE year 1846—the birth-year of both Kate Greenaway and Randolph Caldecott—marked also the genesis of the Christmas card. What was in the first instance a pretty thought and dainty whim, by its twenty-fifth year had become a craze, and has now, another quarter of a century later, fallen into a tenacious and somewhat erratic dotage. The first example of which there is any trace was a private card designed by J. C. Horsley, R.A., for Sir Henry Cole, of the South Kensington Museum, and it proved to be the forerunner of at least two hundred thousand others that were placed upon the market before 1894 in England alone. For five-and-twenty years the designing of them was practically confined to the journeyman artist, who rang the changes on the Christmas Plum-pudding, the Holly and Mistletoe, and on occasional religious reference, with little originality and less art. Later on all that was changed. About 1878 certain manufacturers, printers, and publishers recognised the possibilities which lay in an improved type of production, with the result that in 1882 so great was the boom that ' one firm alone paid in a single year no less a sum than seven thousand pounds for original drawings ' for these cards.[1]

Thereupon arose the Christmas card collector, who vaunted his possessions even as the stamp collector or book-plate collector of

---

[1] See ' Christmas Cards and their Designers, by Gleeson White.' Extra number of the *Studio*, 1894, which is full of interesting information on the subject.

Kate Greenaway

to-day takes pride in his. One of the most ardent is credited with the ownership of 700 volumes, weighing together between six and seven tons and containing 163,000 varieties ! The decade 1878 to 1888 was his happy hunting-time, for it was then that not only were book-illustrators of the highest repute induced to follow an employment which up to that time had been looked upon as merely perfunctory, but established artists, Royal Academicians and others who were popularly supposed to work only for Art's sake and not at all for that of Commerce, vied with one another for the rewards which waited upon artistic success in the new field.

Kate Greenaway had begun the designing of Christmas cards anonymously in the pre-collector days, and her earliest productions, which were no doubt an advance upon most of those which preceded them, are nevertheless interesting rather as curiosities than as works of art. In her valentines she had adopted the slashed doublet and buskin convention ; but the Christmas card was to prove her triumph. Not that she shook herself free from her trammels all at once ; but signs of grace quickly appeared, and the year 1878 found her working on original lines in the front rank of the artists who were taking advantage of the new departure. Before this date her cards seem never to have been signed, and are not easy to identify, as they lack the distinctive characteristics of her later work. As time goes on they bear, if not the initals 'K. G.,' at any rate the unquestionable evidence of her style. Doubtless the difficulty of identifying her early work is due chiefly to the fact that the designs, mainly flower pieces, were only sketched out by her and were given into the hands of more experienced draughtsmen to be finished. What was most noticeable in her work at this period was the remarkable ease with which she adapted her designs to the spaces they were to occupy, whether oblongs, uprights, circles, or ovals.

By this year she was, as *Under the Window* proves, in her own way 'drawing her inspiration from classic forms unfettered by classic conventions,' and her very original designs, coming at a time when the vogue was at its height, went no little way towards increasing her popularity. From this time many of her Christmas cards are well worthy the notice of the collector of beautiful things ; and the fact that her work, done with a single eye to this mode of publication, grew rarer and rarer as time went on gives them the adventitious value of scarcity which

Christmas Cards and Books

sharpens the appetite for acquisition. It is true that Christmas cards bearing her signature continued to appear until late into the 'nineties, but these were usually designs made for her books and afterwards appropriated to other uses. Those of her best period are fully entitled to rank amongst the Art products of the time. These were years when Christmas cards were Christmas cards, designed by Mr. Marcus Stone, R.A., Mr. G. D. Leslie, R.A., Mr. J. Sant, R.A., Mr. W. F. Yeames, R.A., H. Stacy Marks, R.A., J. C. Herbert, R.A., and Sir Edward Poynter, the present President of the Royal Academy. They had not yet developed, as now, into anything from the counterfeit present-ment of an old boot, or a cigar-end, to the *Encyclopædia Britannica*. As Gleeson White wrote, with genuine indignation, in 1894—

> The mass of recent cards, with few notable exceptions, are merely bric-à-brac, and of no more intrinsic merit as to design or colour than half the superfluous trifles of the 'fancy emporium,' the *articles de Paris* in oxidised metal, rococo, gilt plush, and ormolu, which fill the windows of our best and worst shopping streets, and in debased imitations overflow the baskets on the pave-ments outside cheap drapery stores.

Early Sketch for Christmas Card.

Wherefore, to turn back from these to the work of Kate Greenaway at the end of the 'seventies and beginning of the 'eighties is to recognise something of a revelation.

The little drawings of sprites, gnomes, and fairies which, as has been related, attracted the attention of the Rev. W. J. Loftie and of Messrs. Marcus Ward, in Miss Greenaway's first black-and-white exhibition at the Dudley Gallery, and found their way into the *People's Magazine*, were indirectly responsible for at least a hundred separate designs from her brush, all of them reflecting equal credit on the artist and the firm which reproduced them. Some idea of the importance of the output of this house may be gathered from the fact that in 1884 a collection of drawings, done in the main for their Christmas cards, was sold by auction at

75

Kate Greenaway

Messrs. Fosters' Rooms for £1,728 : 12s.[1] In this as in every other field of her work she received the sincerest but to her the most annoying kind of flattery. For example, in 1880 an important house offered £500 in prizes for Christmas card designs, with Sir Coutts Lindsay, Stacy Marks, R.A., and G. H. Boughton, R.A., as judges ; and one of the prizes fell to 'K. Terrell, for designs after the style of Kate Greenaway.' The sale of these Christmas cards ran literally into millions ; and when it is remembered that probably not more than three were designed then for three thousand pictorial postcards put forth to-day, the prodigious popular success of them can easily be realised. These cards, it should be added, were all produced by chromolithography, each one needing, on the average, twelve stones.

In dealing with the iconographies of 'the work of certain artists of importance,' who were represented in the great decade of Christmas card production by more than a single set of cards, Gleeson White rightly accorded to Kate Greenaway the premier place, and wrote :

Miss Kate Greenaway has preserved no complete set of her own designs — nor have her publishers : hence collectors must needs exercise their ingenuity to discover which of the many unsigned cards that appear to be hers are genuine and which are imitations. After the success of her first popular series (issued, as were the majority, by Marcus Ward), it is easy enough to discard the too faithful disciples who never once caught her peculiar charm. But in the earlier of hers, when her manner was less pronounced, even the publishers are not always absolutely certain regarding the authorship of several designs. [2]

---

[1] At this sale Kate Greenaway's illustrations to *Topo* fetched—after the copyright had been used—35 guineas ; whilst others of her pictures sold were 'Three Innocents,' 12 guineas ; 'My Lady and her Pages,' 23 guineas ; 'The Seasons,' 17 guineas ; 'The Time of Roses,' 18 guineas ; 'On the Road to the Ball,' and 'The Fancy Dress Ball,' £28 ; and 'My Lord's Page and my Lady's Maid,' 13 guineas.

[2] 'Those indisputably by Miss Greenaway,' he proceeds, 'include : a set of children, 1878 ; another set, a Page in Red, with a cup, etc. ; children by ponds ; a set of little people in initial letters ; a set of damsels with muffs, and lads in ulsters ; another set of four initials ; a Red Riding Hood set ; an oblong set, with processions of little people ; a tiny set of three ; an upright set of three single figures ; a set of heads ; and a set of "Coachmen." To these may be added the Calendars published by Marcus Ward, as well as the annual "Kate Greenaway's Almanack," published by Geo. Routledge & Sons ; a set in circular panels on small cards, published by Goodall ; a set, "The Four Seasons" ; also a calendar with four designs issued separately as cards, and a few early cards published by Marcus Ward.

'Without very minute and tedious detail, it is not possible to identify even these in written descriptions ; but, unless collectors have at least as many sets (usually four in

Christmas Cards and Books

But this section of her work, important though it was in the early development of the Kate Greenaway we know, and interesting though it is to the collector of her work, was merely a by-path in the direction she was travelling. She was now, in truth, on the high-road to fame and success. The next year (1879) she was hard at work on her *Birthday Book*, a duodecimo volume with verses by Mrs. Sale Barker. It was published in 1880, and 128,000 English, 13,500 French, and 8,500 German copies were placed on the market. For the 382 tiny drawings, 370 of which were minute uncoloured figures, she received £151 : 10s., whilst the royalties (not, of course, received all at once) exceeded £1,100.[1] Every day had its own delightful little pictorial conceit, and each month had a full page in colour in her happiest manner. 'Good Evans!' exclaimed a perfectly respectable newspaper at the sight of them.

Later on, at Mr. Evans's suggestion, Kate Greenaway coloured a certain number of the little wood-engravings, with the idea of publishing them in a separate volume. From these Mr. Evans engraved the colour blocks and bound up a few copies, but no title was decided upon, and the book was never even offered to the publishers. Should one of these little proof copies ever come into the sale-room, some lively bidding may be looked for.

But perhaps the most interesting thing connected with the *Birthday Book* is the fact, which we learn from Mr. Graham Balfour, that Robert Louis Stevenson was first prompted by it to try his hand at those charming verses for children which were afterwards published in the *Child's Garden of Verse*. 'Louis took the *Birthday Book* up one day,' says Mr. Balfour, 'and saying, "These are rather nice rhymes, and I don't think they would be very difficult to do," proceeded to try his hand.'

In this year also Miss Greenaway was commissioned by Messrs. Macmillan & Co. to illustrate a new edition of Miss Yonge's novels. But after finishing four drawings for the *Heir of Redclyffe* and three for *Heartsease*, she threw up the task. She recognised at the end that she was not entirely competent to carry out such work, as she had declared from the beginning her extreme

each series) as I have noted, they may still be certain that the most prized section of their collection is incomplete. How many more can be traced it would be pleasant to discover.'

[1] Of these little drawings in pen-and-ink, many of them scarcely more than an inch high, 292 have lately been offered for sale by a London west-end bookseller, prettily mounted on pages, in an elaborately-bound morocco-covered box, for the sum of £300.

Kate Greenaway

indisposition to enter upon it. The drawings are capital, but hardly appropriate, and excellently as they were cut on wood by Swain, they failed of their effect. For the young man in these drawings Kate impressed her brother John as model; and her father is to be recognised in the frontispiece, in the figure of Percy holding his cherished umbrella over the person of Theodora.

For the same firm Kate also drew, as has been said, a delightful frontispiece for *Amateur Theatricals*, by Mr. Walter Herries Pollock and Lady Pollock in the 'Art at Home Series,' edited by the Rev. W. J. Loftie. Other drawings appeared in *St. Nicholas*, among which should be mentioned illustrations to Tom Hughes' 'Beating the Bounds,' 'Children's Day in St. Paul's,' and Mrs. Dodge's 'Calling the Flowers,' 'The Little Big Woman and the Big Little Girl,' and 'Seeing is Believing.'

The drawing called 'Misses,' which Kate sent this year to the Royal Academy, was less attractive to some than its foregoers. *Fun* fixed upon its title in a critical couplet in the course of a very cutting rhyming review of the exhibition entitled 'The Budget at Burlington House,' and proceeded :

> A picture by Miss Greenaway (we scarcely like a bit of it)
> Is rightly titled 'Misses,' for she hasn't made a hit of it.

The popular interest in Miss Greenaway then and thenceforward may be partly gauged by the great sheaf of applications for biographical information addressed to her by the editors of various magazines, found among her papers. But she hated publicity at all times. Especially did she fear and detest the attentions of interviewers, and she did her best to escape them. In a letter of a later date to Miss Lily Evans she says :

> My mind is dull to-night. I feel like what I was described in one of the notices of the P.V. [Private View], as a gentle, bespectacled, *middle*-aged lady *garbed* in black. Somehow it sounds as if I was like a little mouse. I don't feel gentle at all. See what it is to grow old ! I *have* passed a time avoiding interviewers—no wonder they take revenge !

And when Herr Emil Hannover sought to write a critical and personal study on the artist, he received, as he records, a note from her in which she writes with characteristic reserve and dignity :

> You must wait till I am dead ; till then I wish to live my life privately—like an English gentlewoman.

Christmas Cards and Books

Publishers, too, vied with one another in seeking her services, and a bare list of commissions offered but not taken in the years immediately succeeding would fill pages of this book. Indeed, if we may judge from her correspondence, every amateur who wrote a fairy story or a child's book or a book of verses, and wished to float it on the sea of her popularity, applied to her to illustrate it. One of them thinks that the 'kind praise received from various editors' should be sufficient recommendation. Another flourishes 'seven small children.' Another appeal to her charity and generosity is from a clergyman's wife ; she is in *very* delicate health, her income does not permit of her doing the things which her medical man tells her would greatly benefit her, and so on, and she would be so much obliged if Miss Greenaway would make her verses saleable by illustrating them. Pathetic requests of this sort must have affected her tender heart as deeply as Thackeray's 'Thorns in the Cushion' touched his.

Another, a German composer, puts her verses to music, and with a sense of morality about on a par with his English writes, in the strain well known to successful British authors :

'In Germany every composer has a right over publishing each song by composition without paying any honorary to the poet, therefor the editor would not be obliged to hesitate in publishing your songs in the German translation with melodies. But since it is of importance for me that my composition also *find a spreading in England*,' etc. etc., he offers 'one hundred mark [£5] for twelve of your poems.'

It need hardly be said that to this half-threat, half-insult Kate made no response.

Further evidence of Miss Greenaway's vogue at this time may be gathered from information which Mr. J. Russell Endean has been good enough to provide. He says that shortly after the issue of *Under the Window*, Herr Fischer, of the Royal and Imperial Porcelain Majolica Manufactory, Buda Pesth, showed him half-a-dozen employés, with a copy of the book lying before each of them, at work in the artist's atelier, copying the illustrations upon china plates which had been twice fired, line for line, size for size, and group for group.

To this Herr Fischer himself adds : 'It is a fact that Kate Greenaway was copied in my factory, and I can certainly further affirm that all the books which appeared in the 'eighties were used, and large business was done with the pictures.'

Kate Greenaway

This annexation of copyright British designs by German china manufacturers, however, is in no way unusual. As we write these lines there is brought before us an excellent but wholly unauthorised reproduction upon a porcelain vase decorated with one of Mr. C. Wilhelm's beautiful drawings of dainty animated flowers, a design in which Kate Greenaway would assuredly have rejoiced.

H. Stacy Marks, R.A., it has been said, was one of Miss Greenaway's most valued and helpful friends. The letters of this year that follow show how sincere and kind he was, and how candid a critic. A constant visitor and adviser, and an ardent admirer of her work from early years, he did more than any one to encourage her, to foster her genius, and to bring her into notice. Always seeking eagerly for her criticism of his own work, he was not sparing in his kindly comments on hers. This he held to be not only a duty but, in a sense, a necessity, for he felt that she must justify the advice he had given her to proceed along the path she had discovered for herself, when others, declaring she was blundering into failure, were loudly conjuring her to be more conventional, and to suppress her charming individuality.

H. Stacy Marks, R.A., to Kate Greenaway

October 22, 1879.

Dear Miss Greenaway—Very many thanks for your very pretty and charming book,[1] which has afforded me and my household much pleasure. Where so many designs are delightful, it seems hard to select any special one, but I think, as a happy method of filling up a page, the girls with the shuttlecocks bears the palm ; and how useful is the verse between ! [p. 33].

I like page 41 for its naïve defiance of all rules of composition, and pages 23 and 47 are very sweet.

I am not going to be 'severe,' but I *must* ask you not to repeat those funny little black shadows under the feet of your figures—looking in some places like spurs, in others like tadpoles, in others like short stilts. *Vide* cat and children on page 53 for the last, page 39 for the tadpoles, and pages 10 and 30 for spurs. Why you have done this (much to the detriment of the drawings) in special instances and not in others I can't see. I will only find another fault—the drawing of

---

[1] *Under the Window.*

H. Stacy Marks, R.A.

the *feet* on page 31—the tallest girl's are very funny, but all are queer. A cast of any foot placed a little below the level of the eye would teach you how to foreshorten feet better.

There, I have done! But I know you well enough to feel assured that you would not be content with unqualified praise, and that you are grateful for a little honest criticism.

Don't bother about painting too much. You have a *lay* of your own, and do your best to cultivate it.

Think of the large number of people you charm and delight by these designs compared with those who can afford to buy paintings. You have a special gift and it is your duty in every sense to make the most of it.

By the way, did you write the verses also? If so, there is another feather for your cap, for I know how difficult it is to write verses. for children.

I hope I have not sermonised too much, and thanking you once more for your pleasant, happy book, to which I shall turn again and again, I am, faithfully yours,   H. S. Marks.

H. Stacy Marks to Kate Greenaway

November 3, 1879.

. . . Mr. Ruskin dined here on Thursday last, and spoke in high terms of your feeling for children, etc. I think it not unlikely that you may have a letter from him soon.

One more word of advice—although I almost believe you have too much common-sense to need it—don't let *any* success or praise make you puffed up or conceited, but keep humble and try to perfect yourself more in your art each day—and never sell your independence by hasty or badly considered work.

I have seen so many spoiled by success that I raise my warning voice to you.

And sure enough before three months were out Mr. Ruskin did make it his business to write and give her shrewd and humorous advice. The first letter is dated 1879, but that which follows it shows that this is a mistake : like a great many other people, he found it hard to adopt a new date at the beginning of a new year. Ruskin and Kate Greenaway, whose friendship was soon to ripen into a happy intimacy, shared by his household, did not meet face to face until 1882. He writes in his more fantastic and playful vein.

81   11

Kate Greenaway

JOHN RUSKIN TO KATE GREENAWAY

BRANTWOOD, CONISTON,
Jan. 6th. 1879 [a mistake for 1880].

My dear Miss Greenaway—I lay awake half (no a quarter) of last night thinking of the hundred things I want to say to you–and never shall get said !–and I'm giddy and weary–and now can't say even half or a quarter of one out of the hundred.   They're about you–and your gifts–and your graces–and your fancies–and your–yes–perhaps one or two little tiny faults :–and about other people–children, and grey-haired, and what you could do for them–if you once made up your mind for whom you would do it.   For children *only* for instance ?–or for old people, *me* for instance–and *of* children and old people–whether for those of 1880–only–or of 18–8–9–10–11–12–20–0–0—0—0, etc. etc. etc.   Or more simply annual or perennial.

Well, of the thousand things–it was nearer a thousand than a hundred–this is anyhow the first.   Will you please tell me whether you can only draw these things out of your head–or could, if you chose, draw them with the necessary modifications from nature ?   For instance–Down in Kent the other day I saw many more lovely farm-houses–many more pretty landscapes–than any in your book.   But the farms had, perhaps, a steam-engine in the yard–the landscapes a railroad in the valley.   Now, do you never want to draw such houses and places, as they used to be, and might be ?

That's No. 1.

No. 2 of the thousand.

Do you only draw pretty children out of your head ?   In my parish school there are at least twenty prettier than any in your book–but they are in costumes neither graceful nor comic–they are not like blue china–they are not like mushrooms–they are like–very ill-dressed Angels.   Could you draw groups of these as they *are* ?

No. 3 of the thousand.

Did you ever see a book called Flitters, Tatters, and the Councillor ?[1]

No. 4 of the thousand.

Do you ever see the blue sky ? and when you do, do you like it ?

No. 5.

Is a witch's ride on a broomstick[2] the only chivalry you think it desirable to remind the glorious Nineteenth Century of ?

No. 6.—Do you believe in Fairies ?

No. 7.—In ghosts ?

No. 8.—In Principalities or Powers ?

---

[1] By Miss Laffan, author of *Baubie Clarke* (Blackwood, 1880).
[2] See *Under the Window*, p. 35.

John Ruskin

No. 9.—In Heaven?

No. 10.—In–Any where else?

No. 11.—Did you ever see Chartres Cathedral?

No. 12.—Did you ever study, there or elsewhere, thirteenth century glass?

No. 13.—Do you ever go to the MS. room of the British Museum?

No. 14.—Heavy outline will not go with strong colour–but if so, do you never intend to draw with delicate outline?

No. 15.—Will you please forgive me–and tell me–some of those things I've asked?—Ever gratefully yours, J. RUSKIN.

To this letter Miss Greenaway responded at once, and he writes again :—

JOHN RUSKIN TO KATE GREENAWAY

BRANTWOOD, CONISTON,
Jan. 15th. 1880.

Dear Miss Greenaway—How delightful of you to answer all my questions!–and to read *Fors*! I never dreamed you were one of my readers—and I had rather you read that than anything else of mine, and rather *you* read it than anybody else.

I am so delighted, also with your really liking blue sky–and those actual cottages, and that you've never been abroad. And that's all I can say to-day, but only this, that I think from what you tell me, you will feel with me, in my wanting you to try the experiment of representing any actual piece of nature (however little) as it really is, yet in the modified harmony of colour necessary for printing–making a simple study first as an ordinary water-colour sketch, and then translating it into outline and the few advisable tints, so as to be able to say–The sun was in or out,–it was here, or there, and the gown, or the paling, was of this colour on one side, and of that on the other.

I believe your lovely design and grouping will come out all the brighter and richer for such exercise. And then–when the question of absolute translation is once answered, that of conventional change may be met on its separate terms, securely.—Ever gratefully yours,

J. RUSKIN.

JOHN RUSKIN TO KATE GREENAWAY

BRANTWOOD, CONISTON,
Dec. 7th. /80.

Dear Miss Greenaway—I have just got home and find the lovely little book and the drawing! I had carried your letter in the safest

Kate Greenaway

recess of my desk through all the cathedral towns in Picardy,—thinking every day to get away for home (Now is there any little misery of life worse than a hair in one's best pen ?), and to see my treasure, and I never *got* away ! and now what an ungrateful wretch you must think me !

But—alas—do you know you have done me more grief than good for the moment ? The drawing is so boundlessly more beautiful than the woodcut that I shall have no peace of mind till I've come to see you and seen some more drawings, and told you—face to face—what a great and blessed gift you have—too great, in the ease of it, for you to feel yourself.

These books are lovely things but, as far as I can guess, from looking at this drawing, your proper work would be in glass painting—where your own touch, your own colour, would be safe for ever,—seen, in sacred places, by multitudes—copied, by others, for story books—but *your* whole strength put in pure first perfectness on the enduring material.

Have you ever thought of this ?

Please tell me if you get this note. 1 am so ashamed of not writing before.—Ever your grateful and devoted   J. Ruskin.

John Ruskin to Kate Greenaway

Brantwood, Coniston, Lancashire,
Day after Xmas, 1880.

Dear Miss Greenaway—I have not been able to write because I want to write so much—both of thanks and petition, since your last letter. Petition—not about the promised drawing : though it will be beyond telling precious to me ; I don't want you to work, even for a moment, for *me*—but I do want you never to work a moment but in permanent material and for—' all people, who on earth do dwell.'

I have lying on the table as I write, your little Christmas card, 'Luck go with you, pretty lass.' To my mind it is a greater thing than Raphael's St. Cecilia.

But you must paint it—paint all things—well, and for ever.

Holbein left his bitter legacy to the Eternities—The Dance of Death.

Leave you yours—The Dance of Life.—Ever your grateful and glad
John Ruskin.

Towards the end of this year Stacy Marks again wrote :

. . . I will say no more now than to congratulate you on your success, in which I heartily rejoice—the more so as it does not destroy

Austin Dobson

the simplicity of your nature, or make you relax in your efforts after excellence.

You have found a path for yourself, and though you kindly think I have helped to remove some of the obstacles that beset that path, I can claim no credit myself for having done so.

The year 1880 found her still working on the *Illustrated London News*, and exhibiting and selling her pictures at the Royal Academy ('Little Girl with Fan') and the Dudley Gallery. She also made a drawing, beautifully cut by O. Lacour, for *The Library* (Macmillan), written by Mr. Andrew Lang and Mr. Austin Dobson, to be published in 1881. Concerning this Mr. Dobson wrote :

How I envy you this captivating talent. And how lucky the little people are to get such pictures! I can't help thinking that I should have been a better man if I had had such pleasant play-books in my inartistic childhood. You have a most definite and special walk, and I hope you won't let any one persuade you out of it. I have seen some imitations of you lately which convince me—if indeed I needed conviction—that you have little to fear from rivalry

This year also was published a particularly charming frontispiece to the annual volume of *Little Wide-Awake*, issued by Messrs. Routledge. Other coloured frontispieces and title-pages well worthy of the collector's attention were done for several volumes of the same firm's *Every Girl's Annual*, and *The Girl's Own Paper*. But Kate's output at this period was so great that it is impossible to do more than specify a few of her detached productions. Other events of this year were the translation of her verses in *Under the Window* into German by Frau Käthe Freiligrath-Kröker ; a request from John Hullah, whose acquaintance she had just made, to set some of her 'admirable' verses to music for a new edition of his book on 'Time and Tune'; and an invitation to contribute to the Grosvenor Gallery Exhibition.

The appearance of *Under the Window* (*Am Fenster*) in Germany was hailed with delight by the critics. Herr Trojan, writing in the *National Zeitung*, labelled it 'a small masterpiece of original stamp, out-and-out English, but acceptable to the inhabitants, great and small, of all other civilised nations.' The only objections to it in its new form were the rather too free treatment of the letterpress by the translator and the very unnecessary Germanicising of the children's names.

85

Kate Greenaway

In the same year Miss Greenaway began fully to realise the value of her drawings done for publication, and henceforward made it an inflexible rule to retain the drawings themselves and sell only the *use* of them.

But by far the most important occurrence at this time was the beginning of her personal acquaintance with Mr. Frederick Locker, better known to-day as Frederick Locker-Lampson. He had, as we know, heard of her from Mr. Evans two years earlier, in connection with her verses for *Under the Window*. Now she was to become an intimate friend of the family and a constant visitor at Rowfant and Newhaven Court. Of one of these visits she writes:

> I've been living in very distinguished society. They have a lovely house at Cromer, and it is a beautiful place—such a fine sea and such beautiful ponds and commons, also lots of beautiful houses to be seen about. I went to the most beautiful one I have ever seen—and such a garden, a perfect wonder—such flowers, it looked like June instead of September. There were many flowers I had never seen before; it was a beautiful place.

This year was also notable for what must have been a red-letter day in her life—a red-letter day, it has often been said, in the public life of anybody. Most people like the attention of polite press-notices, but who is not a little bit the prouder when 'the little rascal of Fleet Street' first considers him worthy of his flattering notice? Now for the first time Kate appeared in *Punch*, in an important drawing entitled 'Christmas is Coming!' (Dec. 4, vol. lxxix. p. 254), made by the masterly pencil of Mr. Linley Sambourne. Miss Greenaway heralded the event, or at least the preparations for it, in a letter to Mr. Frederick Locker.

KATE GREENAWAY TO FREDERICK LOCKER

27 Nov. 1880.

I heard again in a hurry from Linley Sambourne, and had to rush off yesterday in a great hurry and get a photo taken; I had to send him simply a negative. So what I shall turn out like I dare not think, even if he could use it at all. I am curious to see what is going to be made of us all—if we are going to have large heads and little bodies, or how we are going to be made funny. . . .

Frederick Locker

I really feel quite cross as I look at the shop windows and see the imitation books. It feels so queer, somehow, to see your ideas taken by some one else and put forth as theirs. I suppose next year they will be all little birthday books, in shape and sort.

[It is clear that Mr. Austin Dobson's assurances had not soothed or convinced her.]

Those little Bewick drawings haunt me—they are so wonderfully different to most that are done. It is a pity there is no way of reproducing such fine work.

In Mr. Sambourne's drawing, Mr. Punch, 'at home,' is invaded by a flight and crowd of artists, writers, and publishers of children's books—by Kate Greenaway, Caldecott, Stacy Marks, Mr. Harrison Weir, Mr. Crane, and Mrs. Sale Barker, by Messrs. Macmillan, William Marcus Ward, Bradbury, Edmund Routledge, De la Rue, Hildesheimer, Duffield, and Walker, all caterers for the little ones, 'for all children,' says *Punch*, in the accompanying text, 'are Mr. Punch's pets. Let's see what you've got,' and forthwith he gives the place of honour to Miss Kate Greenaway, and warmly congratulates her on her *Birthday Book for Children*, 'a most dainty little work and a really happy thought for Christmas.' And a mother and her children are shown listening behind the door to Mr. Punch's declaration.

This was in itself a gratifying evidence of Miss Greenaway's popularity, but that it did not give much satisfaction to her friends is demonstrated by a letter from Miss Anderson, who wrote, 'Thank you so much for sending me the *Punch*. I had the greatest difficulty in finding your portrait. What a horror! It is actionable really!' The fact is, the photograph from which the sketch was made was unflattering in the extreme.

'K. G.' was destined several times to engage *Punch's* attention, but it may safely be said that no press notice ever gave her greater pleasure than that which attended her first appearance in his pages.

Many of Kate's happiest hours were spent in Frederick Locker's company. One day they would go to the National Gallery to gloat over some of their 'darling pictures,' another day to the British Museum, or Noseda's in the Strand to discuss prints, or to Harvey's, the printseller, in St. James's Street. Another day would find them at the Flaxman Gallery ('What a Flaxman gift you have,' he said one day), or at the 'Arts and Crafts Exhibition,' at a private view of the Grosvenor Gallery, or at Colnaghi's to discuss the purchase of a mezzotint. Through him she seems to have become acquainted with Browning and his sister in 1882, and with the Tennyson family, with whom she became on intimate terms. His letters to her, which run into hundreds, teem with

FEAR GOD. & FEAR NOUGHT.

FREDERICK . LOCKER

Book-plate designed for Frederick Locker (F. Locker-Lampson) by Kate Greenaway.

advice, encouragement, and warning. In one of them (Nov. 28, 1882) he says :

It has occurred to me that you are about the only English artist who has ever been the fashion in France. Bonington and Constable are appreciated, but not more than appreciated. I think anybody writing about you should notice this important fact.

That same year she designed a book-plate for him. This was, it seems, with slight alterations reproduced as frontispiece to the edition of his *London Lyrics* published by Scribner in America.

Frederick Locker

She also did book-plates for other members of the family. Discussing them in 1892, he writes:

> There is a mystery about book-plates only known to certain initiated ones, like Lord de Tabley. They must not be pictorial and they must fulfil certain conditions. Now all that you have done for us, and they are many, fully satisfy *my* aspirations.

She also did two coloured portraits of him, now in the possession of Mrs. Locker-Lampson.

In 1883 she was amused to discover that her popularity was so great in Germany that she was claimed there as a German. Even the German poet who was her father was named, and—for Germans are nothing if not circumstantial—it was said that he was obliged to leave Germany in 1848 and went to live in England, where he was many years engaged in a house of business in the City, and that in later years he had returned to Germany. They gave the name of the street (Grüne Weg) in Düsseldorf where she lived, and stated that on publishing her first book Kate translated the name of the street into English and took it as her *nom-de-plume*! Thus is history sometimes made.

Mr. Frederick Locker-Lampson was a great admirer of her art, and when he heard that Ruskin said in 1883 that she should aim at something higher, he laconically, and wisely, warned her to 'Beware.' In the same strain he had written to her the year before :

> You must not be down-hearted about your art, or feel depressed when you gaze at Crane's productions. Each has his or her merit, and there is room for all. All I beg is, that you will not rashly change your style. Vary it, but do not change it.

This advice was called forth by the following letter :—

KATE GREENAWAY TO FREDERICK LOCKER

24 *May*, 1882,

I've been to call on the Caldecotts to-day with Mrs. Evans. My brother showed me some of his (Mr. Caldecott's) new drawings yesterday at Racquet Court. They are so uncommonly clever. The Dish running away with the Spoon—you can't think how much he has made of it. I wish I had such a mind. I'm feeling very low about

Kate Greenaway

my own powers just now, for I have been looking at the originals for the new Crane book. Some of them are literally dreams of beauty. I do wish you could see them. There is one—a long low design of a Harvest Home. I shall try, I think, to get it, but so many are so lovely it is difficult to fix on the best.

I have just got a first proof of my little Almanack (be sure you don't mention anything about it to any one except Mrs. Locker). Mr. Evans wants me to write a little verse to put on a blank page in it. I shall get you to look at it when I have done it.

He inoculated her with his irrepressible love of collecting, and when she came to have a house of her own, acted as her adviser in beautifying it. For example, he wrote in 1882 :

I saw a little Bow figure (china) to-day at the shop to which this card is the address (Fenton and Sons, Holywell Street), a figure as tall as your dancing lady that I gave you. She is in a green jacket. Look at it as you go to the National Gallery on Friday. He asks £2 : 10s. for it and you might get it for £2. It has been injured, but I rather like it, and I think it is genuine, and probably Bow or Chelsea. Now mind you go and see it or I shall be cross. It will only be five minutes out of your way. You will see it in the window.

One day he would send her 'a little stool, not a stool of Repentance, either to sit on or on which to put the books or papers you are reading'; and another day, 'a new edition of my *Lyra Elegantiarum*. It is a hideous book and costs 1s. 6d.' Another day there arrived a flower-stand, 'which comes from Venice, and I hope is decorative'; on another the *Athenæum* (Dec. 1886), which is 'full of your praises'; and on yet another day, a letter in which he says, 'I have told a man to send you two little Stothards which may or may not be pretty, but which are curious from their scarcity. One is called "Just Breeched" and the other "Giving a Bite."'

In return, she showered upon him and his family drawings and copies of her books, in addition to the considerable number which he purchased. Indeed, so generous was she in this respect that in 1883 he wrote :

I was shocked to receive [the drawing], coming as it did after the beautiful drawing you gave Mrs. Locker. Why should you waste your time on me ? It is heart-breaking to think of, when your spare

Frederick Locker

time is so valuable and you have so little of it. You must send me
no more. I say it seriously. No more. I have plenty, plenty to
remember you by, and when I am gone, enough to show my children
the kind feeling you had for me. Work away, but for yourself—for
your new house and for others more worthy.

Her gratitude for attentions paid or gifts presented was
always deeply felt, and prettily acknowledged and expressed.
Thus:

KATE GREENAWAY TO FREDERICK LOCKER

27 Aug: 1880.

. . . The beautiful little red book! I expect I was very horrid
and did not thank you at all, and you thought ' *She* is very ungrateful ;
she might have been a little pleased, when I had taken that trouble to
give her pleasure.'
When people are very very kind—well—when they are very kind,
I think I am so glad I can't say anything to tell them so. And so I
send you now very many thanks for your kindness and the pleasure
you gave me.
I think you will be pleased to know that the *Birthday Book* seems
to be going to turn out a selling success—5,000 for America, 3,000
for Germany, and the rest going off so well that they are ordering
paper for another edition. This first edition is 50,000—so I am
looking forward with rejoicing to future pounds and pennies, uncommonly nice possessions.

He was for ever begging her not to overwork herself, fearing
that her health and bread-winning powers might fail. For
example, he wrote in 1882 :

I hope when you get home you will get to work, but take it
quite easily (say two or three hours a day), and try to be beforehand
with the publishers, etc., and *not let* anything interfere with or stop
your daily moderate work.

Sometimes he feigned jealousy of her devotion to Mr. Ruskin
and others. In 1884 : 'I daresay that Ruskin is sunning his
unworthy self in your smiles. I hope he is impressed with his
good fortune.' In 1885 : 'You must let me be one of your
first visitors to the new house [at Hampstead]. What will you
call it ? The Villa Ruskin or Dobson Lodge, or what ? '

Kate Greenaway

He would get her to colour prints for him, and would watch for commissions for her.

'I saw Pears of Pears' Soap this morning,' he wrote in 1889; 'such a good fellow. Will you do something for him? I am quite serious. I think you might do it without degrading your art.'

They did not always agree in their opinions, but he could make a pretty *amende*. In 1893 he wrote :

I remember we disputed at Cromer. I was irritable and you were —irrational. That is not the right word—but you enunciated opinions that I thought were not sound, and I was stupid enough not to agree with you, for, as Prior says, *you* had the best of the argument, for '*your eyes* were always in the right.' Time is too short for these arguments, at least so I think, so let us have no more.

Occasionally they would discuss more serious topics, and a letter would be drawn from Kate with charming glimpses of self-revelation. For example :

KATE GREENAWAY TO FREDERICK LOCKER

7 *Ap*: 1881.

No, I do not feel angry with the notice of Carlyle—that, I think, expresses very much what I feel—but I do feel angry with the letter, which seems to me commonplace in the extreme, by a man of an utterly different mind. I do like, and I most sincerely hope that whilst I possess life I may venerate and admire with unstinted admiration, this sort of noble and great men. They seem to me to be so far above and beyond ordinary people, so much worth trying to be a little like— and I feel they talk to such unhearing ears. The fact is, most people like to lead the lives that are enjoyment and pleasure to themselves ; and pleasing oneself does not make a noble life. But I must *tell* you what I mean, for I never can write well. . . .

Also, when you come I want you to read a chapter in *Sartor Resartus*. It is called the *Everlasting Yea*. It is beautiful ; and it is when he has given up all selfish feeling for himself and feels in sympathy with the whole world.

Frederick Locker would write special verses for her Christmas cards. He criticised her drawings, interjecting in his letters with curious abruptness and delightful irrelevancy, as though half afraid

Frederick Locker

of his temerity, such remarks as : 'Do you think the Bride sitting under the tree is so feeble that she could not stand up?' or 'Are the young lady's arms (sitting under the tree) like cloth sausages?' and then promptly passing on to other subjects.

At her request he also criticised her verse. Here is an example :—

You ask me to do what Shelley would have had a difficulty in doing. Are you aware that your poem, as it stands, is only not prose because of the inversions? and it has neither rhythm, metre, nor rhyme, excepting 'fun' and 'done,' which is *not* a rhyme to the eye.

'Let me lie quietly in the Sunshine on God's green grass, for the laugh and fun is (? are) over and God's day is nearly done.'

I defy Shelley, or any one, to rhyme those short lines—in the childish language you want. It is not possible. You must either lengthen the lines—or allow yourself a more free and complex diction.

Something like this :

> The sun is warm, so let me lie
> And sweetly rest.
> The grass is soft and that is why
> I like it best.
> The games are over that made us gay—
> And all the fun.
> The sun is dying, so God's fair day
> Is nearly done.

Then he would advise her how to take criticism :—

You must be influenced by what the critics say up to a certain point—but not beyond. It is very annoying to be misunderstood and to see critics trying to show off their own cleverness, but you are now paying the penalty of *success*, and Tennyson suffers from it, and your friend Ruskin and Carlyle and all who make their mark in works of imagination. I *quite* feel what you say about Ruskin. There *does* seem to be a 'holiness' about his words and ideas. I am very glad he telegraphed to you, and wrote. His opinion is worth all the commonplace critics put together, and worth more than the opinion of nineteen out of twenty Royal Academicians.

Again, when one of the critics had complained of the lack of vitality and the woe-begone expression in her children's faces, he consoled her and criticised her together :—

93

Kate Greenaway

Sept. 1881.

I have been thinking over what I said about expression in your faces. I do not think it would suit the style and spirit of your pictures if they were exactly *gay* children—but at present the same sort of complaint might be made about them that is made about Burne-Jones's, and with more reason, for nearly all the subjects you treat of are cheerful, and some playful, and none are classic or tragic. There is no doubt that B.-J. is wrong and the critics are right, but still I am grateful to B.-J. and take thankfully what he gives me, and think it very beautiful, but I cannot but feel its monotony of expression. Any mirth in your pictures should be quite of the subdued kind, such as you see in those delicious pictures of Stothard. Just get out the volume that you have and look at ' Hunt the Slipper ' and many others, and you will see exactly what I want. You also see it in Reynolds, but often overdone, and more overdone in Romney and what I call the 'roguish' school. Leech has often children that look very happy without an absolute smile. You must make your faces look *happy*.

To this she replied in a letter from Pemberton Gardens :—

KATE GREENAWAY TO FREDERICK LOCKER

. . . You are quite right about the expressions. Of course, it is absurd for children to be having a game and for their faces to be plunged in the deepest despair and sadness. I shall bear it in mind, and I hope to do better in my next.

The deep colour you complain of in some is due to hurry, I'm afraid. There was no time to prove this book, and I never had any proof for correction at all, for Mr. Evans said it was impossible, it must go ; and some of the darker ones suffer in consequence. I know you imagine I'm always having them for correction, and sending them back and back again ; but that is not so. . . .

I've found a good subject for you to exercise your energy upon, namely, the Penny Postage stamp. Get the colour changed and you will confer a benefit on everybody. The old Penny Stamp was a good red. Then they changed to a worse ; and now to this detestable purple colour. I never put one on a letter without hating the sight of it. I can't tell you how bitter I feel. They ought to study colour in all things.

I feel a competent judge to-day, because I flatter myself that this morning I have executed a drawing which for colour is—is—is—too —too—too——as I look at it I feel happy. (Compare feeling for postage stamps.)

Frederick Locker

It is a girl walking a baby ; she has an orange spotted dress and a yellow hat with a green wreath round it, and the baby has a white frock with a blue sash and blue toes. Do you see the picture ?

Your little baby girl seems to me as if she ought always to wear a coral necklace and have blue bows to tie up her shoes.

To the same subject of solemn expression in her children Mr. Locker returns in 1882 :

I was looking at your sketch of the 'little giddy laugh,' and I really think it is the only figure of yours I know that has a smile on its face.

He kept a sharp eye on her employers, too, and helped her in business matters. In 1881 he wrote :

—— told me you were engaged on two works for his house, in one of which you were associated with Crane and Caldecott. Now remember you are to be treated on as handsome terms as those two gentlemen or I shall not be satisfied. We must find out what they are to receive.

When his twins were born he called upon her to paint them, embodying his request in the following charming lines :—

Yes, there they lie, so small, so quaint—
  Two mouths, two noses, and two chins—
What painter shall we get to paint
  And glorify the twins ?
To give us all the charm that dwells
  In tiny cloaks and coral bells,
And all those other pleasant spells
Of babyhood ;—and don't forget
The silver mug for either pet ;
  No babe should be without it :
Come, fairy Limner, you can thrill,
Our hearts with pink and daffodil
And white rosette and dimpled frill ;
Come paint our little Jack and Jill—
  And don't be long about it !

And sometimes Kate would take Locker in hand and talk about *his* work.

'So it is a little French poem you have been translating,' she writes. 'I wish you would do more of that sort of thing—and some new *originals* too ; then I would do the illustrations to them.'

95

Kate Greenaway

The proposal was seriously considered for a time, but never was carried into execution—at least, for publication. What happened was this. Locker-Lampson had written a number of poems on his children (published in 1881), and as a surprise present for his wife Kate Greenaway made a series of drawings in a tiny MS. volume, and the poet copied his verses on to the pages in his beautiful handwriting. This, he afterwards told Mrs. Locker-Lampson, was the most anxious experience of his life; for the drawings were done first, and he was in agony all the time lest he should make a mistake or a blot. The result of the collaboration is one of the most exquisite little *bibelots* it is possible to imagine, and the pretty title of it, 'Babies and Blossoms.'

Their delightful friendship lasted for fifteen years, and when he died in 1895 his son wrote to her: 'A son has lost the most dear father a son ever had, and friends the truest friend a friend ever had.'

An equal favourite, too, with Mrs. Locker-Lampson and with her children, to whom in 1883 she had dedicated *Little Ann*, embellishing the page with their four portraits, Miss Greenaway continued her visits after Mr. Locker-Lampson's death. She played hockey with them, and entered heartily into all their games. She 'corrected' Miss Dorothy Locker-Lampson's drawings, and she sent priceless little drawings of her own to Godfrey Locker-Lampson at Eton. Of the last of the visits one of them wrote: 'It was such tremendous fun having you here, and you so enter into our roystering spirits.' And again: 'I wish you were here to join in with your rippling laughter.'

Her attachment for her hostess was very strong, and she would write to 'My dear dear Mrs. Locker' letters full of affection and gratitude and of love for the children. At the same time she was not to be lured from her work, and in thanking Mrs. Locker for her repeated invitations and kindness—'it makes the world so much more beautiful,' she said—she firmly declined to budge; but finding it hard to refuse, she would write to Mr. Locker (April 8, 1882):

Don't let Mrs. Locker ask me to come. Do explain to her; tell her Mrs. Jeune asked me to go to see her and I was obliged to say No. And it all looks so delicious; even about here the trees are so tendrilly and pretty, and it is so sunny and holiday feeling—I long to be out

Frederick Locker

in it all. It is quite an effort to sit at the table bending over my paper. All the little children are out in the gardens and I hear their voices. I even envy the cats as they run along the wall.

She would not only illustrate her letters to Mr. and Mrs. Locker-Lampson with the little pen sketches she bestowed on her other favoured friends, she would now and again embellish them with finished water-colour drawings exquisite in quality. Of these one or two are here reproduced, but they necessarily lose most of their charm in surrendering their beauty of colour.

The last of the letters runs as follows :—

On a Letter to Mrs. Frederick Locker-Lampson.

Dear Mrs. Locker—You see me at the top doing penance in my own particular style, being, according to Mr. Locker's advice—uninfluenced by the works of others. I do not know which bear (black, white, or brown) behaves in the most bearish manner, but I feel I am of that colour ; but please forgive me and let me say thank you very much for your beautiful gift.

You must not think so much of any little sketches I do for you ; it is only my voice saying thank you for all your kindness always. The half of the candle belongs to Mr. Locker for his dear little box.

97

CHAPTER VII

1881–1882

THE EMPRESS FREDERICK, MRS. RICHMOND RITCHIE, RUSKIN,
AND MR. PUNCH—'A DAY IN A CHILD'S LIFE'—'LITTLE
ANN' AND 'MOTHER GOOSE.'

As has already been said, to drive to a palace in a royal carriage to
see a princess had been a dream of Kate's childhood; and in the
year 1881 her baby wish saw its almost complete fulfilment.
Royalties with a small 'r' were now, she said, a matter of course
to her, but of Royalties with a big 'R' she had as yet no
experience.

In her diary of engagements, the entry 'Sunday, July 17,
Crown Princess of Germany,' foretells her first visit to Buckingham Palace. Her own account is not forthcoming, but we have
hint of it in the following quotation from a letter written to her
by Mrs. Richmond Ritchie.

It was just like a fairy tale to hear of you at court with all the
nice little princes and princesses hopping about and asking you to make
enchanting things for them. Mrs. Stanley [1] says they one and all lost
their hearts to you, and to *me* for bringing you to their threshold.

To this Mrs. Ritchie adds :

I remember Miss Greenaway telling me of her visit to the Crown
Prince and Princess at Buckingham Palace, and how cordial they were,
and how the Crown Prince came in and put his hand on his wife's
shoulder and said laughing, 'I am the husband,' as he stood up like a
column by the Princess, who was a little woman.

---

[1] Now Lady St. Helier.

The Empress Frederick

This was the beginning of a friendship which did as much honour to the Imperial lady as to the artist whose worth she was so ready to recognise. Until the Empress's death Kate Greenaway's books, as often as not extra-embellished with original drawings, and her autographed Christmas cards, were always received with appreciative acknowledgments, generally accompanied by some little souvenir in return. They would be accompanied by by letters from the Count Seckendorff such as these sent by the Empress's command : [1]—

COUNT SECKENDORFF TO KATE GREENAWAY

OSBORNE, *Dec. 25th,* 1888.

Dear Miss Kate Greenaway—Her Majesty the Empress Frederick desires me to acknowledge the receipt of your charming new little book, and to say how very kind it was of you to think of her just now at Christmas time. Her Majesty is most grateful to you for your artistic little present.—Believe me, dear Miss Kate Greenaway, very sincerely yours, G. SECKENDORFF.

COUNT SECKENDORFF TO KATE GREENAWAY

THE EMPRESS FREDERICK'S PALACE,
BERLIN, *Jan. 26th,* 1895.

Dear Miss Greenaway—You have had the kindness to send Her Majesty the Empress Frederick such a charming little drawing for Christmas. Her Majesty was delighted with it. The little Almanack is giving her so much pleasure. Will you kindly accept in return a new photo of Her Majesty which I am sending by Royal Messenger to-day?—Believe me, dear Miss Greenaway, very sincerely yours, G. SECKENDORFF.

Of one of these presents Ruskin wrote on December 30, 1884 :

I liked hearing about the present from [the] Princess. I wonder what it can be. I wish I was a Prince and could send you pearls and rubies.

At one time the Empress Frederick showed a personal sympathy not indicated by these formal letters, and during the

---

[1] For authorisation to reproduce these letters we are indebted to the German Ambassador.

Kate Greenaway

period of her great sorrow wrote to Miss Greenaway touchingly and at length ; but that correspondence no longer exists.

About this time Miss Greenaway was introduced at the house of the Hon. Mrs. Stanley to the Princess Christian, whose appreciation of her both personally and as an artist is shown in several letters from this year onwards, preserved by her with affectionate care.

As Mrs. Richmond Ritchie's name has been mentioned, it should be said that for years she and Kate Greenaway were on terms of close intimacy, and although they were not able so frequently to meet in later years, there was always the most cordial regard and love between them. In 1885 there was talk of their 'doing a story together,' but it never came to anything ; yet the idea had evidently been long in their heads, for in 1881 Mrs. Ritchie had written : 'When we write our book it shall be called " Treats," I think, and be all about nice things that happen to little girls— don't you think so ?' It is matter for regret that a proposal so full of charming possibilities was never carried into execution.

In the same year Routledge & Sons published *Mother Goose, or The Old Nursery Rhymes, Illustrated by Kate Greenaway*—one of her daintiest productions, although marred in several instances by crude printer's ink and careless register. Its success, though not equalling that of the *Birthday Book*, was yet very great, 66,000 copies being printed in English, German, and French. The sum of £252 was paid to her for the use of the drawings, and in royalties she received over £650. The book bears on the title-page the baby thrown into a basket of roses which so took Ruskin's fancy. As Mrs. Allingham has said, 'No one could draw roses like Kate Greenaway,' and other critics have compared her drawing of flowers with the work now of Van Huysum and now of Botticelli. Some papers complained that some of the nursery rhymes had been unduly tampered with ; but the illustrations met everywhere with the most cordial praise. An enthusiastic critic exclaimed, 'Should the children of the present generation happen to take into their little curly heads to call together a " monster " meeting—say in the Lowther Arcade—and propose, second, and resolve to erect a great public monument to some favourite goddess, we have a strong conviction that, on a show of tiny hands being taken, the chairman would declare that Miss Kate Greenaway had been unanimously elected for the honour.' It should be remembered that 'correct versions' of nursery rhymes and tales

'A Day in a Child's Life'

vary in different parts of the country, and that every one considers the version of his childhood the true one. Kate Greenaway naturally adopted those she had learnt in London or in Nottinghamshire, and the charge of 'tampering' falls to the ground.

This year she also contributed a charming frontispiece entitled 'Little Fanny' to *Routledge's Christmas Number*, which should not be forgotten by the collector. It was a wonderful shilling's worth for those days, and including as it does contributions by Caldecott, Gustave Doré (then at the zenith of his somewhat evanescent fame), Griset, and Mr. Walter Crane, it is now something of a *trouvaille*.

Another trifle of this year which should not be overlooked is a tail-piece, 'Little Dinky,' done for Locker-Lampson's privately produced selection of his *London Lyrics*.

Kate was now hard at work on the illustrations for *A Day in a Child's Life, Illustrated by Kate Greenaway, Music by Myles B. Foster*, to be published by Messrs. Routledge in 1882.

Concerning its origin Mr. Foster—son of the eminent water-colour painter, Birket Foster—writes:

If I remember rightly, I had already put the whole thing together, and, in fact, I had suggested this as a happy 'follow' to *The Children's Christmas*, by Bob and myself. It seemed such a nice subject for children's music. I culled from books Nos. 1, 3, 4, 5, and 8, asked my friend M. Gibney to write 'Tired,' compounded the rhymes of 'The Lesson' and 'Sleeping' myself, and then showed the whole thing, already set to music, to Mr. Evans, and *he* suggested sending it to K. G., saying that if she liked the idea, she would illustrate it. That I believe to be the commencement. At this time some hundreds of mill-hands at Keighley in Yorkshire and at Holt in Wiltshire were finding pleasure in *The Children's Christmas*, and the thought of their wishes and little needs largely led me on to the work in question, and they performed the *Day in a Child's Life* very prettily in tableaux. It was followed each year by a new work (with my own words)—*Cinderella, Beauty and the Beast, Lampblack*, etc.—but, alas, all these lacked the charm of Kate Greenaway's exquisite art.

Commercially considered, this extremely pretty book was a success, 25,000 copies being issued to the English-speaking world alone, yet the press was not unanimous in its approval. The *Times* especially complained that 'Miss Greenaway seems to be lapsing into rather a lackadaisical prettiness of style. Her

Kate Greenaway

little people are somewhat deficient in vitality. On the whole, we fear we can hardly, for all its prettiness of binding and colouring, recommend her *Day in a Child's Life* as a very cheerful present, nor is the selection of songs which she has illustrated of a much more stimulating order.'

This year on no fewer than three separate occasions *Punch* again turned his attention to Miss Greenaway, all within the space of one month. On December 10, under the heading 'Punch's "Mother Hubbard" Grinaway Christmas Cards,' Mr. Harry Furniss gave a full-page drawing of fourteen grouped cards, the first of which represented Mr. Punch presenting a Christmas card to the Queen and Royal Family, all, saving Her Majesty, being dressed in Greenaway costumes. John Bright appears as Little Jack Horner, picking a 70th plum out of his birthday pie; the Duke of Cambridge in petticoats is riding a cock-horse; Mr. (Lord) Cross as Jack—Jill is in the background—has tumbled down with a pail of 'Thames Water Bill'; Lord Randolph Churchill, as Little Tommy Tattlemouse, is haranguing 'a little house' from the box of the Fourth Party; Sir John Millais is trying a glass slipper on the foot of his own 'Cinderella'; the Duke of Bedford, as 'Mary Mudford quite contrary,' is appreciatively contemplating the untidiness and inhaling the perfume of Covent Garden market; Mr. Fawcett, postmaster-general, as 'Spring-heeled Jack,' is taking a flying leap over the telegraph wires; Mr. Parnell, as the wolf in bed, casts his ogreish eyes on the little figure of Ireland and her basket of neglected Irish Industry; Mr. Gladstone, as the 'Jack,' is chopping down the beanstalk of the Land League; Sir Whittaker Ellis, the new Lord Mayor of London, as Dick Whittington, is issuing invitations from the Mansion House; and other topics of the day are introduced with similar ingenuity.

On December 17, Mr. Linley Sambourne contributed one of his most highly finished drawings, entitled 'The Royal Birthday Book.' Mr. Punch, kneeling in court-dress, receives *Princess Beatrice's Birthday Book* from the Princess herself, an ideally and delightfully draped figure wearing coronet and sandals, the central figure of the composition. Toby stands on guard, crayon-holder in hand, while on the clouds, prominent among other floating figures, like sympathetic familiars, are Kate Greenaway (in Kate Greenaway costume), Caldecott, and Mr. Walter Crane.

102

' Punch '

The accompanying legend runs :

> The Christmas volumes well deserve their gains
> Of Caldecott's, Kate Greenaway's, and Crane's.
> Fair Beatrice, we thank you for your pains.
> *Much Ado About Something,* Act ii. Sc. 3
> (Mr. Punch's Version).

And finally, on December 24, Mr. Furniss gave a second series of four 'Grinaway Christmas Cards,' in which Mr. Edison figures as Aladdin, Britannia as Old Mother Hubbard, Mrs. Langtry as the Sleeping Beauty, and Irving, Ellen Terry, Mrs. Kendal, Charles Warner, Nellie Farren, Bancroft, Toole, Brough, and others as the Girls and Boys coming out to Play. It was all excellent fooling—another indication, if one were needed, that Kate Greenaway's name and method were name and method to conjure with.

The following letter of this year from a highly distinguished authoress who wishes to preserve her anonymity gives a vivid idea of the pleasure which her books brought into innumerable homes :—

October 10, 1881.

Dear Miss Greenaway—Your sweet little white sibylline volumes have again come to delight us all—thank you so very much. H. (aged 3 years) came bundling down, panting, with her book in her pinafore and wildly excited. (I think on the whole she likes 'Jumping Joan' best—but she likes each best.) B. (aged 1½) came in also breathless to look at H.'s book. H. firmly said, 'No, B., you may just look, you mustn't *touch* it.' Then B. was held down by force and we lit the candles, and H. looked at her prize while I looked at mine with B. (only B. and H. *couldn't* understand how the two books could be so exactly alike). Then R. came home and we all exclaimed together, and now we all send you our love and our thanks, dear, again for your beautiful gift.

Are you rested and stronger? Did you have a pleasant summer? We are only just home from a great many clouds and fields and children and dandelions, to find them all again in your sweet incantation.

L. T. told us about your Princesses' visits, which was most thrilling and interesting. Good-night, and thank you again for all of us.

At this time Kate was sending copies of her *Mother Goose* to a few chosen friends, among them to her kind mentor and

103

Kate Greenaway

chief adviser H. Stacy Marks; and the presentation brought her the following critical letter of acknowledgment :—

Oct. 11th, 1881.

Dear Kate Greenaway—Many thanks for your last book. You will get 'tired' of sending me your works sooner than I of receiving them. I have not acknowledged the receipt of this before because I knew you would prefer a letter telling you what I think of your work (even if somewhat critical) to a mere formal one of thanks. I thank you all the same very much, for your work always gives me pleasure—it seems so happy and so fearless of all the conventional rules and ideas that obtain generally about the art.

In many respects you have improved, and the *drawing* is firmer and better. But let me have my fault-finding first, for 'I am nothing if not critical.' You have got rid of the spur-like shadows, but where, even in England, do you see such cabbagy trees as on pages 5, 7, 29 ? You might find a better pattern even in the elm, which *is* cabbagy.

The action of the figure on page 40 is impossible coming down-hill—how about the centre of gravity, madam ? You know I am not conventional, but I am troubled to know why you don't make the hero of your story more conspicuous. Thus on page 47 Tom the Piper's son is the least prominent figure in the composition, and where are the boys ?

Again—the Beggars coming to town are in the far distance, and there's only one dog ! What I mean is, that these two don't tell their story, but I suppose you have some good reason for your treatment.

As instances of fearlessness, I admire the pluck which can place a face directly against a window with each pane made out as on page 12, and the arrangement of the stick in Jack Horner which coincides with his *head* and *both hands*, and as it (the stick) is not continued to the ground we can only suppose it to be resting on the boy's knees.

And now I have done being disagreeable. Despite its little faults, it is a charming book. Your backgrounds of old houses are delightful. The two most pictorial drawings are 'Polly, put the kettle on' and 'Cross-patch.' The latter is especially good and might be painted—the right fore-arm only should be a bit more foreshortened.

A last look gives me a last fault to find—the chins, especially in some of the boys, are still very pointed.

There ! now I have finished, but I don't apologise for telling you the truth from my point of view, because I know you are strong enough to bear it and amiable enough to like it. It will always be a source of

'Little Ann'

pride to me to remember (as you told me) that I was, though in the humblest way, partly instrumental in finding you the way your strength lay.

Ruskin received his copy in a less critical spirit; and a few weeks later he wrote:

JOHN RUSKIN TO KATE GREENAWAY

BRANTWOOD, CONISTON,
Christmas Day, 1881.

My dear Miss Greenaway—You are the first friend to whom I write this morning; and among the few to whom I look for real sympathy and help. You are fast becoming–I believe you are already, except only Edward B. Jones–the helpfullest in showing me that there are yet living souls on earth who can see beauty and peace and Goodwill among men–and rejoice in them.

You have sent me a little choir of such angels as are ready to sing, if we will listen, for Christ's being born–every day.

I trust you may long be spared to do such lovely things, and be an element of the best happiness in every English household that still has an English heart, as you are already in the simpler homes of Germany.

To my mind Ludwig Richter and you are the only real philosophers and ——[1] of the Nineteenth Century.

I'll write more in a day or two about many things that I want to say respecting the possible range of your subjects. I was made so specially happy yesterday by finding Herrick's Grace among the little poems–but they are all delightful.—Ever gratefully and affectionately yours,   J. RUSKIN.

The year 1882 was chiefly occupied with the illustrations for a new edition of that early love of hers, *Little Ann and other Poems*, by Jane and Ann Taylor, a charming production, though slightly marred by certain little faults of drawing which, with all her strict self-training, Miss Greenaway strangely enough never quite overcame. The 'stilt-like' shadows had certainly disappeared, but the feet still sometimes went a little astray, and signs were not wanting here and there that seem to herald the advent of mannerism. But it was a passing phase.

She was now suffering more than ever from imitators, to the vast indignation of her friends and admirers. For example,

---

[1] This word is illegible.

Kate Greenaway

Mr. Locker designates a book entitled *Afternoon Tea* 'a shameful imitation of your manner, [which] if it goes on will tend to disgust the brutal British public and therefore injure you.'

In Belgium especially, where she had a great vogue, not only were her books themselves being imitated, but the illustrations were copied without acknowledgment on to handkerchiefs, plates, vases, caskets, and other objects of commerce, and the copying was so vilely done that they were caricatures rather than reproductions of her work. All this tended, as Mr. Locker truly predicted, to vulgarise the Fairyland which she was creating.

As far as she could Kate combated the evil by refusing to part with the copyright of her works. In 1898 she wrote to Mr. Stuart M. Samuel, M.P., a generous patron for whom she would certainly have strained a point if she could:

> Thank you so very much for the cheque, but I'm so sorry I cannot give you the copyright. I have made it a rule for a long time not to part with the copyright of my drawings, for I have been so copied, my drawings reproduced and sold for advertisements and done in ways I hate.

Nor was Belgium the only offending land. In France and England there were also many manufacturers who recognised the adaptability of her designs for printed fabrics and did not hesitate to 'lift' them for their own purposes. Still, there were honourable exceptions among those who were not prepared to copy or adapt her productions without receiving due permission and offering pecuniary acknowledgment. The offers of most of these, however, she did not care to accept, from a feeling that the 'pot-boiling' character of the work would be derogatory to her art. But apropos of an application by Mr. Powell, of the Whitefriars glassworks, it may be mentioned that the very next year Ruskin himself carried out his expressed intention, and had a drawing of hers of a little girl with a doll 'put on glass,' and wrote of it from Brantwood:

> It will be a nursery window when you are next here, but it might be, as rightly, part of a cathedral window.

A gratifying episode of 1882 was the appearance in the great French art magazine, the *Gazette des Beaux-Arts* (vol. i. pp. 74 *et seq.*) of an article by Monsieur Alfred de Lostalot, in which, whilst recognising particulars in which her work fell short of

Miss Lily Evans

that of Caldecott and Mr. Walter Crane, he yet gave her the
first place for the special qualities of charm and sentiment. And,
after a eulogy too long to quote here, he ends up quaintly—
'Meanwhile I shall lock up the works of W. C., of C., and of
Kate Greenaway in my bookcase with precious care ; unexpected
conclusion : works so precious cannot be left in the hands of
children !'

Kate Greenaway knew exactly what kind of letters children like

On a Letter to Miss Lily Evans.

to receive, and she loved to send them playful missives, instinct with
her love of flowers and animals. An example of such letters,
addressed to the little friend for whom she had so tender an
affection, may be given in illustration.

KATE GREENAWAY TO MISS LILY EVANS

My dear Lily—I have not written to fix a day because I felt I
ought not to spare one just now—or indeed for a little time longer.

Now will you mind waiting a little longer, then my mind will be
more at rest, and we will have a real beautiful day. I'm very sorry

Kate Greenaway

to ask you to wait, but I know you won't mind really. Also more things will be up in the garden and in my boxes of dirt. [Window-boxes for plants, which Miss Evans, as a country child, had never seen before.] I am just going to get pansies in them.

I've a real hope that I do see golden rod coming up at last—or does a witch live in our garden, and is it phlox after all?

Some time after Easter, when you have time to spare, you will get me some more primroses. Those last were real beauties, and lived like anything. In the excitement of coming away I quite forgot to thank Miss —— for all the trouble she took helping to get them for me, so you thank her now.

The kitten has hurt its foot a little. The spring gets into its head and I'm afraid causes it to run on walls with broken glass on the top, or perhaps it attends a dancing class on the quiet and practises too much. Anyhow it is constantly making itself lame, and when it loses the use of a sponge and towel at one go, you can guess how it looks—a little rim of white round its mouth and the rest nicely toned. Good-bye. Love to E. and all, and we will go as soon as ever I can.
K. G.

From a Pencil Sketch in the possession of Lady Pontifex.

CHAPTER VIII

1882 (*continued*) AND 1883

THE RUSKIN AND SEVERN FRIENDSHIP RIPENS—AT BRANTWOOD
—'THE ART OF ENGLAND'—RUSKIN'S ADVICE—KATE GREEN-
AWAY'S FIRST ALMANACK—A GREENAWAY 'BOOM'—MR.
AUSTIN DOBSON.

RUSKIN, as has been seen, took the art of Kate Greenaway very
seriously long before she became personally known to him, and it
is evident, from the portion of a letter found amongst her papers,
probably forwarded to her by the recipient, that he had some
hesitation in opening the correspondence which began after the
dinner with Stacy Marks. The fragment, which runs as follows,
bears no indication either of the recipient's name or of the occasion
of the writing ; but in all probability it was addressed to Mr. Stacy
Marks himself, their common friend.

It is a feeling of the same kind which keeps me from writing to
Miss Greenaway–the oftener I look at her designs, the more I want
a true and deep tone of colour,–and a harmony which should distinctly
represent either sunshine, or shade, or true local colour.—I do not
know how far with black outline this can be done but I would fain
see it attempted. And also I want her to make more serious use of
her talent–and show the lovely things that *are, and* the terrible which
ought to be known instead of mere ugly nonsense, like that brown witch.[1]
—If she would only do what she naturally feels, and would wish to
teach others to feel without any reference to saleableness–she probably
would do lovelier things than any one could tell her–and I could not

---

[1] The lurid and dramatic witch in *Under the Window.*

tell her rightly unless I knew something of her own mind, even what might be immediately suggestive to her, unless perhaps harmfully. Please tell me your own feeling about her things.   J. R.

A correspondence, however, ensued, which led up, on December 29, 1882, to this laconic but all-important entry in her diary : 'Mr. Ruskin came. First time I ever saw him.' His advent had been heralded by the following letter :—

JOHN RUSKIN TO KATE GREENAWAY

27th, Dec. 82.

Dear Miss Greenaway—Friday will do delightfully for me,–even better than to-day–having been tired with Xmas letters and work.

This is a lovely little book–all through–the New and Old Years are chiefly delightful to me. But I wish some of the children had bare feet–and that the shoes of the others weren't *quite* so like mussel-shells.

The drawing on my letter however is perfect ! shoes and all–eyes and lips–unspeakable.—Ever your grateful and devoted

J. RUSKIN.

From the first moment of their meeting a friendship sprang up which grew in strength and mutual appreciation until his death in 1900.

Concerning this interesting first meeting Mrs. Arthur Severn writes :—

I shall never forget his rapturous delight at first making her acquaintance !—and she was indeed one of the sweetest, kindest, and most gifted of women. Lily [Miss Severn] was devoted to her, and we often talk of her and deeply lament her loss. She loved nothing more here [at Coniston] than driving, and was almost childish in the delight it gave her, and with no fear of the horses—and yet she was so timid in other ways.

Henceforth not only did Ruskin and Kate Greenaway con-stantly meet either at Hampstead or at Brantwood, where she paid him several delightful visits, but they carried on a spirited correspondence, which on his side certainly ran to five hundred letters, and on hers to probably double that number. For when, in 1888, illness compelled him to cease writing, Kate made it her kindly business to continue her frequent missives in order to add

'A CALM IN A TEA-CUP.'

Kate Greenaway
26th March
1891

OUT FOR A WALK.

'LUCY LOCKET LOST HER POCKET.'

TWO GIRLS GOING TO SCHOOL.

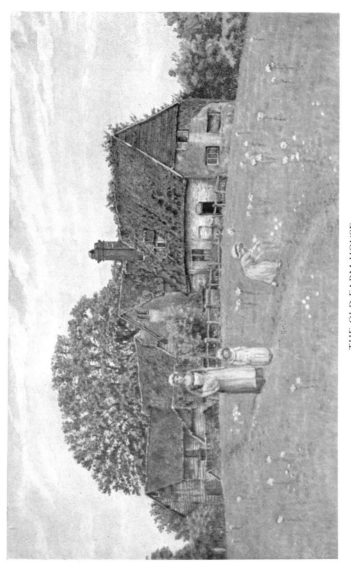

THE OLD FARM-HOUSE.

THE RED BOY.

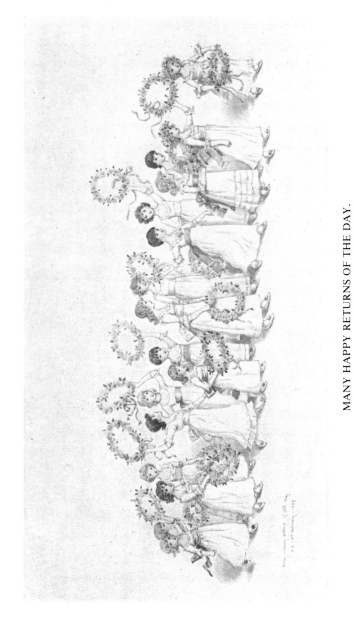

MANY HAPPY RETURNS OF THE DAY.

THE CHERRY WOMAN.

27th Dec. 82

Dear Miss Greenaway

Friday will do delightfully
for me. — even better than today
— having been tired with Xmas
letters & work

This is a lovely little book —
all through — the New and Old
years are chiefly delightful to
me. But I wish some of the
children had bare feet — and
that the shoes of the others
weren't quite so like mussel-shells

The drawing on my letter — however
is perfect! shoes and all — Eyes and
lips — unspeakable!

Ever your grateful and devoted
J Ruskin

Kate Greenaway

to the pleasures and relieve the monotony of a comparatively inactive old age. And in order to amuse and delight him, she illustrated nearly every letter with one sketch at least. A number of these little fancies of her pen have here been reproduced.

Ruskin's letters are full of allusions to his overworked condition, but while fully alive to the golden rule, 'When you have too much to do, don't do it,' he never applied it to himself, and in the end he had to pay the penalty which Nature exacts.

By the kindness of Mr. Ruskin's executors and literary executors—Mrs. Arthur Severn, Mr. George Allen, and Mr. A. Wedderburn, K.C.—we are enabled to take a specified tithe of his side of the correspondence. In the main, his letters will be left to speak for themselves, for the discussion of the side-lights which they throw upon *Præterita* and other of his writings, interesting though it would be, would lead us too far astray.

Miss Greenaway appears to have kept every scrap of Ruskin's writing, and even treasured the numerous telegrams which he sent her on special occasions ; for Ruskin loved the telegraph. He, on the other hand, observant of his own dictum in *Sesame and Lilies*—' Our friends' letters may be delightful or necessary to-day : whether worth keeping or not is to be considered '—seems to have destroyed all of hers save one, which were received prior to 1887. A large proportion of her letters, as has been said, are embellished with charming head- and tail-pieces, to which he makes constant allusion. In her diary for February 8, 1883, appears for the first time the entry ' Birthday J. R.' Henceforward the day is always so marked, and—a sacred memory to her—is so continued even after his death.

In March she received an invitation to Coniston, and she wrote to Mrs. Severn, Ruskin's cousin and adopted daughter, to accept.

11 PEMBERTON GARDENS, HOLLOWAY, N.,
8 *March* 1883.

Dear Mrs. Severn—You are very very kind, and Mr. Ruskin is very very kind, and I look forward with very great pleasure to the time I shall pass with you. . . . And, please, you are not to make so much of me, for I am not in the least a frog Princess. Wouldn't it be nice if I were, to emerge suddenly, brilliant and splendid ?

In May she paid her first visit to Brantwood, and found herself all at once plunged into an atmosphere of thought and art

The Ruskin Friendship

and literature which was to her alike new and exhilarating. That she was somewhat bewildered by her new experiences is shown by the following quotations from letters to Mrs. Evans and her daughter :—

Kate Greenaway to Mrs. Evans

It was all altered (my coming here) in such a hurry, and since I have been here I have had so little time, or I should have written sooner, but the days do go. After breakfast I am allowed (which is a great favour) to go into the study and see all sorts of beautiful things, with little talks and remarks from Mr. Ruskin as he writes ; then we go drives, walks, or on the lake till tea-time. Then it is dinner-time ; then he reads us something nice or talks in the most beautiful manner. Words can hardly say the sort of man he is—perfect—simply. . . . I do not know yet when I shall come home—they want me to stay a month, but I shall not stay nearly so long as that.

And again :

Everything is confused, I never know day or date. I'm always looking at books or pictures. I am absorbed into a new world altogether. I'm sorry to say it has turned so wet ; we have to stay in and there are no more hills or lake or streams. I shall be up next week. I'm feeling very bad that I am not up now, but Mr. Ruskin wants me to stay, wants me to tell him things about colour, and puts it in such a way I can't well leave, and the few days won't make much difference.

On her return home she writes to Miss Lily Evans :—

My dear Lily—Enjoyments seem pouring in upon you—mine are over for a time—for you see I am home again, and it was so lovely up there, you can't think. You know how I admire things—well I did such a lot. There was such lots to admire—such wild wide stretches of country and then such mountains—such mossy trees and stones— such a lake—such a shore—such pictures—such books—my mind was entirely content and satisfied, and I miss it all so much, and grumble and grumble like you did when you came home from Scarborough.

Johnny was the worm that bore it for a while, then he turned, and said I just wanted taken to a road in the East End of London for a while—then I should have all the ridiculous nonsense knocked out of my head and look upon Hampstead [1] with gratitude.—*I daresay.* It's all very fine, isn't it ? when you just come home.

---

[1] The Greenaways were contemplating moving from Holloway to Hampstead.

Kate Greenaway

And really you are coming out, dining out at the B. F.'s[1] really ! I've just got a little note with

To meet the PRINCE and PRINCESS CHRISTIAN.

Mrs. JEUNE.

At Home.   Early.

Quite fashionable ! I think I'll pass it on to you. You shall be K. G. for once, for you are coming out and growing up quite dreadfully. Where is Caroline now ? [Miss Lily Evans' favourite doll]. But it don't matter, for you're very like the old Lily after all.

So good-bye, dear, with my dearest love.   K. G.

This year (1883) Ruskin accepted his second call to the Oxford Professorship, which had been interrupted in 1879 by ill-health, and forthwith he gave his first series of lectures on 'The Art of England,' already quoted from. The following extracts from letters to Kate dated 'Oxford, 11th May '83' and 'Herne Hill, 17th May '83,' hint at his forthcoming lecture on 'Mrs. Allingham and Kate Greenaway.'

I only got here this afternoon out of Derbyshire, and found your lovely little note waiting and it made me partly happy–and partly sorry–but chiefly the first–for indeed I look forward to your working at Coniston without any acute sense of being tortured next time–when you really can get settled on those stones—(which are much better drawn than any you ever did before)—and I can stay to keep the cows in order ! My old Chamouni guide told me once I was fit for nothing else.

I can't write a word but this to-night.—I'll think over the drawing-cleaning ; perhaps it will be safest to trust it only to you–there's plenty of time, for *your* lecture isn't till the 23rd,—we shall have had our tea long before that.

I can't part with the drawings to be india Rd [india-rubbered] —having them by me helps me so, and I'm going to put those which I show—(I'm only going to show what I *speak* of, to prevent carelessness in looking) under raised mounts which will quite hide soiled edges.

I am very anxious to know what you have been thinking about— colour, and skies, since you got over the first indignation at my tyrannies !—and I've ever so much to say about the daughter of Heth[2]

---

[1] Birket Fosters.   [2] William Black's novel, published in 1871.

114

The Ruskin Friendship

—this chiefly, that you never need think I can like a tragic novel—
and this is either teazing or tragedy all through.

The Scotch too, is execrable—and all the younger brothers are
merely like bolsters in a pantomime—put there to be kicked or tumbled
over. Black *has* some quiet sense of humour in more refined elements
—but is merely clumsy in pantomime.

So many thanks for the large print—but the next you choose *must*
be cheerful.

On June 7th, he writes from Herne Hill :—

You are *not* to put any more sugar-plums of sketches in your
letters—as if they weren't sweet enough without. Besides, I can't
have you wasting your time and wits in that scattered dew of fancy.—
You must really gather yourself into a real rivulet between banks in
perspective—and reflect everything truly that you see.

You absurd Kate to think I was tired of the drawings. I was only
tired of seeing the corners unfinished—you're nearly as bad as me, that
way. Now be a good girl and draw some flowers that won't look as if
their leaves had been in curlpapers all night—and some more chairs than
that one chair—with the shade all right and the legs all square—and
then I'll tell you what you must do next.

Again on the 15th, from Oxford :—

I'm thinking of you every day and a great part of the day long,
whenever I get out into the fields, more and more anxious every day
that you should resolve on a summer's work of utter veracity—drawing
—no matter what,—*but* as it *is*.

I am certain all your imagination would expand afterwards, like—
a rosebud. But especially I do want some children as they are,
—and that you should be able to draw a pretty one without mittens,
and that you should be more interested in phases of character. I want
your exquisite feeling given to teach—not merely to amuse.

Miss Alexander's book [1] will delight you—but it is *all* chiaroscuro—
or rather chiar with no oscuro—while you will always think and see
in colour.

I'm going to do a bit of 'Kate' glass—directly, for some English
hall in fairyland.

You'll soon have proof of the lecture on you !

---

[1] By his American friend, Miss Francesca Alexander, the exquisite artist of *The
Roadside Songs of Tuscany* and the charming writer and poet who to this day with her
mother are residents of Florence, famous for their charity, kindliness, and hospitality.

Kate Greenaway

On June 17th, he writes from Oxford :—

What a lovely little bit of dark grounded grace! and the two pencils are delicious—but the feet *are* getting *too* small.

It's delightful to me beyond telling that you do yourself feel the need of a time of obedience to the 'everlasting Yea' of Things.—What I meant by phases of character was—in painting, what Scott or Shakespeare give in words,—the differences in loveliness which are endless in humanity. Those little girls who were playing at being in church must have been so different from little girls who were tormented by being at church.

Yes, it is very sad that I can't get done here,—but there are three years of absence to redeem, and being allowed in my own department to have my own way entirely, it is a very stringent duty to do the best I can. And just think what the arrangements of a system of teaching in connection with a great University means, or *should* mean.

I have mounted, for the present, 25 of the Mother Goose drawings beside the plates, and put them in a cabinet by themselves, among our loan series. People are immensely interested in them, and feel the difference between drawing and plate quite as you would like them to. Every drawing has its own sliding frame and glass so that they are *absolutely* safe, as far as handling is concerned.

On a Letter to Ruskin.

You must hear a little more about Miss A.'s before you see them; I shall very soon have a proof of lecture for you.

And from Brantwood on the 22nd :—

What lovely, lovely things these are, that have come to-day—the tambourine and the looking out to sea.—But your own eyes ought to have been three times as big—on your eyes be it—and I don't understand the doggie carrying the maulstick—because I've never seen you with a pet in a blue riband—and the first thing I should have done would have been to order the feathers out of your hat ! . . .

It was nice, that, of the gentleman and friendship—and yet it wasn't. How dogged the English are in thinking that you can't praise anybody honestly.

I got tired at Oxford and had to run down here for some rest—but shall be up again in a week or two and I hope in the mean time to get some things organised for engraving some of the line sketches

The Ruskin Friendship

in line, and the moment this bad weather is past, I shall expect to hear of the progress of the River. I saw a boy in a brown jacket with a yellow basket in his hand–looking up wistfully at the sky–in the main street of Worcester–he wanted only a Kate to draw him and would have been immortal.

At the end of June Monsieur Ernest Chesneau had written to Ruskin asking him for K. G.'s portrait and particulars of her life for an article in a French publication. Alluding to this he writes from Brantwood on July 4th,

> I kept the portrait till I could scarcely bear to part with it. But it's gone to-day,—and I've wreaked my jealousy on M. Chesneau by three pages of abuse of the whole French nation and Academy.

By this time enthusiastic admirers among foreign critics were many. There were M. Arsène Alexandre and M. Jules Girardin of Paris, Dr. Muther of Breslau, M. A. C. Loffelt, art-critic of the Dutch Journal, *The Fatherland*, and Dr. J. Zurcher of Amsterdam. And Karl Emich, Count of Leiningen-Westerburg, was among the keenest of them all. Even so Parisian a personage as Alexandre Dumas *fils*, who in 1881 had acquired one of her pictures, was sensitively responsive to her essentially English art. The agent through whom he purchased the drawing wrote to her :—' Your talent is still more appreciated in Paris than in London. A proof of it is that all the *imitations* made of your works, which are sold here, have not any success in Paris at all, where something else but nice book-binding is required '—the suggestion being that, unlike the thick-headed Saxon, the artistic Gaul could discriminate unfailingly between the original and imitations—a two-edged compliment which Kate might appreciate as best she could.

Ruskin was much concerned at Kate Greenaway's occasional lack of the sense of form. He did not want her to study anatomy, but was for ever begging her in his letters to make studies from the nude figure as the only way. But on this matter she was stubborn : she had had enough of nude studies at her own studio and at Heatherley's. Here are two of his numerous letters on the subject :—

BRANTWOOD [1883].

I'm beginning *really* to have hopes of you. This terrific sunset shows what a burden those red and yellow wafers have been on your

117

Kate Greenaway

conscience. Now, do be a good girl for once, and send me a little sunset as you know *now* how to do it—reversing everything you used to do.

—Then secondly,—I'm in great happiness to-day thinking that M. Chesneau must have got that lovely Kate this morning, and be in a state words won't express the ecstasy of. Then thirdly—As we've got so far as taking off hats, I trust we may in time get to taking off just a little more—say, mittens—and then—perhaps—even—shoes!—and (for fairies) even—stockings—And—then—

My dear Kate,—(see my third lecture sent you to-day)—it *is* absolutely necessary for you to be—now—sometimes, Classical.— I return you—though heartbrokenly (for the day)—one of those three sylphs, come this morning.

Will you—(it's all for your own good!) make her stand up, and then draw her for me without her hat—and, without her shoes,— because of the heels) and without her mittens, and without her—frock and its frill? And let me see exactly how tall she is—and how—round. [Note written in pencil: 'Do nothing of the kind. J. R. S.'] It will be *so* good of—and for—you—And to, and for—me.

After finishing this letter, he has turned it over and written:—

Finished right side yesterday. Posted 6th. That naughty Joan got hold of it—never mind her—you see, she doesn't like the word 'round'—that's all.

Who, conversant with Miss Greenaway's work, can doubt that Ruskin's advice was entirely right and sound?

Ruskin to Kate Greenaway

Brantwood, 10*th July* /83.

You really are as good as gold—heavenly gold of the clouds, to be so patient—and to send me such lovely things—but I'll try to make them of real use to you with the *public.*—The cloud fairies are LOVELY and I'll have them put in a glass window the moment I'm sure of my workman.—(I'm waiting in great anxiety for the result of the first trial—I am not anxious about the colour—but about the drawing of the features and hair exactly right on the larger scale.) And so also the milkgirl, *tidied* the least bit about the feet, shall be glassed—in better than mirror.

The sunset is a delight to me and all that you say of what you

The Ruskin Friendship

used to feel, and will again. All that is necessary is some consistent attention to the facts of colour and cloud form.—Make slight pencil memoranda of these, the next pretty one you see. Have you a small sketch-book always in your pocket?

You ought to make notes of groups of children, and of more full faces than you—face—usually. The profile is becoming conventional.

I have never told you about Villette *etc.*—They are full of clever-ness but are extremely harmful to you in their morbid excitement; and they are entirely third-rate as literature.—You should read nothing but Shakespeare, at present.

—And—you should go to some watering place in August with fine sands, and draw no end of bare feet,—and—what else the Graces unveil in the train of the Sea Goddess.

Again on the same subject he writes on the 26th,

I want you to go to Boulogne and take a course of fishwives and wading children.

And once more :—

The dancing girls are delightful but you *are* getting a little mannered and I shall press you hard for sea study. No winter work will take its place. I want the blue of the sea for you and the running action of the bare feet.

RUSKIN TO KATE GREENAWAY

BRANTWOOD, [*Sept.*] 6*th*, [1883].

What a lovely letter I've got this morning! I can't but think that lake-pond must be a divine one I know between Dorking and St. Catherine's, Guildford—the springs of it, and indeed *any* chalk springs at their rising, beat *our* rainfall streams all to mud, they are so celestially purified by their purgatory under the chalk. Also *they* are of *green* water! while ours are—*purple*!!!

If only, some day, *next year* you could come fresh to them *with* a sketch-book!

But all you have been seeing is boundlessly helpful and good for you, and the motives of the sketches you send to-day are unsurpassable and I must have you carry them out when you get to work again.

The news of Scarborough fills me with delight also. I shall prob-ably then be at Abbotsford—and to get a little sketch from you at the breakfast table there! fancy!

I hope my letter about the engraving will show you how I felt

119

Kate Greenaway

what *you* did !—But you've no notion what can be done yet, when I've got the man into harness. His dotting tint is execrable, but we *must* have clear line tints often.

And in the same strain—

19th Sept. [1883].

Yes, I know well how tired you are, and I do hope you'll play on the sands and do nothing but what the children do—all day long. As soon as you are yourself again I'll tell you exactly what I want about the drawings. There was work enough for a *week* in that *one* of the girl with brown background, alone.—And you ought to do nothing but patches of colour with a brush big enough to tar a boat with for months to come.

Then *Fors Clavigera* appeared embellished for the first time with a headpiece from Kate Greenaway's pencil—a charming little girl watching the sun set across the sea. This was followed by a sweet and dainty little dancing maiden as headpiece to Letter 93, headpiece and tailpiece to Letter 94, headpiece to Letter 95, and full-page frontispiece to Letter 96. In the last-named a dancing babe of fortune leads by the hand a still more fascinating babe in rags—the rags and babe as clean and sweet as are all the rags and babes in K. G.'s child-Utopia—whilst a dainty lady tripping in the rear impartially scatters roses over them from a basket under her arm. The drawings in no way illustrated the text; they were wholly adventitious decorations.

These are the only K. G. drawings published by Ruskin, saving those to *Dame Wiggins*, of which some account appears in the next chapter, although others were engraved. These last, or some of them, are included in the later volumes of the noble Library Edition of Ruskin's works. The engravings in *Fors* were executed by Roffe. Their appearance on the printed page without any sign of a plate-mark is at first sight very puzzling, but this is accounted for by the extravagant size of the plates, which were, by Ruskin's special orders, made larger than the page upon which they were destined to be printed.

The only one of the 'Letters' in which Kate Greenaway is referred to by name is No. 94, 'Retrospect.' Ruskin is insisting upon the proper work for women, 'scrubbing furniture, dusting walls, sweeping floors, making the beds, washing up the crockery, ditto the children, and whipping them when they want it, etc. etc.' Then he goes on with advice as to plain work :

The Ruskin Friendship

Get Miss Stanley's book, which gives you the elements of this work at Whitelands,—(I hope, however, to get Miss Greenaway to sketch us a pattern frock or two, instead of the trimmed water-butts of Miss Stanley's present diagrams).

In the following extract from a letter of November 12, he refers to the scheme which he had in his mind for reproducing her coloured work in a more satisfactory way than could be done by the printing press. K. G. was to make coloured drawings which were to be printed in outline and then coloured by hand in facsimile — a method frequently used, but nowhere so successfully on a large scale as in France. Ruskin himself had her engravings in some copies of *Fors* coloured by hand in this manner.

On November 12th, he writes:—

This maid of the muffin is beyond, beyond! I *must* engrave *her* for a lovely *Fors* on toasting forks.

The colouring of Miss Primrose and all others must be done for a quite full and frank payment, enabling the colourist to count her day's work as a comfortable and profitable one. Each must be done as attentively and perfectly–while as simply–as possible.

It ought only to be *part* of the colourist's day's work–else it would be sickeningly monotonous–there will never be any pressure or hurry of her–the price being simply so much per score or hundred as she can deliver them.

The next letter refers to *Little Ann*.

STACY MARKS TO KATE GREENAWAY

Dec. 31, 1883.

I won't allow the year to pass away without thanking you for what is, I think, on the whole, I might say entirely, your *best book*. The drawing is better and I think there is more feeling for *grace* in the figures than in the earlier works.

I have put it away carefully in my 'Greenaway Collection' where it will always be a valued item.

Your work should be all the more popular after all Ruskin has said of it. He has dined with us once or twice before he left for Coniston and we have more than once talked of you.

He is a singular and wayward genius. I tried to get him to admire Caldecott but it was no use—and he had not a word to say for Keene or Sambourne.

Kate Greenaway

The following extract from a letter of Ruskin's dated ' Brantwood, 26th December '83 ' refers to the headpiece of Letter 93 of *Fors* :—

I shan't go to sleep over your note to-day.

But I have no words any more than if I *was* asleep, to tell you how marvellous I think these drawings. No one has ever done anything equal to them in pure grace of movement–no one in exquisiteness of dainty design–I tremble now to ask you to draw in any other way.

As for the gift of them, I had never such a treasure given me, in my life–but it is not for me only. I am sure that these drawings will be [valued] endlessly and everywhere if I can get them engraved the least rightly,—the sight of them alters one's thoughts of all the world.

The little beauty with the note, alone, would have made a Christmas for me.

I hope you will like the use I've made of one of your little dance-maidens–I think her glory of simplicity comes well alone.

The beginning of 1883 had seen the publication of Kate Greenaway's first Almanack. Published at one shilling by George Routledge & Sons, and of course engraved and printed in colours by Mr. Edmund Evans, it achieved an enormous success, some 90,000 copies being sold in England, America, France, and Germany. It was succeeded by an almanack every year (with but one exception, 1896) until 1897, the last being published by Mr. Dent. The illustrations were printed on sheets with blank spaces for the letterpress, in which English, French, or German was inserted as the market demanded. There are various little conceits about these charming productions which are calculated to appeal to the ' licquorish chapman of such wares '; so that complete sets of them already fetch respectable sums from the collectors of beautiful books, especially when they have not been divested of the paper envelopes or wrappers in which they were originally issued.

A Manchester bookseller who invested in three hundred copies had a startling experience. Almost within the week he was gratified to find that his stock was exhausted. Subsequently he was visited by a would-be purchaser who tendered three pence for as many copies. In response he protested that the selling price was one shilling apiece, when his customer informed him that the book was selling at that moment in Piccadilly—Piccadilly, Manchester—at the price of one penny. And enquiry not only

The Kate Greenaway ' Boom '

proved the statement to be correct but also elicited the fact that the books in question were the property of this very bookseller, the rapid disappearance of whose stock had been primarily due not to sales but to theft.

It has been said—let us admit, with a little exaggeration—that Kate Greenaway dressed the children of two continents. In such measure as it is true, this was mainly due to the fact that her almanacks found a regular sale in France, from which America and Europe so largely take their cue in feminine matters sartorial.

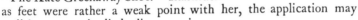

There was now a Greenaway boom, just as we have since seen a Trilby boom, and amongst other amusing compliments this year a firm of shoemakers approached the artist with a request to allow them to christen a special boot for children which they were putting on the market ' The Kate Greenaway Shoe.' Inasmuch as feet were rather a weak point with her, the application may well have proved a little disconcerting.

Towards the end of the year a proposal was afoot that Miss Greenaway should issue a volume of selected poems, with illustrations from her pencil, and Mrs. Severn proffered her aid, if it were desired, in making the choice. To this amiable offer her friend replied :—

KATE GREENAWAY TO MRS. ARTHUR SEVERN

11 PEMBERTON GARDENS, HOLLOWAY, N.,
29th Dec. 1883.

My dear Mrs. Severn— . . . And now about the book suggestion. Such a book is thought of, even planned out ; and it rested between the choice of that and one other to be the next year's book. The other one was decided, as we thought the poetry book would be the best last. But I'll talk to you about it, and please don't say anything about it till I've seen you. I don't want it known that I'm going to do a poetry book. It is an understood thing that I do NOT mention the names of any book going to be done till it is brought out—and this book is to be poems of my own selection. I can only do those that get into my mind of themselves—my own pets and favourites. But so many thanks all the same for writing that long letter about it. . . . With love,—Yours affectionately,   K. G.

This was followed, a little more than a month later, by a further note on the subject :—

KATE GREENAWAY TO MRS. ARTHUR SEVERN

11 PEMBERTON GARDENS, HOLLOWAY, N.,
2nd Feb. 1884.

Dearest Mrs. Severn—The verses have come in safety—one or two are quite new to me, and would be exactly what I'd like to put in. They are all nice, but I doubt if in some cases the copyrights could be obtained, and some of them are a little too much about children. Children, I find, like to know about other things—or what other children did—but not about children in an abstract sort of way. That belongs to older people.

I wonder if you remember what poem you liked best when you were a child? I can remember, well, some I liked,—'How Horatius kept the Bridge'—I used to love that. Then 'The Wreck of the Hesperus,' 'The Pied Piper,' 'The Rope Walk,' 'The Thoughts of Youth.' But I'm afraid I had a great many loves—indeed, and so I do now. I find something to like in most things. With love, and hoping soon to see you,—Yours sincerely,   K. G.

In the summer of 1883 a charming collaboration took place in the pages of the *Magazine of Art* (which was then under the editorship of W. E. Henley) between Kate Greenaway and a poet in whose tender, exquisite, and dainty art she took infinite delight— Mr. Austin Dobson. Earlier in the year an article in that magazine on 'Art in the Nursery' had paid homage to the work of Miss Greenaway, along with that of Walter Crane, Randolph Caldecott, Miss Lizzie Lawson, and M. Ernest Griset. But Kate is the heroine of the band, and the 'peculiar quality of cherubic dowdiness' of her youngsters, the winsomeness of the babies' solemn flirtation under an immense umbrella, and similar fascinating scenes, received the appreciation that was their due. Then in a number of the magazine that contained contributions by Robert Louis Stevenson, Cosmo Monkhouse, Leader Scott, Mr. W. C. Brownell, and others, Kate Greenaway contributed her charming page-drawing in which Mr. Austin Dobson's equally delicious

HOME-BEAUTY.

Poem by Austin Dobson.   Drawing by Kate Greenaway.

Reduced from the *Magazine of Art*, 1883, by permission of the publishers,
Messrs. Cassell & Co.

Kate Greenaway

verses were set. The drawing, here reproduced, naturally suffers greatly from the necessary reduction in size : lines are thickened, the exquisite drawing of faces, of eyes and mouths and dimpled chins, and the dainty gradations of the pencil strokes, are inevitably impaired if not lost. But the grace of the composition, the pretty grouping, the sweet childish attitudes, remain intact ; and the verses, written in in our reproduction by Mr. Dobson's own hand, though here too small in scale to be easily read, match the design in playful elegance. They run as follows :—

HOME-BEAUTY

Mine be a cot,' for the hours of play,
Of the kind that is built by Miss Greenaway,
Where the walls are low, and the roofs are red,
And the birds are gay in the blue o'erhead ;
And the dear little figures, in frocks and frills,
Go roaming about at their own sweet wills,
And play with the pups, and reprove the calves,
And do nought in the world (but Work) by halves,
From ' Hunt the Slipper ' and ' Riddle-me-ree '
To watching the cat in the apple-tree.

O Art of the Household ! Men may prate
Of their ways 'intense' and Italianate,—
They may soar on their wings of sense, and float
To the *au-delà* and dim remote,—
Till the last sun sink in the last-lit West,
'Tis the Art at the Door that will please the best ;
To the end of Time 'twill be still the same,
For the Earth first laughed when the children came !

CHAPTER IX

1884–1885

THE industry of Kate Greenaway during the years 1884 and 1885
added considerably to the growing list of her works.   First there
were the two *Almanacks*, which, save for the enlarged *format* of
that of 1884—an experiment not repeated—showed a distinct
advance on the first.

That for 1884 certainly did not please Ruskin, for he wrote :—

> I find Baxter [1] thinks the almanack beautiful ! if that's any consola-
> tion to you–but *I* divide the figures of it simply into the Hobblers
> and the Kickers, see August, March, June, and November for the
> hobblers (or shamblers) and the rest for kickers with the one variety
> of Straddler in October.

But the public was otherwise-minded and bought over 90,000
of the combined issues !   Then a new experiment was tried in the
shape of four calendars, all for 1884 ; but these proved a financial
failure and had no successors, and the designs were afterwards
for the most part adapted to Christmas cards and issued by
Goodall & Sons.   They are only mentioned here for the sake of
completeness, and although they contain some of Miss Greenaway's most charming work, they are but trifles by the side of
the more ambitious publications of these two prolific years.

Of these the *Language of Flowers* first claims attention with

---

[1] Ruskin's body-servant.

Kate Greenaway

an edition of 19,500 copies. Half of these went to America, which country henceforth was to prove to K. G. a client even better than England. This, like the Almanack, failed to please Ruskin, who wrote on Oct. 8th with his usual directness :—

> You are working at present wholly in vain. There is *no* joy and very, very little interest in any of these Flower book subjects, and they look as if you had nothing to paint them with but starch and camomile tea.

The fact is that the book was printed on unsuitable paper and much effect was thereby lost; still the illustrations, although not always very apposite, include some of the daintiest and most exquisitely drawn figures and flowers she ever produced.

Undeterred by Ruskin's denunciation Miss Greenaway sent a copy of it to Mrs. Severn with the following pathetic little note :—

KATE GREENAWAY TO MRS. ARTHUR SEVERN

11 PEMBERTON GARDENS, HOLLOWAY, N.,
9th Nov. 1884.

I've been thinking of you so often for days past. I send you my little book. Mr. Ruskin thinks it very bad. He says he's ashamed to show it to any one—I hope it won't affect you so fearfully. I am very disgusted myself—*only* I *don't* feel *I am* so much to blame as the printers, who have literally blotted every picture out.

But, anyhow, you'll think I mean well in sending it you, don't you? And you—do you feel quite strong and well again now? . . . Remember, when there is a chance I might see you, I'd be *very very very* glad and delighted.—Yours affectionately, K. G.

Then came *Kate Greenaway's Painting-Book* which, although it consisted of blocks brought together from *Under the Window, Kate Greenaway's Birthday Book, A Day in a Child's Life, Marigold Garden,* and *Mother Goose,* had nevertheless a great and deserved success, and set at least forty thousand children painting away at her delightful designs.

This was followed by *Mavor's Spelling-Book,* surely, as now illustrated by K. G., one of the most inspiring school-books ever published for children, with the beautifully engraved cuts printed in brown in the text. Ruskin wrote of it : 'Spelling Book ever so nice—But do children really learn to spell like that? I never did.' To which it may be added that his own experience is given in *Præterita*, vol. viii. p. 20 (1900 ed.).

Oddly enough the success of the venture was comparatively small, only 5,000 copies being called for. But when, seeing that there was no great demand, the publishers issued the capital letters alone in a tiny square 48mo volume entitled *Kate Greenaway's Alphabet*, the vagaries of book-buying were curiously exemplified by the fact that the circulation reached the more than respectable total of 24,500 copies.[1] Mr. Evans, with whom the idea of illustrating *Mavor* originated, proposed that Caldecott should be associated with Kate Greenaway in the work, but to this, in spite of her great admiration for her friend, she would on no account consent.

Half the number of the illustrations were engraved on wood as usual by Mr. Evans. The rest were reproduced by process and, says Mr. Evans, with characteristic fair-mindedness, neither K. G. nor Caldecott could at the time say which they considered the more satisfactory. Kate was much amused and gratified by the notice in the *Athenæum*, which waxed eloquent, and even facetious, over the book. After comparing the little designs to those of Stothard, and declaring that under Miss Greenaway's guidance three-syllable words become quite easy, it proceeds :

It is quite evident that the artist is not yet equal to four syllables —at least she has left the section which is devoted to those monsters without an illustration of any kind. Perhaps she, like ourselves, believes no boy ever gets to four syllables in *Mavor*, and thinks it useless to illustrate that stage of learning.

The drawings to *Mavor* had a further destiny ; for several of them were used, with the addition of colour and in reduced size, to provide illustrations to the *Almanack* of 1889, while the *Almanack* of 1895 (much against Miss Greenaway's desire) was entirely made up of them. Very beautiful they looked ; but it is more than probable that the public detected the employment of 'old matter' and that the commercial failure which attended the publication that year was at least the partial cause for the annual issue of the little work being suspended.

But the most important addition to the output of these years, that which added largely to the artist's reputation, was *Marigold Garden*, in which she was once more author and illustrator in one.

[1] This includes an edition of 2,000, published by Hachette & Cie., of Paris.

Kate Greenaway

For an expensive book the sales were very large, England taking 6,500, America 7,500, and France 3,500 copies. The charm of the book lies in itself, in spite of halting verse or summary perspective. Any description of it here would be inadequate : it must be seen to be fully appreciated.

The year 1885 also saw the publication of *Dame Wiggins of Lee and her Seven Wonderful Cats. A Humorous Tale. Written principally by a Lady of Ninety*, edited with additional verses by Ruskin, and with some new illustrations by Kate Greenaway. These nursery rhymes had first seen the light in 1823 with the woodcuts coloured by hand. In the present edition these were facsimiled in outline and left, as Ruskin says in the preface, for 'clever children . . . to colour in their own way.' Of his and K. G.'s part in the republication he says :

> I have added the rhymes on the third, fourth, eighth and ninth pages–the kindness of Miss Greenaway supplying the needful illustrations. But my rhymes do not ring like the real ones ; and I would not allow Miss Greenaway to subdue the grace of her first sketches to the formality of the earlier work.

A further edition of the little book was published in 1897 by Mr. George Allen.

In the letters preceding the publication of *Dame Wiggins*, which by the way in *Præterita* Ruskin designates his 'calf-milk of books on the lighter side,' we find several references to K. G.'s illustrations.

In May he writes : 'Don't bother yourself with Dame Wiggins –it's the cats you'll break down in.' But his prophecy proved wrong, for on July 5 he confesses 'you never shewed such sense in anything as in doing those cats ' ; and again on the 11th, 'The cats are gone to be wood-cutted just as they are–they can't be better ' ; and again on the 29th, alluding to a further proposed collaboration : 'We'll do that book together of course–I'll write a story about perpetual spring–but–however are you to learn what a lamb's like ? However after those D. W. cats I feel that nothing's impossible.'

About this time Miss Greenaway for the first and we believe the only time listened to the voice of the journalist for the purposes of an article on her art in an American magazine entitled *The Continent*. Her hatred of publicity was not in any way overcome, but she felt that as the article was inevitable 'facts were

' Kate Greenaway's Birthday Book '

preferable to fiction.' Moreover, by reason of her consent, she was in a position to impose restrictions, and she made it a cardinal condition that such particulars as 'what she takes to eat before sitting down to her work,' and personalities of every sort, should be rigorously excluded. She may have been influenced to give certain authoritative information in consequence of a former experience, when a 'lady interviewer' of an American journal— a lady whom she had declined to receive—published an 'interview' that was an invention from beginning to end. Later on Miss Greenaway met the Editor of the publication and seized the opportunity to state the facts, when he professed, and doubtless felt, much indignation at the imposition which had been practised upon him and the public.

Then also occurred the fishing episode to which allusion has been made in an early chapter. It is a curious commentary on the fable of the man and his ass that even Kate Greenaway's tender and humane designs could not escape fault-finding on ethical grounds from a hypercritical admirer of her art.

'How is it,' he wrote, 'that there are several lovely publications of yours that I am prevented from treating my little friends to on account of the fascination of the angling scenes which so often occur in them? . . . Do you not think there is no necessity for *encouraging* children to take pleasure in killing animals?'

He had been foolish enough to object to some such innocent illustration as that of the little boy fishing, on October 14 of the *Birthday Book*, whereto is appended a verse for which, by the way, Kate was not responsible :

What is this boy fishing for ?
What does he hope to get ?
He hopes to get a very fine fish,
But I think he will get wet.

To this remonstrance she replied to the effect that Providence had ordained a state of war between man and the lower animals and that we must take a good many things as we find them.

131

Kate Greenaway

The Ruskin letters of 1884 are full of interest. Criticism, appreciation, good-humoured chaff, and sadness, jostle one another at every turn. A standing joke is K. G.'s supposed jealousy of Miss Alexander and her exquisite work. In April she had asked for her autograph, and he writes in fun, for he could not have been serious in his criticism :—

Much you'd care for one of Miss Alexander's letters–on 'principles of chiaroscuro' and the like. She's drawing very badly just now–there's a little bonne-bouche for you.

In several letters he returns to the old charge and rallies her :—

Thanks–more than usual–and *much* more, for the little drawing–an *effort* in the right direction ! But quite seriously, and all *my* wishes out of the court, you MUST learn to draw something more of girls than their necks and arms ! ! You must go to the sea-side, and be resolved that–if nothing else be pretty–at least the ankles shall be.

Anon he mixes judicious praise and blame, rarely giving her jam without a pinch of medicine in it.

RUSKIN TO KATE GREENAWAY

BRANTWOOD [*Jan. 7th*, 1884].

It's not 'horrid bad' but it is not at all good.
When ARE YOU going to be GOOD and send me a study of anything from nature–the coalscuttle or the dustpan–or a towel on a clothes screen–or the hearthrug on the back of a chair.
I'm very cruel, but here's half a year I've been waiting for a bit of Common sense— !
And I've nothing but rain and storm all day–I never saw the place so dreadful,–but if you'll only paint me the coalscuttle or the towel it will be a solace.—Don't you think you ought to know when you do well or ill without asking me ?–I am very glad to hear of that instinct for greater things, though.

RUSKIN TO KATE GREENAWAY

BRANTWOOD [*April 20th*, 1884].

Yes, I am really very sorry about the sore throat. You had better take it fairly in hand at once, lie by, and foment and otherwise get

Ruskin Correspondence

yourself to rights at once. You can't work while you are ill like this. But this cloud lady is very lovely, and you really MUST draw *her* again for me without any clothes, because you've suggested a perfect coalheaver's leg, which I can't think you meant! and you *must* draw your figures now undraped for a while—Nobody wants anatomy,–but you can't get on without Form.

I'll send her back to have her gown taken off as soon as you're able to work again, meantime I've sent you two photographs from Francesca [1]–only don't show them about, because I want them not to be seen till my text is ready.

Again on May 1st, he writes:—

Indeed the drawing is lovely, beyond all thanks or believableness or conceivableness and gives me boundless pleasure, and all sorts of hope of a wonderful future for you. But it is of no use to ask me how things are to stand out. You never had any trouble in making them do so when you had power of colour enough–but you can't make these tender lines stand out, unless you finished the whole in that key, and that ought only to be done of the real size. What you ABSOLUTELY need is a quantity of practice from things as they *are*–and hitherto you have ABSOLUTELY refused ever to draw any of them so.

On July 6th, referring to an illustration she is engaged on for *Marigold Garden*, he adds instruction to praise:

You're a good girl to draw that leaf. The four princesses in green tower [2] will be delightful but the *first thing* you have to do in this leafy world is to learn to paint a leaf green, of its full size, at one blow, as a fresco painter does it on a background, with the loaded brush opening by pressure to the leaf's full breadth and closing to its point.

Again on the 9th:—

I knew you could do it, if you only would. That's been what's making me so what you call angry lately. This is as good as well can be. Only, remember brown is only to be used for actual earth, and where plants grow close to it or for brown dark leaves etc., not as shadow. And there's already more delineation than I at present want you to spend time in.

And on the 25th he continues his instruction:—

The ivy is very beautiful and you have taken no end of useful trouble with it, but the colour is vapid and the leaves too shiny.

---

[1] Miss Francesca Alexander.   [2] Page 22 of *Marigold Garden*.

Kate Greenaway

Shine is always vulgar except on hair and water–it spoils leaves as much as it does flesh–and even jewels are better without it. I shall return you this study which you will find very useful and I've sent you two more sods to-day, more to be enjoyed than painted–if you like to do a bit of one, well and good.

I am glad to hear of the oil work–but it is winter work not summer. I can't think how you can bear to spoil summer air with it.

On October 18, he says :—

You must like Turner as soon as you see landscape completely. His affectations—or prejudices, I do not wish or expect you to like—any more than I should have expected him to like roses drawn like truffles.

Then he finds that he has been expecting too much, counting on physical powers with which Kate has not been endowed.

I have not enough allowed for your being nearsighted but shall like to see what you do see. At any rate near or far off, study of the relation of moss [1] is indispensable.

Those hot colours of flowers are very lovely–you can do as many as you like–only not dull things mixed with Naples yellow.

Look well at the foot of Correggio's Venus, and at the weeds in Mantegna's foreground.

For the same reason Ruskin has more 'sods' cut and packed off to her to paint.

Not to tease you–but they'll go on growing and being pleasant companions. As regards colour, no one of course sees it quite rightly. We have all our flaws and prejudices of sight, only, be convinced there is a RIGHT, mathematically commensurable with nature, and you will soon get to care for no 'opinions,' but feel that you have become daily more true.

So she promptly sets to work to paint one of the sods, and he is so delighted that he flashes off a telegram—

The sod is quite lovely, the best bit of groundwork I ever got done, so many thanks, but don't tire yourself so again.

---

[1] A water-colour drawing of 'Rock, Moss, and Ivy' by K. G. is now in the Sheffield Museum. Of its origin the catalogue says 'The sketch was made by Miss Greenaway in consequence of Mr. Ruskin having told her one day at Brantwood, that she could draw pretty children daintily enough but she couldn't make a drawing of that rock. Miss Greenaway hastily produced this study of it, and presented it to Mr. Ruskin.'

Ruskin Correspondence

On great occasions, he gives her unqualified praise, which unqualified praise it may be noted not infrequently coincides with an improved condition in his health.

11*th. Feb.*, 84.

I did not answer your question which of the girlies I liked best because it was unanswerable, yet something is to be said anent it.

Of course the Queen of them all is the little one in front–but she's just a month or six weeks too young for *me*. Then there's the staff bearer on the right (—the left, as they come) turning round ! ! !– but she's just three days and a minute or two too *old* for me. Then there's the divine one with the dark hair, and the beatific one with the brown,–but I think *they*'ve both got lovers already and have only come to please the rest, and wouldn't be mine if I prayed them ever so. Then there is the little led beauty who is ruby and diamond in one,– but–but,–not quite'tall enough, again–I think the wisest choice will be the pale one between the beatific and the divine !

But they're all ineffable !–I think you never did a more marvellous piece of beauty and it's a treasure to me like a caught dream.

I wonder how you can bear to think of drawing *me*–and how you mean to do it !

Sitting always tires me a good deal, but perhaps John will let me lie down in his room for a quarter of an hour before tea.

Of this portrait he writes later in an undated letter of the same year :—

I was with some saucy girls yesterday and I was saying how proud I was to have my portrait drawn by you–but only I had been so sleepy !

If the portrait was ever done, there is now no trace of it.

RUSKIN TO KATE GREENAWAY

BRANTWOOD, 20*th*, *July* [1884]
(an entirely cloudless morning and I wonderfully well).

I am more cheered and helped by your success in this drawing than by anything that has happened to me for years ;–it is what I have been praying and preaching to everybody and *never* could get done !

135

Kate Greenaway

I was nearly certain the power was in you, but never thought it would come out at a single true effort!

—The idea of your not seeing chiaroscuro!–the ins and outs of these leaves are the most rightly intricate and deep I ever saw–and the fern drawing at the one stroke is marvellous.

It's a short post this morning and I've a lot to get ready for it–but I've such lovely plans in my head for all you say in your last two letters —And I'll forgive you the pig!–but we must draw dogs a little better. And we must learn just the rudiments of perspective–and draw feet and ankles,–and,—a little above,–and purple and blue things–and–the Sun not like a drop of sealing wax,–and then—Well,–we'll do all that first, won't we?

RUSKIN TO KATE GREENAWAY

BRANTWOOD [*July 22nd*, 1884].

The little hippopotamus with the curly tail *is* lovely, and the explosive sun promises a lovely day, and it is so *very* joyful news to me that you like doing trees and see them all leaves and are going to do feet and ankles and be so good. There's no saying what wonderful things you may do, all in an instant, when once you've fought your way through the strait gate. And you will have the joy of delighting many more people beside me; and of doing more good than any English artist ever yet did. And I'll put *you* in some of my books soon, as well as Miss A. and very thankfully.

But you must have a few more sods, you know.

One of the 'lovely plans' he has in his head is 'a book on botany for you and me to do together—you do the plates and I the text—a hand-book of field botany. It will be such a rest for you and such a help for–everybody!–chiefly me.'

But it comes to nothing, for he finds that some one has taken the wind out of their sails and writes on Easter Day of the following year :—

Something less strong than the Lamp-post. But I am ever so much more strong. . . .

But oh, we're both cut out with our flower book—Here's a perfect primrose of a clergyman brought out such a book of flowers! beats us all to sticks–buds and roots. I've got to write to him instantly and it's short post.

Another plan is to paint with her 'some things at Brantwood like Luca and the Old Masters–and cut out those dab and dash

136

people. I felt when I came out of the Academy as if my coat must be all over splashes.'

If the Academy did not please, the Grosvenor of that year had no better fortune, for on May 3 he writes :—

I was so curious to see those Grosvenor pictures that I went in with Joan yesterday and got a glimpse.—The only picture there worth looking at is Millais' Lorne,[1] and his straddling girl is a fright,[2] and his Lady Campbell[3] a horror.—As for that somebody in the sea,[4] what did I tell you about model drawing ?—People are getting absolutely brutified by it. There's another nearly as bad in the Suffolk St.[5] In the great mediæval times, painters could draw people dressed or undressed just as they chose–without the smallest weakness, shame, or conceit. Now, there is scarcely a foolish or bad feeling in one's head or body, that isn't made worse in the model-room. I scratched nearly every picture through in my catalogue yesterday.

Another plan was that they should both set to work to paint 'a purple kingfisher.'

Couldn't you go to Mr. Fletcher and ask him to introduce you to Dr. Gunther, and ask Dr. Gunther to show you an Abyssinian kingfisher, and give you any one you like to draw out in a good light ?

Sometimes Ruskin is betrayed into writing about himself. For example on March 20th, from Brantwood, when for the time being not only all the world seems wrong but in Professor Clifford's poignant words even 'The Great Companion' seems dead :

I didn't tell you if I was well—I'm not : nor have I been for some time,–a very steady gloom on me ; not stomach depression but the sadness of deliberately preparing for the close of life—drawing in, or giving up, all one's plans—thinking of one's beloved places, I shall never be there again–and so on. A great deal of the time I *have* lost in the mere friction of life–scarcely any sense of Peace,—And no hope of any life to come. I forget it all more in the theatre than anywhere—cathedrals are no good any more !

Mind you go and see Claudian ![6]

---

[1] Portrait of the present Duke of Argyll.
[2] Portrait of Lady Campbell when a little girl—Miss Nina Lehmann.   Painted in 1865.   [3] Lady Campbell (Miss Nina Lehmann) on her marriage.
[4] 'Aphrodite' by Philip Calderon, R.A.   [5] The Society of British Artists.
[6] For *Claudian*—the play produced by Wilson Barrett, who acted the title-rôle—Ruskin had a prodigious and rather unaccountable admiration.   To one of the present

Kate Greenaway

And on Dec. 1st, from Oxford:—

I've been in a hard battle here these eight weeks,–the atheistic scientists all against me, and the young men careless and everything going wrong–so that I have had to fight with sadness and anger in all my work. My last lecture is to be given to-morrow but I have been feeling more tired in this cold weather, and the correspondence is terrible. I have never a moment to draw or do anything I like–except throw myself on my bed and rest, or listen to any good music if I can get it quietly.

From among his more general and less didactic epistles three may be given as examples.

RUSKIN TO KATE GREENAWAY

BRANTWOOD, 23 *Jan.* /84.

. . . You must try to like the Alexanders–for they are Heaven's own doing–as much as Heaven ever allows to be seen of it.

I ought to be ' good ' about everything, for good people love me,–and have loved.

Here is the strangest thing has come to me to-day.

L——[1] was–I have told you have not I–a saint in her way,–and was constant in the habit of prayer.

One evening—I may have told you this before, but it is better to have it in writing,—being out at a friend's house where there were a good many people–more or less known to her and to each other–one coming in told suddenly that L——'s chief girl friend (she knew before of her illness) was at the point of death.

There was a clergyman at the party and L—— asked him to pray for her friend–but he was taken aback being among all the young people, said he could not.—'Then'—said L——, (only 18 at that time) '*I* must.' —She made the whole company kneel down–and prayed so that they *could* not but join with her.

And the girl was saved. Afterwards I used to see her, often enough. She married, to L——'s great delight–a Highland religious squire–and she with her husband came to see me here, with their two

writers, he said during the run of the piece : ' I admired it so much that I went to see it three times out of pure enjoyment of it, although as a rule I cannot sit out a tragic play. It is not only that it is the most beautifully mounted piece I ever saw, but it is that every feeling that is expressed in the play, and every law of morality that is taught in it, is entirely right.'

[1] A young lady who died young. Her fine character and sweet disposition Ruskin greatly admired.

Ruskin Correspondence

children, boy and girl,–three years ago. Since then the children have remembered me, and sent me a card, for themselves at Christmas, this last year, to which I returned a letter of thanks addressed to D—— and F——. My letter found little F—— on her death-bed. Her Father writes to me–yesterday, 'I think you will be pleased to know that your letter addressed to D—— and F—— gave my darling in her pain a bright smile.'—And he encloses to me an *envelope* which F—— had addressed to me in return. But the letter–never, and yet–she has written one she knew not. For the envelope is written in L——'s hand! I could not tell the difference except in the letter J. of the beginning.

Is not this a pretty little story?

RUSKIN TO KATE GREENAWAY

BRANTWOOD [*March 3rd*, 1884].

No wonder I couldn't understand about the letters–here's one enclosed which ought to have been at Witley almost in time to receive you and has lain in my unanswered letter heap till an hour ago!

I'm so delighted about your beginning to like purple and blue flowers, though it's only for my sake. Not that I'm not proud of being able to make you like things! . . . .

I think flowers in *my* order of liking would come nearly like this,

> Wild rose
> Alpine rose
> Alpine gentian
> White Lily
> Purple Flag
> Purple convolvulus
> Carnation—all the tribe
> Pansy, all the tribe
> Thistle—all the tribe
> Daisy and Hyacinth
> Snowdrop and Crocus

I only put the last so low because they have such an unfair advantage over all the rest in coming first,–and of course I've some out of the way pets like the oxalis and anagallis but then *they* have an unfair advantage in always growing in pretty places. The wood anemone should go with the daisy, and the 'Blossoms' apple and almond–hawthorn and cherry, have of course a separate queendom.

I must really go and look for that lovely girl you gave me with basket of pansies!

139

Kate Greenaway

Brantwood [*March 22nd*, 1884].

What a nice letter—and I'm so pleased that your Father was surprised, and that Johnnie liked 'Unto This Last'–and that you think you'll like some more. I think I tired myself with trying to draw your little girlie yesterday–she's *so* hard, and I'm as lazy to-day as ever I can be, and don't care for anything but a French Novel, about police! And I'm ashamed to read it at 3 in the afternoon–and it's wet–and I can't do St. George's accounts–and I should like some tea and muffins–and–there are no muffins in Coniston. . . . .
I feel so listless because there's no time left now to do anything.

Oh dear, think how happy you are with all that power of drawing–and ages to come to work in and paint Floras and Norahs and Fairies and Mary's and Goddesses and–bodices–oh me, when will you do me one without any ?

I must take to my French novel, there's no help for it—Mercy on us, and it's two hours to teatime ! and the room so quiet, and all my books and things about me—and I can't do a thing—
Wouldn't you like a photograph of me like that ?

No doubt, it is difficult to help feeling at times that Ruskin's admiration for K. G. partakes too much of hyperbole. And yet we cannot but confess that as he was honest in welcoming the Pre-Raphaelites so was he honest in his greeting of her. He was weary of the artificial pedantry of those who had elaborated an artistic code ' with titles and sub-titles applicable to every form of [art] and tyrannous over every mode of sentiment,' and he acclaimed an exquisite small voice, which sang its little song in its own sweet tone of purity and in its own tender unconventional way. What he meant was in no wise that she was cleverer than other people. He over and over again tells her one way or another that she was no great executant. But she had that rarer gift of seeing old things through new eyes and giving artistic expression with curious and delightful success to these newer and fresher views. And as Ruskin was by nature vehement and by practice a controversialist, he could scarcely resist being led from time to time into italicizing his words and emphasizing his verdicts.

In the meanwhile the warmest affection had ripened between Mr. Ruskin's cousin and adopted daughter, Mrs. Arthur Severn,

Friendship for Mrs. Arthur Severn

and Kate Greenaway. Like most others, Kate had been fascinated by the charm, goodness, and ability of Mrs. Severn ; and so enlisted her sympathy that when her friend fell ill, Kate opened her heart to her, like a child :—

11 PEMBERTON GARDENS, HOLLOWAY, N.,
Wednesday [10 *Dec.* 1884].

Dearest Mrs. Severn,—

Poor Dear. I'm so sorry. I hope it will be as short in staying as it seems severe.

I'm so sorry.

I think I will put off coming till next week, for then, I hope, I'll be stronger. I am very unwell again to-day—so absurdly weak.

And you, too, would not be well enough to see me this week. It is such hard work, isn't it, talking when you don't feel well. Not that I can or will say I felt that with regard to you, you always seem so cheerful and comforting—that you'd do me good at any time. Poor Dear.

But I will write again, and I'll hope to see you quite recovered. My mother is very ill, too, with a bad cold and cough.

Good-bye. How sweet of you to write to me at all, feeling so ill. I hope you're feeling better this morning. With, Dearest, lots of love, Your affectionate, K. G.

I'm *very, very, very sorry.*
Poor Dear.

A little later on when Mrs. Severn's young sons were about to be sent to their first boarding school, Kate sent a characteristic note of sympathy :—

My dearest Mrs. Severn— . . . I wonder if I shall see you to-morrow at the R. A. I shall be there till nearly 4—but I remember. Your boys are going to-morrow I hope you won't feel it dreadfully. But I should think they will be happy there. It is so much nicer than quite a strange school and strange people. Please feel they will be very happy. . . . Your very affectionate　　K. G.

And for Mrs. Severn's little daughter, Violet, Kate Greenaway composed the doleful history of a naughty girl, such as most delights the mind of a tiny child. That characteristic booklet, delightfully sketched in pencil and colour, Miss Violet Severn has kindly allowed to be reproduced here.

141

CHAPTER X

1885 AND 1886

THE MOVE TO FROGNAL—RUSKIN : LETTERS AND CONFIDENCES,
PRAISE AND BLAME, HIS ILLNESS—MRS. ALLINGHAM

On Monday, February 16th, 1885, Miss Greenaway moved to
Frognal, into the house designed for her by Mr. Norman Shaw,
her home until her death. Of her experiences as a house-builder
she has left no record, and Mr. Norman Shaw kept none of her
letters. As there were so few neighbouring houses at the time,
and as some number was necessary, the architect suggested the
adoption of ' 50,' for it was unlikely that a higher number would
eventually be reached. When in due time the other plots were
filled up, Miss Greenaway's house became No. 39, and to that it
was altered. This detail, trivial as it is, is mentioned, as the reader
might be misled into believing that Miss Greenaway had at some
unspecified time changed her Hampstead home.

The scheme did not commend itself to Ruskin. On the 1st
of the previous October he had written from Kenmure Castle:—

I could not get your dainty letter until to-day. The two sweeties
in it are indeed beautiful, and only need to be painted larger to become
a most glorious picture. I must stand over you while you paint them
again with a big brush. But I am aghast at the house at Hampstead
and quite resolved that you *shan't* live in London. Of course if you
had stayed at Scarborough you would have begun drawing the children
at the shore, and that was just what I wanted.—But wait till I come
and talk to you–I'll make your life a burden to you if you live in
London ! If you had come to Norwood instead of Hampstead, there
would have been some sense in it–I've no patience with you.

And you must give up drawing round hats. It's the hats that

142

THE TWINS.

Two pages from the little MS. volume, measuring about 3¼ × 2½ inches, entitled 'Babies and Blossoms.' Drawn by Kate Greenaway and written by Frederick Locker. (In the possession of Mrs. Locker-Lampson.)

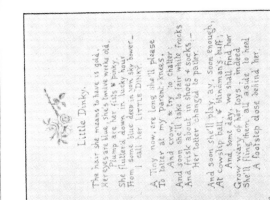

LITTLE DINKY.

Two pages from the little MS. volume, measuring about $3\frac{1}{4} \times 2\frac{1}{2}$ inches, entitled 'Babies and Blossoms.' Drawn by Kate Greenaway and written by Frederick Locker. (In the possession of Mrs. Locker-Lampson.)

FROM CAREFULLY EXECUTED WATER-COLOUR DRAWINGS ON LETTERS
ADDRESSED TO MRS. FREDERICK LOCKER-LAMPSON.

FROM A WATER-COLOUR DRAWING ON A LETTER ADDRESSED TO
MRS. FREDERICK LOCKER-LAMPSON.

KATE GREENAWAY'S HOME, 39, FROGNAL, HAMPSTEAD.

Designed for Kate Greenaway by R. Norman Shaw, R.A.

TEA-ROOM LEADING OUT FROM THE STUDIO, 39, FROGNAL, HAMPSTEAD.

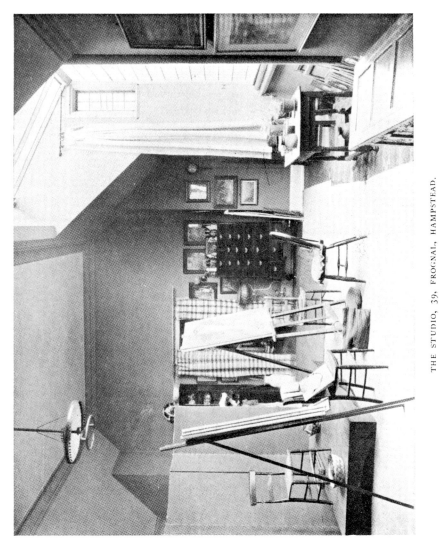

THE STUDIO, 39, FROGNAL, HAMPSTEAD.

'ROVER.'   MR. JOHN GREENAWAY'S RETRIEVER.

For ten years Kate Greenaway's faithful companion.

The Move to Frognal

always save you from having to do a background–and I'm not going to be put off with them any more.

Just prior to the move Ruskin wrote :—

You're not going to call your house a Villa ! ?—Could you call it Kate's State–or Kitty's Green–or Katherine's Nest,–or Brownie's Cell–or Camomile Court–or Lassie's Leisure–or the Romp's Rest–or–something of that sort ?

And again :—

I will take real care about the addresses–but I really must have a pretty one for the New House–you don't suppose I'm going to write Frognal every day of my life—It might as well be Dognal–Hognal–Lognal–I won't.   If it is to be I'll have it printed ! ! !

But Kate saved him the trouble, for thenceforward she kept him supplied with sheaves of envelopes addressed to herself in her own handwriting.

The day before the actual flitting he took care to write a letter to welcome her in the new house.

BRANTWOOD, 15 *February* 1885.

I hope you are beginning by this time in the afternoon to be very happy in thinking you're really at home on the Hill, now,–and that you will find all the drawers slide nicely, corners fit and firesides cosy, and that the flowers are behaving prettily, and the chimnies–draw–as well as you.—That's a new pun, all my own–only think ! It isn't a very complimentary one–but indeed–the first thing to be seriously thought of in a new house is chimnies,–one can knock windows out–or partitions down–build out oriels–and throw up turrets–but never make a chimney go that don't choose.

Anyhow—I am glad you are settled somewhere–and that I shan't have my letters to direct nobody knows where.—And let us bid, both, farewell to hollow ways, that lead only to disappointment–and know what we're about,–and not think truths teazing, but enjoy each other's sympathy and admiration–and think always–how nice we are !

No sooner was she settled than she began to receive uninvited attentions.   On the 4th March she wrote to Mrs. Severn :—

There was a horrid man drawing the outside [of the house] all day. So I suppose he is cribbing Mr. Shaw's design, and going to put my house up somewhere else, who knows where.

143

Kate Greenaway

Her friends were not all entirely satisfied with it. On 25th March she wrote :—

My dearest Mrs. Severn,—

Mr. Locker came to see this new studio yesterday. He said, 'What a frightful *falling off* from the *old one*.' Isn't that sad ?—but I fear true.

But she was pleased to think that although it was not so pretty as her last studio, it was larger, lighter, and altogether more practical.

The household included Kate's father and mother and her brother, John Greenaway. Mr. Greenaway was still practising as a wood-engraver, with an office in the City ; Mr. John Greenaway was the sub-editor of the *Journal of the Chemical Society*, a post he holds at the present time ; while Mrs. Greenaway managed the domestic affairs. Of the routine of Miss Greenaway's life at this time Mr. John Greenaway writes :—

Of my sister at work, we saw very little. She very wisely made it a fixed rule that, during working hours, no one should come into the studio save on matters of urgency. Her great working time was the morning, so she was always an early riser and finished breakfast by eight o'clock. Her most important work was done between then and luncheon time (1 o'clock). Practically she never went out in the morning. After luncheon she usually worked for an hour or two, unless she was going out anywhere for the afternoon ; and then went for a walk on the Heath, and came back to tea. The evenings up to eight o'clock, when we had a meal that was a sort of compromise between dinner and supper, were spent in letter-writing, making dresses for models, occasionally working out schemes and rough sketches for projected books and such-like things ; but all finished work was done in the morning or afternoon. In the summer too, a good deal of this time was spent in the garden seeing to her flowers. After supper she generally lay on a sofa and read until she went to bed at about 10 o'clock.

She could not stand late hours and seldom went out in the evening. For the same reason she very seldom dined out. Tea-time was always her time for going out to see friends, or for them to see her.

The change of abode was a great success ; but in Miss Greenaway's correspondence we have at this period frequent references to domestic worries and minor troubles. For instance, she writes to Miss Evans :—

> It is quite tragic about all your servants going. Have you got a cook yet? You get a better chance of hearing something about them before you engage them than we do.
> I almost HATE ours! They pretended they could do such a lot. You would have thought that *one* was used to distinguished beings the way she went on. *We* felt quite vulgar. She spoke of the puddings as sweets and when I tried to convey to her mind that in our house they were called puddings she said, 'Ah! I see! you prefer comfort to style!' which is quite true, I do—only I don't get it at her hands, and as for *style!*—unless it consists in a nice coating of dirt over everything, I don't know where that is either. I hope your fate won't be such.

The work of 1885 has been described in the last chapter. It only remains to complete the year's record by extracts from Ruskin's letters, which in consequence of another severe illness break off abruptly on May the 22nd.

He had now retired into seclusion at Brantwood, where he was as happy as failing health would permit in the company of Mrs. Arthur Severn, the 'Joan' of the letters, and her husband and family who lived with him.

Now it was that he set to work on that remarkable fragment of autobiography published at intervals under the title of *Præterita*, to which allusion has already been made ; and he speaks of it in the following extracts from letters of this period :—

RUSKIN TO KATE GREENAWAY

BRANTWOOD, *4th, Jan.* (1885).

It was nice hearing of your being made such a grand Lioness of, at the tea–and of people's praising me to you because they had found out you liked it–and of Lady Airlie and old times.
. . . . . I've begun my autobiography–it will be so dull !, and so meek ! !–you never did !
I write a little bit every morning and am going to label old things it refers to–little drawings and printings and the like. I'm not going to talk of anybody more disagreeable than myself–so there will be nothing for people to snap and growl at. What shall I say about people who I think liked me ? that they were very foolish ?
I got a dainty little letter from my fifteener to-day, and have felt a

Kate Greenaway

little better ever since. She's at the seaside and says there's nothing on the shore–I've told her to look–and that I should like to write the 'Natural History of a dull Beach.'

RUSKIN TO KATE GREENAWAY

BRANTWOOD, *7th, Jan.* 1885.

The auto won't be a pretty book at all, but merely an account of the business and general meaning of my life. As I work at it every morning, (about half an hour only) I have very bitter feelings about the waste of years and years in merely looking at things–all I've got to say is–I went there–and saw–that. But did nothing. If only I had gone on drawing plants–or clouds–or—.

He is still full of interest in her work, unsparing of criticism and reproof where he considers them needful. On Jan. 2nd :

You are always straining after a fancy instead of doing the thing as it is. Never mind its being pretty or ugly, but get as much as you can of the facts in a few minutes and you will find strength and ease and new fancy and new right coming all together.

On Jan. 29th :—

I think the reason Miss A.[1] puzzles you is that you never make quite a sincere study, you are always making a pretence of striving for an ideal.

I want you to learn nature perfectly–then Miss A. will not puzzle you—though you will do quite different things. I am so glad you like Holbein.

And on Jan. 4th :—

I'm very glad you want to paint like Gainsborough.

But you must not try for it—He is inimitable, and yet a bad master. Keep steadily to deep colour and Carpaccio–with white porcelain and Luca—You may try a Gainsborough every now and then for play.

But he can also be unstinting of praise. On Feb. 8th :—

This is quite the most beautiful and delightful drawing you've ever given me, and I accept it with the more joy that it shows me all your powers are in the utmost fineness and fulness, and that you are steadily gaining in all that is best–and indeed will do many things— heaven sparing you and keeping your heart in peace,—more than [have] ever yet been seen in all human dreams.

---

[1] Miss Francesca Alexander.

146

Ruskin Correspondence

On April 7th :—

Ah ! just wait till you see ! *I'm* quite crushed !—Never knew such pink and blue could be found in Boxes—and not a touch of camomile anywhere ! and not a single leaf in an attitude !

Well—those anemones are a thing to tell of ! What a heavenly place London might be—if there was nobody in it.

Yes, you SHALL draw the tulip this time—if there's a bit of possible tulip in you. I have my doubts !

And on May 1st :—

I never was so much pleased with any drawing yet as with this, for it is complete in *idea*, and might become a consummate picture, with very little effort more, nor were ever faces more lovely than those of the central girl and the one on her right hand. You must paint me this some day—in Mays to come, when you're doing all sorts of lovely things at Brantwood, and the books give you no more trouble and yet bring you in showers of gold like the celandines.

And I'll try not to tease. It's too sweet of you doing this lovely thing for me.

And—what pleases me best of all's the beauty of the rhyme. It is higher in rhythmic power and quality than anything I've read of yours, and is in the entirely best *style* of poetry.—I believe the half of your power is not shown yet.

You have given me a very happy Mayday.

Suddenly we get a glimpse of his tender feeling for, and pretty sympathy with, her beloved flower :—

Oxalis out everywhere—wanting to be drawn. They say they'd like to feel how it feels, for they never were drawn in their lives.

For a moment he returns, on July 3rd, to the old subject of drawing from the nude and incidentally shows that he looks upon her as an exception to what he considers should be the general rule :—

What *you* have first to do is to learn to draw ankles and feet because you are one of the instances the enemy have of the necessity of the nude.

The moment you have any leisure for study—feet—feet—and arms. No more shoes, come what will of it.—To the seashore—as soon as may be—Until you come to Brant [*i.e.* Brantwood].

147

Kate Greenaway

And every now and again Ruskin shows his unabated enthusiasm for new knowledge and his gusto for new studies :—

. . . . Please ask Johnnie what colour frozen hydrogen is, and if transparent or opaque. The rascally chemistry book gives me six pages of bad drawings of machines,–and supplies me with a picture–to aid my imagination–of a man in badly made breeches turning a wheel !–but does not tell me whether even liquid hydrogen is transparent or not,–they only say it is 'steel-blue.'

On July 26 :—

This has been a very bright day to me, not least in the thoughts of this–but in other ways very fortunate and helpful,—I've found out why clouds float, for one thing ! ! !–and think what a big thing *that* is !

In reply to Kate's request for information on the cloud discovery he writes on July 28th :—

Clouds float because the particles of water in them get warmed by the sun, and warm the air in the little holes between them–then that air expands and carries them up. When they cool it comes down and then they stick together and come down altogether.

But Miss Greenaway was not yet satisfied, so to appease her curiosity he makes further answer on July 29th :—

Clouds are warmer or colder according to the general temperature of the air–but always enable the sun to warm the air within them, in the fine weather when they float high. I have yet to learn all about the wet weather on this new condition myself.

The following letters of the year speak for themselves :—

Ruskin to Kate Greenaway

Brantwood, 15 *Jan.* 85.

You say in one of–four !–unanswered [letters], you wonder how far I see you as you see yourself ? No one sees us as we see ourselves–all that first concerns us must be the care that we do see ourselves as far as possible rightly.

In general, young people (and children, like you) know very little of themselves ; yet *something* that nobody else can know. *My* knowledge of people is extremely limited, continually mistaken–and what is

148

Ruskin Correspondence

founded on experience, chiefly of young girls,—and this is nearly useless in your case, for you are mixed child and woman,—and therefore extremely puzzling to me.

But I think you may safely conclude that—putting aside the artistic power which is unique in its way, the rest of you will probably be seen more truly by an old man of—165, which is about my age, than by yourself—at almost any age you ever come to.

I note with sorrow that the weather bothers you. So it does me—but when the pretty times come, *you* can enjoy them, *I* can't.

Though I do a little like to see snow against blue sky still—to-day there's plenty of both. . . . . . .

You and your publishers are both and all geese.—You put as much work into that Language of Flowers as would have served three years bookmaking if you had only drawn boldly, coloured truly, and given 6 for 60 pages. The public will always pay a shilling for a penny's worth of what it likes,—it won't pay a penny for a pound's worth of camomile tea. *You* draw—let *me* colour next time !

RUSKIN TO KATE GREENAWAY

BRANTWOOD, 19 *Jan.* 85.

The book I send to-day is of course much more completed in shade than your outlines ever need, or ought to be, but I believe you would find extreme benefit in getting into the habit of studying from nature with the pen point in this manner and forcing yourself to complete the study of a head, cap, hair and all—whether it succeeded or not to your mind, in the time you now give to draw the profile of lips and chin.

You never need fear losing refinement,—you would gain steadily in fancy, knowledge and power of expression of solid form, and complex character. Note especially in these drawings that their expressional power depends on the rightness, not the delicacy of their lines, and is itself most subtle where *they* are most forcible. In the recording angels, pages 22, 23, the face of 23 is beautiful because its lines are distinct—22 fails wholly because the faint proof of the plate has dimmed them.

Tell me what the publishers ' propose ' now, that I may sympathise in your indignation—and ' propose ' something very different.

I can scarcely conceive any sale paying the expenses of such a book as the Language of Flowers—but think you could produce one easily with the original outlay of—say at the outsidest, £500, which you would sell 50,000 of at a shilling each in a month.

Tell me how you like this little head and tail piece herewith. I'm going to use them for a little separate pamphlet on schools.

149

Kate Greenaway

$\frac{1}{4}$ past two P.M. 13 *Feb.* 85. BRANTWOOD.

Am I busy? Well—you shall just hear what I've done to-day.

7–$\frac{1}{2}$ past, Coffee. Read Northcote's conversations marking extracts for lecture.

$\frac{1}{2}$ 7–8. Dress.

8–$\frac{1}{2}$ past, Write two pages of autobiography.

$\frac{1}{2}$ past 8–$\frac{1}{4}$ 9. Lesson to Jane Anne on spelling and aspiration. Advise her to get out of the habit of spelling at, hat.

$\frac{1}{4}$ 9–half past. Correct press of chapter of Modern Painters.

$\frac{1}{2}$ 9–$\frac{1}{2}$ 10. Breakfast–read letters–devise answers to smash a book-seller, and please an evangelical clergyman–also to make Kate under-stand what I'm about and put Joan's mind at ease. . . . . .

Wished I had been at the Circus. Tried to fancy Clemmie 'all eyes.' Thought a little mouth and neck might be as well besides. Pulled grape hyacinth out of box, and put it in water. Why isn't it blue?

$\frac{1}{2}$ 10. Set to work again. Finished revise of M. P. chapter. Then took up Miss Alex. next number. Fitted pages etc. Wrote to Miss A. to advise her of proof coming.

Wrote to Clergyman and Joan and smashed bookseller.

$\frac{1}{2}$ 12. Examined chess game by correspondence. Sent enemy a move. Don't think she's much chance left.

1. Looked out some crystals, ' Irish Diamonds' for school at Cork. Meditated on enclosed mistress' and pupils' letters–still to be answered before resting—Query, how?

$\frac{1}{4}$ past one. Lunch. Peasoup.

$\frac{1}{4}$ to two. Meditate letter to Colonel Brackenbury on the Bride of Abydos. Meditate what's to be said to K.

2. Baxter comes in–receives directions for manifold parcels and Irish diamonds–think I may as well write this, thus. Wild rainy day. Wrote Col. Brackenbury while your ink was drying to turn leaves– now for Irish Governess,–and my mineralogist–and that's all!

WHIT-BLACK MONDAY, 85
[*May* 26, LONDON].

I was down to very low tide to-day, and am still, but partly rested, still my head not serving me,–the driving about town continually tires me fearfully,–then I get vexed to be tired–then I can't eat because I'm vexed–then I can't sleep and so it goes on. I've been thinking rather

Ruskin's Illness

sorrowfully over the Marigold Garden, which is no garden, but a mystification–the rather that I saw a real marigold garden at Mr. Hooper's the wood engraver's on Thursday and was amazed. And I mourn over your not showing me things till it's too late to do anything less, or more.

I'm at the saddest part of my autobiography–and think extremely little of myself—then and now—I was sulky and quarrelled with all life –just because I couldn't get the one thing I chose to fancy.— *Now*–I can get nothing I fancy–all the world ebbing away, and the only question for me now–What next?

If you could only change souls with me for five minutes !—What a wise Kate you would be, when you got your own fanciful one back again.

The melancholy tone of the last letter was a pathetic prelude to the very serious illness of this year, of which we find in her laconic diary the following unusually concise entries :—

July 31. He is much worse to-day.
Aug. 11. Still as ill.
  ,,   13. No change yet, still so quiet.
  ,,   14. Slightly better.
  ,,   15. Still better.
  ,,   19. Still better and downstairs.
  ,,   24. Still getting better but so slowly.
  ,,   25. Still better.
  ,,   26. First drive.
  ,,   28. Out in garden alone.

By January of the next year (1886) Mr. Ruskin had sufficiently recovered to resume work on his autobiography and wrote on the 22nd :—

I am so very thankful you like this eighth number so much, for I was afraid it would begin to shock people. I have great pleasure in the thing myself—it is so much easier and simpler to say things face to face like that, than as an author. The ninth has come out very prettily, I think—

Again on the 27th :—

I am so very very glad you like Præterita–for it is–as you say– the 'natural' me–only of course peeled carefully—It is different from what else I write because–you know–I seldom have had to describe any but heroic–or evil–characters–and this watercress character is so much easier to do–and credible and tasteable by everybody's own lips.

Kate Greenaway

And on Feb. 23rd :—

It *is* lovely of you thinking of illustrating the life–I am greatly set up in the thought of it. But wait a while. I hope it will be all more or less graceful. But I fear it will not be cheerful enough. I'll try and keep it as Katish as–the *very* truth can be.

Clotilde is still living, (I believe)–Baronne Du Quesne,–a managing châtelaine in mid-France.

On March 30 he is still insistent with criticism :—

I can only answer to-day the important question about the green lady—' You mean she doesn't stand right ? '

—My dear, I mean much worse than that. I mean there's nothing of her to stand with ! She has no waist–no thighs–no legs–no feet.—There's nothing under the dress at all. . . . . . You recollect I hope that when you were here, I told you you had never *drawn* a bit of drapery in your life.

When you are inclined to try to do so–go and copy as well as you can a bit of St. Jerome's in the Nat. Gall.–and copy a bit of photograph–if you are ashamed to paint in the gallery, and send it me.

I gave you a task to do at the same time–which you never did–but went and gathered my best cherries instead–which I wanted for my own eating–and expected me to be pleased with your trying to paint them !

But soon she is made happier by unqualified praise :—

On a Letter to Ruskin.

You never did anything more lovely than the little flowers to the poem–and the poem itself is most lovely in its outflow from the heart. I am very thankful to have set the heart free again–and I hope that your great genius will soon have joy in its own power.

This year Ruskin was occupying much of his leisure by working on drawings which he had made in early life. Beginning by sending them to K. G. for criticism, he ended by insisting on her keeping for herself one out of every ten, finding much amusement in guessing which would be her choice week by week. The whole thing was a pretty contest in generosity between the great critic and his devoted admirer.

Ruskin Correspondence

On May 21 he writes :—

If you only knew the delight it is to me to send either you or Johnnie anything that you like ! But—not to worry you with the thought of their coming out of my drawers, I shall send Johnnie some only to look at and send back at leisure.—

You're a nice Katie–you–to talk of generosity–after giving me about £2000 worth of drawings as if they were leaves off the trees.

And on June 8 :—

You cannot think what a real comfort and help it is to me that you see anything in my drawings. They are all such mere hints of what I want to do, or syllables of what I saw, that I never think–or at least never thought, they could give the least pleasure to any one but myself–and that you–especially who draw so clearly, should understand the confused scratches of them is very wonderful and joyful to me.

I had fixed on the road through the water for you, out of that lot in my own mind ;–it *is* like you, and it's so nice that you found it out,–and that you like the hazy castle of Annecy too. But it shall be Abingdon this time—It will be very amusing to me to see which you like, out of each ten ; but I think I shall know now pretty well.

Ruskin is still full of schemes of collaboration which, in his opinion, will draw out her best powers so that her gifts may be made more useful to others.

RUSKIN TO KATE GREENAWAY

BRANTWOOD, 27 *April* 86.

It has been a perfect and thrice lovely April morning–absolutely calm, with dew on fields, and the wood anemones full out everywhere : and now coming in, before breakfast, I get your delicious letter about Beauty and the Beast,–I am so very thankful that you like it so– and will do it. For I want intensely to bring one out for you– *your* book–I your publisher, charging you printing and paper only. Hitherto I'm sure your father and Johnnie must think I've been simply swindling you out of your best drawings and–a good deal more.

But now I want you to choose me the purest old form of the story– to do–such illustrations as you feel like doing.—Pencil sketch first at ease. Then–separately, a quite severe ink line–cheaply and without error cuttable–with no bother to either of us,–so much plain shade as you like. To be published without colour, octavo, but with design

Kate Greenaway

for a grand hand-coloured quarto edition afterwards. I'll write a preface—and perhaps with your help, venture on an additional incident or two?

Yesterday was lovely too—and I couldn't sit down to my letters— nor get the book sent.

It is about Sir Philip Sidney and an older friend of his at Vienna— mostly in letters.[1] Read only what you like—there's lots of entirely useless politics which shouldn't have been printed. But you will find things in it—and it is of all things good for you to be brought into living company of these *good* people of old days. . . . . . .

And again on May 7th :—

I wonder if you could put in writing about any particular face—what it is that makes it pretty?   What curl of mouth, what lifting of eyelid, and the like—and what part of it you do first.

I think a new stimulus might be given to drawing in general by teaching some simple principles to girls about drawing each other's faces.

Then there is a recurrence of his illness and a three months' cessation of letters.   In his rambling talk he is heard to say, 'The only person I am sorry to disappoint is poor Miss Greenaway.'

Now again we find pathetic little notes in her diary :—

July 5. Heard this morning he is ill. Had a letter from him.
July 6. Not quite so ill to-day.
July 10. Still ill.
July 14. A little better now.

By September he is at the seaside and again able to use his pen, although too weary and depressed even to make use of that 'Natural History of a dull Beach' which he carried in his mind but which was destined never to be written.

Ruskin to Kate Greenaway

Sunday [*Sep.* 19, 1886].

I'm sending two miles that you may get your—this—whatever you call it—it isn't a letter—and I dare say you won't get it.   I haven't got yours—they won't give anything to anybody on Sunday !—and I'm sure

---

[1] *The Correspondence of Sir Philip Sidney and Hubert Languet.   Now first collected and translated from the Latin with Notes and Memoir of Sidney.* By Stewart A. Pears (London, William Pickering, 1845).

Ruskin Correspondence

yours is a beauty—in the post office over the hill there, and I can't get
it and I've nothing to do and I can't think of anything to think of,—
and the sea has no waves in it—and the sand has no shells in it—and
the shells—oystershells—at lunch had no oysters in them bigger than that
[a rough drawing of a small oyster] in a shell—and *that* wouldn't
come out!

And the wind's whistling through the keyhole—and I ought to go
out—and don't want to—and here's Baxter coming to say I must, and to
take '*this*' to Morecambe.

Much good may it do you.

Soon however he is full of a new plan and once more anxious
for her co-operation :—

Ruskin to Kate Greenaway

Brantwood,
Saturday [Nov. 2, 1886].

It rejoices me so that you enjoy those old master drawings.

It comes, in the very moment when I wanted it—this British M.
enthusiasm of yours.

I'm going to set up a girls' drawing school in London—a room
where nice young girls can go—and find no disagreeable people or
ugly pictures. They must all be introduced by some of my own
sweetest friends—by K. G., by Lilias T.[1] by Margaret B. J.[2] —by my
own sec. Lolly[3]—or by such as ever and anon may be enrolled as
Honorary Students.

And I want you at once to choose, and buy for me beginning with
enclosed cheque, all the drawings by the old masters reproduced to
your good pleasure—Whatever you like, I shall—and the school will be
far happier and more confident in your choice ratified by mine.

And I will talk over every bit of the plan with you—as you have
time to think of it.

—I'm not quite sure I shall like *this* American book as well as Bret
Harte—but am thankful for anything to make me laugh,—if it does.

This year (1886), besides the *Almanack* of which 45,000 copies
were issued, the American sales doubling those of England, and a
large number of designs for Christmas Cards, *A Apple Pie*,
published by George Routledge & Sons, had a gratifying success.

---

[1] Miss Trotter.   [2] Miss Burne-Jones.
[3] Laurence Hilliard, Ruskin's secretary.

Kate Greenaway

England took 7,000 copies, America 3,500, and France 3,000. But it did not by any means meet with Ruskin's approval, and on Nov. 9 he writes from Brantwood :—

Ruskin to Kate Greenaway

I am considerably vexed about Apple Pie. I really think you ought seriously to consult me before determining on the lettering of things so important—

The titles are simply bill-sticking of the vulgarest sort, over the drawings—nor is there one of those that has the least melodious charm as a colour design–while the feet–from merely shapeless are becoming literal paddles or flappers–and in the pretty–though ungrammatical– 'Eat it' are real deformities.

All your faults are gaining on you, every hour that you don't fight them—

I have a plan in my head for organising a girls' Academy under you ! (a fine mistress you'll make–truly–) Lilias Trotter and Miss Alexander for the Dons, or Donnas of it–and with every book and engraving that I can buy for it–of noble types–with as much of cast-drawing, and coin [1]–as you can use,–and two or three general laws of mine to live under ! and spending my last breath in trying to get some good into you !

The next letter refers to an advance copy of *The Queen of the Pirate Isle, by Bret Harte, Illustrated by Kate Greenaway*, with many charming coloured engravings, yet in our opinion certainly not deserving his estimate of it as 'the best thing she had ever done.' The fact is the drawings are treated in a more natural and less quaint and decorative manner than was common with her : and that is what her mentor had always been clamouring for.

Ruskin to Kate Greenaway

Brantwood [*Nov.* 14, 1886].

Waiting for post in expectation of Bret Harte. My dear, you must always send me all you do. If I don't like it–the public will,– if I do–there's always one more pleasure in my disconsolate life.

---

[1] Ruskin had much faith in the educational value of drawings from Greek coins of the finest period.

Brantwood,
Coniston. Lancashire.
Nov 9th 86

I am considerably
bored about Apple Pie.
I really think you oughts
semidly to consult me before
determining on the lettering
of things so important —
The titles are simple
bill-sticking of the vulgarest
sort, over the drawings
— nor is there one of those
that has the least melodious
charm as a colour design —
while the

157

feet – from merely shapeless –
are becoming literal
paddles a flappers – and
in the pretty – though
ungrammatical "Eat it"
are real deformities

All your faults are gaining
on you, every hour thats
you don't fight them –

I have a plan in my head
for organizing a girls Academy
under you – (a fine mistress –
you'll make – truly –) Lilias
Trotter – and Miss Alexander

THE.NAUGHTY. LITTLE
GIRL
WHO·WENT TO SEE HER
GRANDMAMA

Once there was a little girl. and one
nice fine afternoon. Her mama said her
nurse might take her to have tea with
her Grandmama — if the little girl would
promise to be a very good little girl indeed
for I'm sorry to tell you she was often a
very bad little girl — indeed — and did
all sorts of things she ought not to do.
but she said she would be a very
nice child indeed to day — so she had her

A FACSIMILE OF THE ORIGINAL FOUR-PAGE CHILD STORY
Written and illustrated by Kate Greenaway for Miss Violet Severn, now in Miss Severn's possession.

Her Grandmama - was ever so kind - and said now my Dear You may Play in the Garden till tea time but dont touch anything - oh no said the little Girl -

Now her Grandmama had a fine Gooseberry Trees. and the first thing the naughty Girl did was to Pick lots of her Grandmothers favourite Gooseberries

Then her Grandmothers had a nice Cat it didn't like to run - it liked to sit still in the Sun. - now she got a big long stick and made it run very fast - the Cat was very Angry - and very indignant - and very Offended and it did wish it could talk - and tell her Grandmama. How Fast it? Naughty little Girl had made her run.

Then the chickens had "all gone" to have a nice comfortable rest on a bough - she fetched the long stick again and poked them all off - they wished they could tell her Grandmother too -

Then - she turned over the Bee-hive - and all the Bees ran away. Oh you naughty little Girl -

bonnet Put on and said Good bye to her mother.
now mind You are very good said her
mamma. Oh Yes
mama. said the
little Girl.

But there - as soon as she had got
a little way - she ran away from
her Nurse and ran after a
Poor little Butterfly. With her
Parasool.

Then her Grandmamma. had some very nice Rhubarb growing in
the Garden. her Grandmamma. liked Rhubarb tart very much - but
she never had any tart For her dinner - Oh no - for the naughty
Girl Put it all down the well.

Then. she got some large stones. and
sat upon. the seat and. Oh she was
too she dropped. them on to Peoples
heads as they passed by. over the wall.

Her Grandmother - never let her Play in the Garden again
and I think it served her right dont you —— The Pony
was never made to run so fast any more - but sat
in the sun and enjoyed itself all day long -
The kind Grandmama - had nice Gooseberry and
Rhubarb Tarts - for her dinner next year -
the chickens' were never Potted off again

And what was the end of the
naughty Girl - Oh she - had to sit still -
and do lessons - and the Cat laughed when
she heard it - because - she didnt like a
long stick to come after - her - and the
chickens said - Cock a doodle doo - we
dont want any more of you - they meant -
the bad little Girl -

So she went on doing mischief - and tore
her Frocks - and never said if you Please and
never said thankyou - and walked in the mud -
and bit off the ends of her Glove fingers - always -
for she was dreadfull naughty - —— the End — KG

TAKING IN THE ROSES.

THE GARDEN SEAT.

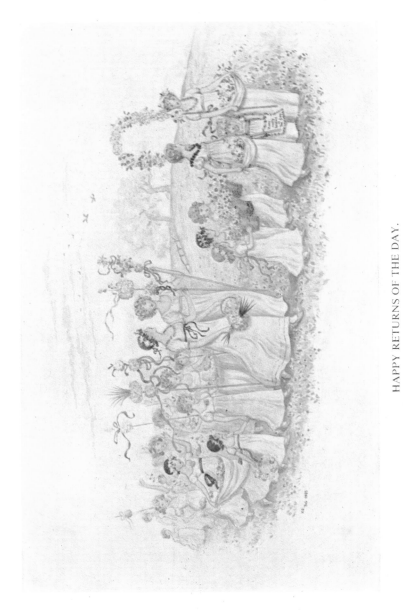

HAPPY RETURNS OF THE DAY.

COTTAGES.

for the Doris, or Donnas? it — and
will every book and burgeons that
I can bring for it — ? noble type —
— with as much ? easy — cheering, and
can — as you can use. — and tears or those
several leaves of mine & live under; and
speeding my little breath in trying
to get some good into you?
       Ever yours

          VR.

159

Kate Greenaway

And you ought to feel that when I do like it–nobody likes it so much !–nor half nor a quarter so much.

Yes, it has come–you're a dear good Katie–and it's lovely. The best thing you have ever done–it is so *real* and natural. I do hope the public will feel with me for once–yes, and for twice–and many times to come.

It is all delightful, and the text also–and the print. You may do more in colour however, next time.

Then there comes a note of criticism and a note of praise.

Of criticism, harking back to *A Apple Pie*, in reply to a sort of good-natured protest from his resolute victim :—

But I never *do* scold you ! never think of such a thing ! I only say I'm–sorry. I have no idea what state of mind you are in when you draw stockings down at the heel, and shoes with the right foot in the left and the left in the right–and legs lumpy at the shins–and shaky at the knees. And when, ever–did you put red letters like the bills of a pantomime–in any of *my* drawings ? and why do it to the public ?

Of praise which in this case has been unduly withheld :—

I've never told you how much I liked a long blue nymph with a branch of roses who came a month ago. It is a heavenly little puckered blue gown with such a lovely spotty-puckery waistband and collar, and a microscopic and microcosmic cross of a brooch, most beautiful to behold. What is she waving her rosebranch for ? and what is she saying ?

Then comes the only letter written by Miss Greenaway to Ruskin before 1887 and preserved by him, and it is followed by a few letters of a general character from him to her.

KATE GREENAWAY TO RUSKIN

50, FROGNAL, 30 *Nov.* 1886.

Yesterday was such a nice day. I had your letter in the morning—then the sun came out—then I went to see Mrs. Allingham in the afternoon who was in town for a few days—with such a lot of beautiful drawings——they *were* lovely—the most truthful, the most like things really look—and the most lovely likeness. I've felt envious all the hours since—there was one cottage and garden with a deep background

Ruskin Correspondence

of pines—it was a marvel of painting—then such a rose bush—then, a divine little picture—of her own beautiful little boy sitting on a garden seat with a girl picking red currants—and a background of deep laurels. You can't think the beauty of it—and *many many many* more—all so lovely, so beautiful. She asked me could I tell her anything—give her advice—and I could not help saying, I can give you nothing but entire praise and the deepest admiration.

She asked after you,—and she said she had often wished to give you a little drawing—but she didn't know if you would be pleased to have it—I don't think I left any doubt in her mind. She asked me what subject I thought you would like best—I said I fancied a pretty little girl with a little cottage or cottage garden—so I hope it will come to pass—I think it will.—You will be so pleased, *only you will like it better than mine*, but Mrs. Allingham is the nicest of people. I always feel I like her so much whenever I see her. And I wish you could have seen those drawings yesterday for they would have been a deep joy to you. She is going to have an exhibition of 40 in London soon. You ought to see them.

Well—I hope you're feeling better. I hope I will have a letter in the morning. I have enjoyed the *Præterita* very much, it is so cheering to have it coming again—

Ruskin to Kate Greenaway

BRANTWOOD, 1*st* Dec. '86.

That *is* delightrul hearing about Mrs. Allingham. I'm so very glad she's so nice as to want to give me a picture. Please tell her there couldn't be anything more delicious to me–both in the sense of friendship and in the possession.

I am very thankful she is doing–as you say–in beauty, and so much besides.

And it is right that you should be a little envious of her realisation– while yet you should be most thankful for your own gift of endless imagination. The realism is in your power whenever you choose.

Ruskin to Kate Greenaway

BRANTWOOD [*Dec.* 12, 1886].

I *do* like *you* to have the books I have cared for,–and–too securely I say–there is no chance of my ever wanting to read these more. My only pleasures now are in actual nature or art–not in visions.

All national costumes, as far as I know, are modern. The con-

Kate Greenaway

ditions of trade established after the 16th century changed everything, and there can be no more consistent art like that which delights you so justly. But the peasant *instincts* are as old as–500 B.C., through it all–and I have seen a half naked beggar's brat in Rome throw a vine branch round his head, like a Greek Bacchus.

And you do more beautiful things yourself, in their way, than ever were done before,–but I should like you to be more amongst 'the *colour* of the colours.'

No, I'm not feeling stronger, but I'm strong enough for all I've to do.

On a Letter to Ruskin.

CHAPTER XI

1887–1890

KATE GREENAWAY AS A CORRESPONDENT—HER LETTERS TO
RUSKIN—HER FRIENDS—LEARNING PERSPECTIVE—RUSKIN'S
LAST LETTERS—'THE PIED PIPER OF HAMELIN'—MRS.
ALLINGHAM, R.W.S.—THE 'BOOK OF GAMES'—ELECTED TO
THE ROYAL INSTITUTE OF PAINTERS IN WATER-COLOURS—
PARIS EXHIBITION—DEATH OF MR. JOHN GREENAWAY, SR.

On a Letter to
Ruskin.

THE most important publications of the year
1887 were *The Queen of the Pirate Isle* (Chatto),
already mentioned ; the *Almanack,* oblong instead
of upright as were all the others, of which over
37,000 copies were sold ; and *Queen Victoria's
Jubilee Garland,* made up of illustrations collected from earlier books.

From this year forward Ruskin made it a
practice to preserve at any rate the majority of
Miss Greenaway's letters.[1] On his side, however, the correspondence was soon destined to
cease, and so in place of the interchange of

---

[1] It was Mr. Ruskin's practice to destroy everything not of
special interest to him or what was unlikely to be of use. On
one occasion the present writer sent him by request certain early
proofs of etched plates, the coppers of which were in the Professor's possession. After a time, on being requested to return
them, he replied that he had destroyed them—'How else do you
think I could do my work if I litter my house with such?'—
and offered by way of compensation to have as many proofs pulled as his disconsolate
correspondent might desire.

Kate Greenaway

thought, which would have afforded stimulating reading, we have to content ourselves with what was in the end to be carried on as a monologue.

The earliest of these letters do not lend themselves to extended quotation. It is only later, when Kate made it part of her day's work to take her share in relieving the tedium of the aged Professor's unoccupied days, that they assume any real importance to the reader.

The key-note of these epistles is their artlessness. She has a child's heart at forty and 'lives with her girlhood as with a little sister.' As we read them the words 'How *naïf*' are for ever on our lips. From time to time we come upon a luminous point and a touch of bright humour, but for the most part the letters are lacking in grip and *verve*. Languid too, they often are, the consequence doubtless of the conscientiousness with which she spent herself in her work, especially when her health during the last ten years of her life was far from robust. And yet with all their shortcomings they have a very real interest and are redolent of her strong personality.

They are instinct, too, with the scent of flowers, the love of trees, the fascinations of her garden, of sunsets and beauties of earth and sky; full, too, of her dog Rover, whom her friends the Allhusens twit her with calling 'Wover'—indeed hardly a letter goes without a chapter, or at least a verse, of Rover's biography, from which a book entitled *The Diary of a Dog* might easily be compiled. They are full of what she is reading (as we might expect, she is always inveighing against the unhappy endings of books)—and tell in detail what she is working at; full of pictures she has seen which wanted 'a Ruskin for their proper criticism'; full of her favourite model 'Mary'—'we always have a merry time, I think we are both made to laugh a good deal'; full of her love of nature—'the garden is full of pictures but I can't get time to do them'; and again, 'when the sun shines I can smell the grass growing'; full of the seasons—'they have got mixed up this year; poor spring has got badly treated or else had an aspiring mind and tried to take too much of the year for her own property—anyhow here is winter again'; full of her friends, the Locker-Lampsons, the du Mauriers, Lady Jeune, 'one of the kindest people in all the world,' and her daughter, now Mrs. Allhusen, the Tennysons, and the beautiful Mrs. Stuart Samuel, 'spring personified dressed in blue and violet—a real Beauty she is and very nice'; full of

Kate Greenaway as Correspondent

playful allusions to the pedantic conversations of Miss Edgeworth's
Harry and Lucy, which she and Ruskin had read and laughed
over together. And they are full of the summer and winter
exhibitions—'no one now says a good word for the Academy
though they all want to be made R.A.'s'; full of the pictures
she intends to paint—'I have often wished lately to paint a picture
of Night—it looks so beautiful out of my window—the yellow
lights in the windows—the stars in the sky. I think I shall do
a little angel rushing along in it, I want to do it as a background
to something. If I could but do a della Robbia angel—with that
look—those curls'; and again, 'Don't you love a market, a real
country one, where the stalls are so pretty with pears and plums
and little sage cheeses and long rolls of butter? For years I
have been going to paint such a market stall. One day—I
suppose—one day I shall.' And yet again they describe lovely
gardens which she has visited; and old houses to which she has
made pilgrimages.

One day there is a touch of sensitiveness:—'I am often
amused at the women who sell the violets—they so often smell
them before presenting them to the purchaser
—this is not always an attraction.' Another
day she touches off a portrait:—'My sister's
little girl is good to contemplate. Her profile
is like a *cheerful* Burne-Jones.'

Now she airs a prejudice:—'I wish
there were no worms in the garden. I *am*
so frightened when I sow things to see them
turn up. I know they are useful but they
are not nice-looking. I do not dislike many
things, but a worm I have a repulsion for.'

And now she pays one of her rare visits
to the theatre—a great event in her quiet
life:—'I went to see *Rebellious Susan*—not a
deep play—very interesting—very cleverly
acted. But I like going deeper into
things, I think I like deeper motives for
things than what Society *thinks.*' Then
she tells of the trouble she takes over her
pictures:—'I am doing Cinderella carry-

'VIOLETS, SIR?'
On a Letter to Ruskin.

ing in the Pumpkin to her fairy godmother—you don't see the
godmother. I have put a row of scarlet beans as a background.

165

Kate Greenaway

I am going to grow a row in the garden on purpose.' And now she wants what she can't have :—'I wish you a very happy Birthday. I wish I was going to be there to see all the lovely flowers you are going to have. If I were there you should ask me to tea—I think—yes, I think you ought to ask me to tea—and we'd have raspberry jam for tea—a muffin, some violets—and a Turner to look at—oh yes, I think you should ask me to tea.'

That is the kind of letter she writes—dwelling but a moment on this or that point, irresponsible, sportive, sometimes gay, less often grave, delightful to the receiver but rarely with sufficient ' body' for the unsympathetic coldness of printer's ink.

The drawings which embellished them are charming in their spontaneity, and who can wonder at the half-heartedness of Ruskin's protest when he writes :—

—In trying to prevent you wasting your time on me I have never told you how much I do enjoy these little drawings. They are an immense addition to the best pleasures of my life and give me continual interest and new thought.

Little marvel that such a protest prompted her to become even more lavish than before. What a delight these letters were to him when ill-health made any written response impracticable may be gathered from Mrs. Severn's reiterated announcements :—

'The Professor is absorbed with delight in your letter.'—
' Your letters are always so interesting and a real pleasure to *him*.'
—'How grateful I ever am for your *untiring goodness* to him. Your letters really are one of the *great* pleasures of his life.'—
' Your lovely letter with the sweet little people looking from the ridge of the hill at the rising sun so delighted Di Pa.[1] He looked at it long and lovingly and kept repeating " Beautiful ! beautiful ! beautiful ! " ' And when he was ill in 1897 :—' Your letters (the only ones he at present has) he much enjoys.'

These letters were full of passing allusions to her friends, of whom she now had many amongst persons distinguished in art and society. She was slow at forming intimacies but she was tenacious of them when made. As she wrote to her friend of many years' standing, the Hon. Mrs. Sutton Nelthorpe, in 1896 :

I'm sorry now that I can see you so seldom.—That's me, so slow at getting to want a person and then wanting them so much.

---

[1] Di Pa was the pet name Ruskin bore at that time in his immediate family circle.

Her Friends

To mention only a few of her friends, there were Mrs. Miller, Miss Violet Dickinson, the Stuart Samuels, Lady Dorothy Nevill, Lady Jeune, Lady Victoria Herbert, Rev. W. J. Loftie, Stacy Marks, the du Mauriers, Mrs. Allhusen, Mrs. Richmond Ritchie, the Edmund Evans', Mr. Norman Shaw, Mr. Austin Dobson, the Locker-Lampsons, Lady Mayo, the Hon. Gerald and Lady Maria Ponsonby, the Hon. Mrs. Sutton Nelthorpe, Mrs. Allingham, the Duchess of St. Albans, Lady Ashburton, the Tennysons, Mrs. Arthur Severn, her daughters, the Misses Lily and Violet Severn, and her husband, Mr. Arthur Severn, R.I., Miss Vyvyan, and Miss Fripp. Miss Vyvyan, like Mrs. Basil Martineau and Mrs. Ridley Corbet (wife of the distinguished painter, the late M. Ridley Corbet, A.R.A.), was a fellow-student of Kate's; Miss Fripp was niece of the well-known member of the Royal Water-Colour Society. With Mrs. Garrett Anderson, M.D., for some years from 1887 her medical adviser, she was very friendly. With Mr. Anderson, too; and also with Miss Mary Anderson, Kate was on the most intimate terms during her life at Hampstead.

In March of this year Ruskin set himself the task of teaching her perspective in about a dozen consecutive letters. He had often alluded to the matter, but now he fills his letters with diagrams of cubes and gables and arches, sparing no pains to make things plain to her and setting her tasks which she most faithfully performed. The technical parts of these letters would here be out of place but some of the side issues suggested by them will bear quotation.

To tell the truth, the perspective in her drawings is often very deficient, and the calm violation of its laws in some of her earlier work was due, not to quaintness as people thought, but to real inability to master it. She would innocently make independent sketches of pretty cottages, real or imagined, and then calmly group them together, with little or no correction or bringing into harmony, as a background for a composition of playing children. In her earlier years her father would often put these portions of her design into proper perspective, and later on her brother John. Indeed, at her first exhibition a critic was examining a drawing from *Under the Window*, and as he looked it over, he exclaimed to a friend, first in amazement and then in anger, 'She has one point of sight here, and another here! and here! and here!! Why, she has five distinct points of sight!'

167

Kate Greenaway

Afterwards her brother would reduce the whole to correctness for her to re-draw. So when Ruskin began to educate her in a branch of art which, by the way, is neglected and loathed by not a few of the greatest of the world's painters, she explained to him how she was in this respect in the excellent care of her brother. Mr. John Greenaway, by the way, always believed that his sister's curious inaccuracy was due to her short-sightedness; as she would approach too closely to the objects she drew, and so 'got them out.'

Thereupon, on March 8, Ruskin writes: 'I like Johnnie's sticking himself up to teach you perspective! I never believed you'd learn it, or I'd have taught it you here, and been done with it. Anyhow–don't you let him teaze you any more and just mind this to begin with.' Here follow diagrams and explanation, and he goes on 'That's enough for to-day. Three more scribbles will teach you all you'll ever need to know.'

Two days later he returns to the subject :—' There's no fear of your forgetting perspective, any more than forgetting how to dance. One can't help it when one knows. The next rule you have to learn is more than half way. One never *uses* the rules, one only feels them–and defies if one likes–like John Bellini. But we should first know and enjoy them.'

The last words refer to the following passage which he had written the day before, when sending her a copy he had had made for her of Bellini's picture :—

'The Globe picture is one of a series done by John Bellini of the Gods and Goddesses of good and evil to man.[1] She is the sacred Venus–Venus always rises out of the sea, but this one out of laughing sea of unknown depth. She holds the world in her arms, changed into heaven.'

On March 12 he says, apropos of her work on the *Pied Piper*, 'Finished the rats, have you! but you ought to do dozens of rats in perspective with radiating tails.' Here he draws a rough example of what he means and continues :—' I believe the perfection of perspective is only recent. It was first applied to Italian Art by Paul Uccello (Paul the Bird–because he drew birds so well and many). He went off his head with his love of perfection–and Leonardo and Raphael spoiled a lot of pictures with it, to show they knew it. Now the next thing you have to be clear

---

[1] 'Venus, Mistress of the World'—one of the series of allegorical subjects by Giovanni Bellini in the Academy of Fine Arts in Venice.

Perspective and Bellini

of in perspective is that–the Heavenly Venus is out of it. You couldn't see her and the high horizon at once. But as she sees all round the world there are no laws of perspective for her.'

Not unnaturally, perhaps, Miss Greenaway claims for herself the same licence or privilege of abstention as Bellini was allowed, so on March 17th Ruskin replies:—'I didn't answer your question "Why may not I defy Perspective as well as John Bellini?" Not because you are less—but because defying is a quite different thing from running against. Perspective won't put up with you–if you tread on her toes–but will concede half her power to you if you can look her in the eyes. I won't tell you more till you're across that river.'

Two other extracts from Ruskin's letters, and the record of this year is complete.

Ruskin to Kate Greenaway

Brantwood,
Monday 23 [Jan. 1887].

I'm still quite well thank God, and as prudent as can be–and have been enjoying my own drawings! and think I shan't mind much if there's a fault or two in your's!

But we will have it out about suns and moons like straw hats! and shoes like butter boats–and lilies crumpled like pocket-handkerchiefs, and frocks chopped up instead of folded. I've got a whole cupboard full of dolls for lay figures and five hundred plates of costume–to be Kate Greenawayed.

Ruskin to Kate Greenaway

Brantwood [April 4, 1887].

The anemones are here–and quite lovely, but you know they're not like those wild ones of Italy and wither ever so much sooner.

I'm enjoying my botany again–but on the whole I think it's very absurd of flowers not to be prettier! How they might all grow up into lovely trees–and pinks grow like almond blossom, and violets everywhere like daisies, tulips climb about like Virginian creeper–and not stand staring just as if they'd been just stuck into the ground.—Fancy a house all in a mantle of tulips.—And how many new shapes they might invent! . . . . And why aren't there Water Roses as well as Water Lilies?

169

Kate Greenaway

In the early part of the year Kate Greenaway seems to have designed a cover for *The Peace of Polissena*, by Miss Francesca Alexander, a 'Part' of *Christ's Folk in the Apennine*, edited and partly written by Ruskin—a graceful reply to her supposed but of course entirely imaginary jealousy of that lady's work—but it does not appear to have been used. This may have been a result of the return of the Master's illness which again laid him low in the spring of 1887.

In January of 1888 we find him sufficiently recovered to write the following pathetic letters from Sandgate, whither he had gone to recuperate.

In other letters of this period he complains that he has hardly strength to answer hers, and that he is sadly oppressed by the cold which oppresses her. He praises her for her appreciation of Donatello, and says that Donatello would have appreciated Kate Greenaway. But he qualifies his praise by telling her that she would do far more beautiful things if she would not allow herself to be hurried away by the new thoughts which crowd upon her and hinder her from fully realising *any*.

Then he falls foul of modern novels, of which he is having a surfeit through the circulating library. Some of the books for girls he finds passably good but deplores the fashion, which began with *Misunderstood*, of breaking children's backs, so that one never knows what is going to happen to them when they go out walking !

RUSKIN TO KATE GREENAWAY

[SANDGATE] 27 *Jan.* 88.

You cannot conceive how in my present state, I envy–that is to say only in the strongest way, long for–the least vestige of imagination, such as yours. When nothing shows itself to me–all day long–but the dull room or the wild sea and I think what it must be to you to have far sight into dreamlands of truth–and to be able to see such scenes of the most exquisite grace and life and quaint vivacity–whether you draw them or not, what a blessing to have them there–at your call. And then I stopped and have been lying back in my chair the last quarter of an hour,–thinking–If I could only let you feel for only a quarter of an hour what it is to have no imagination–no power of calling up lovely things–no guidance of pencil point along the visionary line–Oh how thankful you would be to find your mind again.

And what lovely work you have spent–where no one will ever see

170

'Processions'

it but poor me—on the lightest of your messages. Do you remember the invitation sent by the girl holding the muffin high on her toasting fork? You never did a more careful or perfect profile. And the clusters of beauty in those festival or farewell ones?

Well, I had joy out of them—such as you meant—and more than ever I could tell you, nor do I ever cease to rejoice at and wonder at them,—but with such sorrow that they are not all in a great lovely book, for all the world's New Years and Easter days.

You might do a book of Festas, one of these days—with such processions!

By 'processions' are meant the long drawings with a bevy of following maids, and sometimes of boys too, of which one or two examples are included in this book. They contain some of Miss Greenaway's most careful and dainty work in drawing, colour, and composition, but, unfortunately, are so large that they have suffered great reduction.

RUSKIN TO KATE GREENAWAY

[SANDGATE] 17 Feb. 88.

It's just as bad here as everywhere else—there are no birds but sea-gulls and sparrows—there is snow everywhere—and north-east wind on the hills,—but none on the sea—which is as dull as the Regent's Canal. But I was very glad of the flower letter yesterday,—and the chicken-broth one to-day, only I can't remember that cat whom I had to teach to like cream. I believe it *is* an acquired taste—and that most cats can conceive nothing better than milk. I am puzzled by Jim's inattention to drops left on the tablecloth—he cleans his saucer scrupulously, but I've never seen him lap up, or touch up, a spilt drop. He is an extremely graceful grey striped fat cushion of a cat,—with extremely winning ways of lying on his back on my knee, with his head anywhere and his paws everywhere.

But he hasn't much conversation and our best times are I believe when we both fall asleep.

He says he yearns for 'Pipers,' alluding, of course, to drawings for '*The Pied Piper of Hamelin*, by Robert Browning, with 35 Illustrations by Kate Greenaway. Engraved and printed in colours by Edmund Evans,' which George Routledge & Sons were just publishing. The book, which was charming throughout, save for a poor drawing on page 31 and a curious solecism on page 39, met with immediate and gratifying success. Stacy

171

Kate Greenaway

Marks wrote :—'You have far exceeded my expectations in carrying through what must have been a strange and difficult task.' Ruskin spoke of it as the grandest thing she had ever done. An American admirer wrote enthusiastically :—'You have more followers in the States than ever the Pied Piper of Hamelin had.' She sold the original drawings for a large sum to Messrs. Palmer & Howe of Manchester.

On Feb. 23 Ruskin writes :—

> The Piper came by the 11 post—ten minutes after my note left this morning. I only expected outline proofs, so you may judge how pleased I was.
>
> It is all as good and nice as it can be, and you really have got through your rats with credit–and the Piper is sublime–and the children lovely. But I am more disappointed in the 'Paradise' than I expected to be–a *real* view of Hampstead ponds in spring would have been more celestial to me than this customary flat of yours with the trees stuck into it at regular distances—And not a Peacock !–nor a flying horse ! !

The only other publications of the year were the sixth *Almanack*, of which 20,000 out of 37,500 copies went to America and 6,500 to France, and a contribution to *The American Queen*. There were also private commissions executed for Lady Dorothy Nevill, Lady Northcote, and Mr. Ponsonby.

But the crowning event of 1888 was the friendship which she now formed with Mrs. Allingham. Sixteen years before they had worked side by side as students, but since then their paths had diverged. The account of their intimacy will best be told in that delightful artist's own words :—

> It must have been in 1872 or 1873 that I first met Kate Greenaway at an evening class at the Slade School (which I only attended for three months). I had given up my student work at the R.A. schools— (she doubtless had then left Kensington) for drawing on the wood in my own studio.
>
> I was not formally introduced to her till several years after I was married, when I met her at an evening party at Tennyson's — in Belgrave Square, I think. Mr. Frederick Locker presented me to her, and we had a pleasant talk, I remember. In 1881, we went to live at Witley in Surrey, and among our kindest neighbours were Mr. and Mrs. Edmund Evans, with whom Kate often came to stay.
>
> For several years we (K. and I) had merely pleasant friendly meetings without in any way becoming intimate. I think it was in the

Mrs. Allingham's Recollections

spring of 1888 that we went out painting together in the copses near Witley and became really *friends*. In the autumn of that year we removed to Hampstead, and it was always a pleasure to visit Kate in her beautiful home and to sit and chat with her by the hour in her cosy little tea-room or in the great studio full of interesting things. When the time came for saying good-night, she would always come down to the hall-door and generally put on a hat hanging in the hall and come as far as the gate for more friendly last words.

One day in the autumn of 1889 we went to Pinner together on an exploring expedition for subjects, and were delighted with some of the old cottages we saw there. I had been pressing her ever since our spring time together at Witley to share with me some of the joys of painting out of doors. Another day we went farther afield—to Chesham and Amersham. She was delighted with the beauty of the country and the picturesque old towns—especially with the 'backs' at Amersham and the river with its border of willows and little cottage gardens and back yards. As evening drew on and black clouds warned us that a storm was imminent, we hailed a baker's cart that was going towards our station and we agreed that it gave us a capital view of the country over the high hedges.

In the spring of 1890 I took my children to Freshwater, Isle of Wight, and found rooms near us for Kate. She and I went out painting together daily, either to some of the pretty old thatched cottages around Farringford or to the old dairy in the grounds, when we often had a friendly visit from the great poet himself, or from Mr. Hallam Tennyson, with an invitation to come up to tea.

During the summer of that year (1890) we continued our outdoor work together, generally taking an early train from Finchley Road to Pinner, for the day. She was always scrupulously thoughtful for the convenience and feelings of the owners of the farm or cottage we wished to paint, with the consequence that *we* were made welcome to sit in the garden or orchard where *others* were refused admittance.

I am afraid that her short sight must have greatly added to the difficulty of out-door painting for her. I remember her exclaiming one day at Pinner, 'What am I to do? When I look at the roof it is all a red blur—when I put on my spectacles I see every crack in the tiles.'

Though we often sat side by side, painting the same object (generally silently—for she was a very earnest, hard worker—and perhaps I was, too), it seemed to me that there was little likeness between our drawings—especially after the completion in the studio. But she was one of the most sensitive of creatures and I think she felt that it might be wiser for both of us to discontinue the practice of working from the same subjects, so, after that summer of 1890, we did

173

Kate Greenaway

not go out painting any more together. Whether days or months passed between our meetings, I was always sure of the same hearty greeting from her.

The last time I saw her was Feb. 28, 1901, at the Fine Art Society. I thought she looked fairly well, and seemed so, though she spoke of having felt tired sometimes. But she said nothing of the serious illness of the year before. It was not possible to have much talk then. I became exceedingly busy just after that time, and in May went abroad—and when later on in the year I called at her house, I was told she was not well enough to see friends.

Her work remains for all to see and enjoy. Of herself, I can truly say that she was one of the most honest, straightforward, and kindly of women : a sympathetic, true, and steadfast friend.

The year 1889 produced, besides the *Almanack*, which by now had become an institution, *Kate Greenaway's Book of Games*—with, as a matter of course, Mr. Evans as engraver and printer, and G. Routledge & Sons as publishers—and ' *The Royal Progress of King Pepito*, written by Beatrice F. Cresswell, illustrated by Kate Greenaway,' and published by the Society for Promoting Christian Knowledge. Of each of these books nearly ten thousand copies were issued. The *Book of Games*, in which she could choose her own subjects and follow her own bent, found K. G., if not at her best, at least happy and unrestrained, while with *King Pepito* it was otherwise. As was usually the case with her, she found it hard to assimilate another's ideas. The inelasticity of story-book illustrating seemed to paralyse her pencil and she became mannered and conventional.

This year she was elected a member of the Royal Institute of Painters in Water-Colours, and was moreover represented by thirteen frames of drawings in the British Section of the International Exhibition at Paris.[1] These were greatly admired, and elicited the following, amongst innumerable other tributes of praise :—

Son genre a été une innovation et une preuve de bravoure, comme tous les actes d'indépendance dans l'ordre moral et artistique.

Lancer au milieu d'une société blasée, ces échappés de nurseries, vêtus à la mode bizarre et charmante qu'on appelle maintenant ' la Greenaway,' était à coup sûr original. . . . . .

---

[1] These comprised designs from the *Almanack* for 1884, and drawings from *Marigold Garden*, the *Language of Flowers*, and *Little Ann.*

Ruskin's Last Letters

> Les œuvres de l'aquarelliste anglaise jettent-elles là une note fraîche
> et gaie, et font-elles l'effet d'un enfant dans un intérieur de vieux,
> d'un oiseau égaré dans un cloître. . . . . .
> L'usateur des Almanachs semble avoir une préférence marquée pour
> certaines couleurs : elle excelle dans l'usage du blanc, du rose, et du vert.
> Avec leur emploi, elle arrive à des teintes effacées d'un effet charmant.
> Ses tons évoquent l'image des pendules à fleurs et des soies anciennes,
> des vieilles faïences à paysages et des céladonnades à la Watteau, toutes
> ces choses, comme elles nous arrivent maintenant, mangées de soleil,
> vieilles d'un siècle et pourtant encore délicieusement jolies, ainsi que
> les aquarelles qui en réveillent le souvenir.

Since the spring of 1888 there had been no letters from Ruskin,
who had made his last foreign tour to France, Switzerland, and
Italy in the vain hope of renewing his health.   Now in the spring
of 1889 he was back at Brantwood with ten pathetic years before
him of growing infirmity.   In May he was well enough to write
to Miss Greenaway the following letters, which were to be the
last he was ever to send.   In the course of the following month
he produced a chapter of *Præterita* and then his literary career
was closed.

RUSKIN TO KATE GREENAWAY

BRANTWOOD *May-day* 1889.

I've been a-maying with you all day,–coming upon one beautiful
thing after another in my drawer, so long unopened–most thankfully
to-day unlocked again–and sending balm and rose and lily sweetness
all through the old study.   What exquisite drawings those were you
did just before I fell so ill,–the children passing under the flower arch–
&c.! and Joan tells me you are doing *such* lovely things now with
such backgrounds,–grander than ever, and of course the Piper is the
best book you ever did–the Piper himself unsurpassable–and I feel as
if he had piped me back out of the hill again, and would give some
spring times yet to rejoice in your lovely work and its witness to them.
I do hope much, now–the change is greater and deeper for good
than it has ever been before, but I have to watch almost every breath
lest I should fall back again.
I wonder if you would care to come down in the wild rose time–
and draw a branch or two, with the blue hills seen through them, and
perhaps study a little falling water–or running–in the green shadows.
I wouldn't set you to horrid work in the study, you should even draw
any quantity of those things that you liked–in the forenoon–and have

175

Kate Greenaway

tea in the study, and perhaps we could go on with the Swiss fish story !
and I've some psalter work in hand that I want you to help me in-
tebbily,—and poor Joanie will be so thankful to have somebody to look
after me a little, as well as her :—and so—perhaps you'll come, won't
you ?

I am so very thankful that you can come—and still care to come—!
I was so afraid you might have some work on hand that would hinder
you—but now, I do trust that you will be quite happy, for indeed you
will find here, when you are at liberty to do what you like best,—the
exact things that become most tractable in their infinite beauty.   You
are doing great work already—some of the pages of the Piper are
magnificent pictures, though with a white background—you will be led
by the blue mountains and in the green glens to a deeper colour-
melody—and—to how much else—there is no calculating.   Please bring
the primrose picture !—it will be the intensest delight to me and in
looking over your drawings again, (how many do you think there are
in my Kate drawer, now—besides those in the cabinets ?) I feel more
than ever—I might almost say twice as much as I used to, their
altogether unrivalled loveliness.

And I think, as soon as you have seen all the exhibitions, and
feel able to pack your country dresses and sacrifice London gaieties
for monastic peace in art and nature, that you should really come ;
the roses will soon be here—and the gentians and hyacinths will
certainly be here before you—and it is best, while all things bid fair
for us, to take Fortune at her word.

I trust that my health will go on improving—but I might take cold,
or Joanie might—or the children.   At present we're all right and I
want you to come as soon as may be.

I *am* so sorry you can't come sooner, to see the gentians—but I suppose
they contrive ways of growing them now even in London.   But I have
a cluster of nine,—in a little glass in the study bow window—you know
where *that* is ? !—three little roses pretending to be peach blossoms
in another little glass on my table, and beside them a cluster of
' myrtilla cara '—if you don't know what that is, it's just jealousy and I'll
make you paint some—where your easel shan't tumble, nor your colours
be overflown—I don't a bit know what's the right word—Shakespeare's
no authority, is he nowadays ?—and next the Myrtilla Cara who is
in her sweetest pride and humility of fruit-like blossom, there's a
cluster of the most beautiful pyrus I ever saw—it is almost white, I

Ruskin's Last Letter

suppose with the cold and rain, where it blooms on the outside wall, but on my table–brought in by Joanie, it has become glowing red–not in the least like a rose–but yet not in the least vulgar–like a lady wearing a scarlet cloak–and with its own grand laurel-like leaves.

Well, if you can't come yet you can't–but you must read a little bit of *me* every day–to keep you steady against the horrible mob of animals calling themselves painters, nowadays (–I could paint better than they by merely throwing my ink bottle at them–if I thought them *worth* the ink). But take my Ariadne Florentina–and read for to-morrow the 112th paragraph, p. 94–and in the appendix, the 244th page down to 'steam whistle.'—Post's going–and I must not begin any special appendix to Katie–except that she must not plague herself with endeavours to realise the impossible—Her first, and easy duty is to catch the beautiful expressions of *real* children.

BRANTWOOD, 14 *May*, 1889.

I am so very happy you are teaching yourself French. It is the greatest addition you can give to the happiness of your life,–some day I hope–old as I am–to see you drawing French children–and listening to them !

And you must learn a little Latin too ! only to enjoy the nomenclature of Proserpina. Please take it down and read pages 227, 228, about Myrtilla cara–and just look at my type of all perfection, the Angel Raphael's left hand in the great Perugino,–it will refresh you and contrast, ever more brightly and richly, with modern mud and pewter.— But– . . . . . . the idea of asking why a hand is so difficult ! Why it's ever so much harder than even a foot–and for an *arm*–nobody ever could *paint* a girl's arm yet–from elbow to wrist.—It's not quite fair to show you these two *tries* of yours–but yet, the moral of them is that you must cure yourself of thinking so much of hair and hats and parasols–and attend *first*, (for some time to come) to toes–fingers– and wrists.

Thus ended, so far as Ruskin was concerned, a correspondence which had not only been one of the greatest pleasures of Kate Greenaway's life, but had been above all a healthy stimulus and a liberal education.

The following year, 1890, which saw no publication calling for notice other than the *Almanack*, was clouded by the death of her father, Mr. Greenaway, on August 26th. He was one of those honourable, hard-working, competent servants of the public who, content to do their work quietly, look for no fame and no reward beyond the right to live and earn an honest livelihood for

177   23

Kate Greenaway

themselves and their dependants. Mr. Mason Jackson of the *Illustrated London News* paid him a fitting tribute when he wrote :—

I have known Mr. Greenaway so long and admired his sterling qualities so much that I feel I have lost another of my valued friends. His family will have the satisfaction of feeling that he has left behind him an unblemished character and a respected name.

Ever ready to help in charitable undertakings, although almost driven to her wits' end to get through work which had to be done, Kate this year designed a cover for the album of the Bazaar held in aid of the ' New Hospital for Women ' ; such contributions she felt due to a public from whom she had received so handsome a recognition. Very different, however, were the feelings she expressed towards the methods of certain journals of getting something for nothing, and over these she would wax exceedingly indignant. There were those who solicited her for an (unremunerated) opinion ' as a representative woman on the servant question,' or for a few lines on ' why I like painting for children,' or for ' the briefest message to our readers in a series of timely words or messages from men and women distinguished in politics, literature, and art ' ; or for a ' gratuitous product of your skill—which would give you a magnificent advertisement and result materially to your renown and prosperity ' !

To signalise her election she contributed to the Royal Institute of Painters in Water-Colours four exhibits— ' A Portrait of a Little Boy,' ' An Angel visited the Green Earth,' ' Boy with Basket of Apples,' and ' Head of a Boy ' ; and she exhibited also a portrait of a little lad at the Royal Academy.

CHAPTER XII

1891-1895

FOR the last year or two Kate Greenaway had shown unmistakable signs of failing energy, and in 1891 her friend Mr. Anderson of the Orient Line sought to persuade her to take a sea-voyage on the steam-ship *Garonne* : it must not be sup-posed, however, that she was yet showing the first symptoms of the illness which was to terminate ten years later in her death. She published no work this year except the *Almanack* and, though scarcely worthy of repeated mention, the title-page designed for *The Orient Guide*, as a graceful acknowledgment of Mr. Anderson's kindly friendship. At the Royal Academy she was represented by a 'Girl's Head,' and at the Royal Institute by 'An Old Farm House' and 'A Cottage in Surrey.'

On a Letter to Ruskin.

But the year was far from being un-eventful, for now for the first time she determined to hold a 'one-man' exhibi-tion of her water-colour drawings at the Gallery of the Fine Art Society, at 148, New Bond Street.

179

Kate Greenaway

The exhibition was highly successful. The town flocked to see the originals of the designs which had charmed it for so many years in the reproductions, and greatly was the world surprised at the infinite tenderness, delicacy, and grace of her execution, and the wealth of her invention. Sir Frederick Leighton purchased two of her pictures and others followed suit to the amount of more than £1,350. (The net sum which came to her was £964.) For the first time the general public and the critics had the opportunity of assigning to Kate Greenaway her rightful place amongst contemporary artists. She had appeared in most of the important exhibitions in London and the provinces, and her pictures had almost invariably found purchasers, but these occasional exhibits had been comparatively few. Now her work could be gauged in bulk and there was a chorus of approval. Not that too much stress must be laid upon that. Even now, some years after her death, there is some contention as to exactly where she stands. As Mr. Lionel Robinson asked at the time—did she found a school or did she only start a fashion? was hers but a passing *ad captandum* popularity or does her art contain the true elements of immortality?

The following letters of this year exhibit her perennial love of spring flowers, with which Lady Mayo now constantly supplied her, in return for which on this occasion she sent a drawing of St. John's wort, bluebell, and apple-blossom ; and we recognise once more her fastidious terror lest she should receive payment for what was not precisely to the taste of her clients.

KATE GREENAWAY TO LADY MAYO

Dear Lady Mayo—Your lovely flowers have just come. It is too good of you to have such kind thought and remembrance of me. I thank you very much. I think nothing gives me such joy and delight as spring flowers, and after this long, long winter how delightful it is to have them back again. The springs always come late to us here ; it is such a cold place. I am just now going into Surrey to paint primroses.

I feel I must send you a flower also. I wish it could be as lovely as yours !—With kind regards and again thanks, yours very sincerely,

KATE GREENAWAY.

The following letter probably refers to the first of a set of tiny water-colour portraits of children executed for Mr. Ponsonby

The Hon. Gerald Ponsonby

which show what she might have accomplished if she had set herself seriously to the painting of miniatures :—

KATE GREENAWAY TO MR. PONSONBY

50, FROGNAL, HAMPSTEAD, N.W.,
5th October 1891.

Dear Mr. Ponsonby—I am long in sending you the drawing, and now I do send it, I am afraid you will feel it very unsatisfactory ; I feel it so myself—it is so much more difficult to me—doing a Portrait than a purely fancy drawing. Now I can't make up my mind if it requires more darks or not. If you feel that let me have it back and I will put them in. I am rather afraid to do more. I have puzzled over it until I don't know what it wants really. But one thing is certain, you must not have it if you do not care for it. I should be so sorry if you did,—it would really pain me and you know it would not matter in the least. I should be the gainer—having had such a pleasant time with you and a pretty little girl to draw—so please be very sure you don't keep it if it is not what you wish.

The African marigolds are still beautiful—the memories of Christchurch and Poole are still vivid—I did so very much like seeing them. I believe seeing old towns and villages *are* my greatest enjoyments,—if only I did not make such abject sketches. I saw the salmon-coloured house on my way home.—With kind regards, yours sincerely,

KATE GREENAWAY.

For the next nine years (1892-1900) there were no new publications with Kate Greenaway's name on the title-page with the exception of the Almanacks. These were published in 1892, 3, 4, and 5 by George Routledge & Sons as heretofore. In 1896 there was none : perhaps, as we have said, because that for 1895 had been 'made up'—much against K. G.'s will—from old and comparatively unsuccessful work ; still, as we see later, an application was made to Miss Greenaway for an almanack, but she was indisposed to do it. In 1897 the last was published by J. M. Dent & Co. Of these charming booklets complete sets are now not easy to obtain, and readily fetch four or five times their original cost.

In 1892 there was a small exhibition of twenty of her watercolours by Messrs. Van Baerle in Glasgow, and an important commission executed for the Dowager Lady Ashburton.

In 1893 five of her drawings were sold at the Columbian Exhibition, Chicago, for forty-five guineas. These were the

181

Kate Greenaway

title-page to *Marigold Garden*, 'The Mulberry Bush,' 'Girl drawing a Chaise,' 'Little Girlie,' and 'Little Phyllis.' The Almanack drawings of this year were disposed of through Messrs. Palmer, Howe & Co. of Manchester to Mr. David Walker of Middleton in the neighbourhood of that city, with special and exclusive permission to reproduce them as designs for 'sanitary wall-papers.' Kate was delighted with the results and many a nursery is now gay with these charming productions.[1]

The modern passion for book-plate collecting was at this time at its height and Kate came in for her meed of praise at the hands of Mr. Egerton Castle in his *English Book-plates* of this year, and at the hands, too, of Miss Norna Labouchere in her *Ladies' Book-plates*, of two years later. In the former are reproduced those designed by Miss Greenaway for 'Frederick Locker' and his son 'Godfrey Locker-Lampson,' and in the latter for 'Dorothy Locker-Lampson' and 'Sarah Nickson.' Amongst others for whom she designed book-plates may be mentioned Lady Victoria Herbert, Miss Vera Samuel (a child's book-plate), Mrs. J. Black, and Mr. Stuart M. Samuel. Most of those mentioned are here reproduced.

Although the publications of these closing years of her life were scanty it must not be supposed that K. G. allowed her pencil and brush to be idle. This was far from the case. It is true that her work done for reproduction was nearly at an end, but she was devoting herself with unabated enthusiasm, so far as her health would allow, to the more congenial task of painting small easel pictures in water-colour in view of future exhibitions at the Fine Art Society's gallery.

The following letter shows her hard at work for her next public appearance, and the entry of this year, the only entry in her long range of laconic diaries of an introspective nature—'To remember to keep resolution firmly and to think how much can be made of Art and Life,'—demonstrates the spirit in which she was working.

KATE GREENAWAY TO MR. PONSONBY

50, FROGNAL, HAMPSTEAD, N.W.,
29th Dec. 1893.

Dear Mr. Ponsonby—I believe the Exhibition is finally settled at LAST—drawings to be sent in on the 15th, and Private View to take

---

[1] Reproduced as end-papers of this volume.

'The Ladies' Home Journal'

place on the 20th. . . . . . . And it is nice weather to get on in! Black night here the last three days. . . . . . Mr. Huish of course changes the date about nine times. First they couldn't, then they could. First the small room and then the big one. HE suggested Palms to fill up the corners. Think of my poor little works floating about in that big room. I wrote a beautiful letter, suggesting that a considerable amount of Palms seemed inevitable — but the letter was not allowed to be sent, my brother considered it FLIPPANT and unbusiness-like. I thought this rather hard, as I had abstained from remarking that a few apple trees or roses might be more in accordance with the sentiment of my drawings than plants of an Oriental character. However I am going to have the small room. Shall you be still in London? Nothing will get finished if this fog lasts.

I was desperately [sorry] not to see the tree—but there was no help. I wrote to Lady Maria in so much of a hurry—I hope I explained clearly, and that I am hoping to come to tea when a leisure afternoon comes to Lady Maria to have me.

I wish you and Lady Maria a very happy New Year.—Yours sincerely,   Kate Greenaway.

I'm too delighted that the shops are once more open—and that the Post comes and goes.

The exhibition opened on January 22, and the gross proceeds were £1,067 : 16s. (net £799). The most important works were 'The Green Seat' (40 guineas), 'The Stick Fire' (35 guineas), 'The Cherry Woman' (40 guineas), 'The little Go-Cart' (36 guineas), 'Cottages' (45 guineas), 'Jack and Jill' (20 guineas), 'The Fable of the Girl and her Milk Pail' (40 guineas), 'Lucy Locket' (30 guineas), 'Standing for her Picture' (25 guineas), 'Two Little Sisters' (25 guineas), 'The Toy Horse' (25 guineas), 'Belinda' (25 guineas), 'Down the Steps' (25 guineas), 'Apple Trees' (55 guineas), 'Over the Tea' (35 guineas), 'A Spring Copse' (40 guineas), 'The Old Steps' (35 guineas), 'Under the Rose Tree' (25 guineas), 'At a Garden Door' (35 guineas), and 'A Buttercup Field' (£30).

This year she began her connection with *The Ladies' Home Journal*, published in Philadelphia, which, with its circulation of 700,000, did much to enlarge her circle of American admirers. The connection lasted through four numbers and proved highly remunerative. Thirty pounds was paid her per page for the serial rights only of seven or eight beautiful little pen-and-ink drawings illustrating delightful verses by Miss Laura E. Richards. They

Kate Greenaway

were executed in her happiest vein and they not only show no
falling off either in invention or execution but an absolute advance
in the free use of the pen. The only other published work of this
year which calls for mention is the coloured drawing 'A Sailor's
Wife' reproduced in the December number of *The English
Illustrated Magazine*. It is ambitious in treatment, but illustrates
the artist's limitations, although much of its failure is due to the
crudeness of the colour-printing.

The fact is that her genius for drawing for the press had now
grown fitful, and that she felt this herself is proved by her refusal
at this time to undertake the illustration of Messrs. Longman's
Reading Books for elementary schools, which a few years earlier
would have made a very strong appeal to her. Doubtless, too, her
health had much to do with it and disinclined her to bind herself
to the dates and exactions which it is incumbent on publishers
to set.

After two years' absence from the walls of the Royal Institute
she was now again represented by the portrait of 'A Girl,' which
was the forerunner of an unbroken series of exhibits until 1897.

On February the 2nd, the little circle at Frognal was further
sadly reduced by the deeply-mourned death of Mrs. Greenaway,
of whose fine and sterling character the reader has caught glimpses
in the earlier chapters. The strain of this sorrow coming immediately after the exhaustion consequent upon the exhibition of her
pictures, resulted in some months of broken health, and it was not
until May that Miss Greenaway found herself again fit for work.

Soon after her mother's death she wrote :—

KATE GREENAWAY TO MR. PONSONBY

50, FROGNAL, HAMPSTEAD, N.W.,
10*th* Feb. 1894.

Dear Mr. Ponsonby—Thank you so much for your kind letter.
You and Lady Maria have been so KIND. I can't tell you HOW much
it has been to me to feel I have such friends as you always are to me.
We certainly do feel desolate and strange, but I know in time the very
dreadful feeling will pass off, though I also know life must be for
ever a different feeling, for I have never felt the same since my
father died. . . . . . .
I am sorry you also have had a sad loss—I have seen many notices
of it in the Papers. The longer I live the less I understand the scheme
of life that comprises so much sadness in it. I wish we could under-

Lady Maria Ponsonby

stand more. Will you tell Lady Maria I am so looking forward to seeing her? I feel like Lady Dorothy, who once, when you had gone abroad, said she was glad you had rainy weather because you should have stayed in London.—Yours sincerely,   KATE GREENAWAY.

After a visit to Mr. and Mrs. Locker-Lampson at Rowfant to recuperate her health she wrote:—

KATE GREENAWAY TO LADY MARIA PONSONBY

39, FROGNAL, 9 *May* 1894.

Dear Lady Maria Ponsonby—I have had you and Mr. Ponsonby so much in my mind for the last two weeks—and I feel so much I would like to write to you, but don't you trouble to write to me, if you are too busy. It is a pleasure to write to you—anyhow.

I think I feel to my real friends as I do to my favourite books— they get into my mind after a separation and I am impelled to write to them or read them as the case may be.

I think of one of Mr. Locker-Lampson's favourite stories of Carlyle, who said to Mr. Allingham—'Have a care, Allingham, have a care— there's a danger of your making yourself a bit of a bore.'

These are not quite the words—the original ones are better put.— I fear that danger as regards myself.

I came home from Rowfant last week. I had a nice time. I think I am feeling stronger, but sometimes I do not feel very well, but of course it is rather a slow process, and it requires patience, which quality I don't possess.

Are you coming to Green Street this month? will you allow the bore to come and see you, as soon as you do, one afternoon? *It will be nice to see you again.* I think about you so often.

The Pictures are not much this year—I mean at the New Gallery and the Academy, but I've only seen both in a dense crowd so it is hardly fair to say—but the Modern Art strikes me as very FUNNY. I would like to go with Mr. Ponsonby to the R.A. I'd like to see the effect on him of certain Productions—I am sure you would feel the same (shall I call it *lovely* delight) as I do—in viewing these works of art.—I suppose I've grown old and old-fashioned—but really you never saw such creatures as disport themselves on these canvases. You go and look, and let me go with you.

Will you tell Mr. Ponsonby the garden has been made so *tidy* that I shall venture to take him round it when he next comes to Hampstead? The woodbine and carnations are alive and look as if they will do well.

I am at work again now—my ideas are coming back to me. I

185   24

Kate Greenaway

feel as if I'd been in the earth for the winter and was beginning to wake up.

We have such gloomy skies every day, it spoils the lovely spring look; if only it would rain and be done with it! You see I grumble. It does me good.

I do hope you will soon be in town, and *do let me come to tea soon.*—With kind regards to Mr. Ponsonby, your affectionate
KATE GREENAWAY.

And to Lady Mayo, who had again sent her some spring flowers :—

KATE GREENAWAY TO LADY MAYO

Dear Lady Mayo—What lovely flowers! I thank you so much. There are two of my dearest loves—tulips and that beautiful double white narcissus. But I have entirely succumbed to the fascinations of a new beauty, the lovely greeny white ranunculus, the pale lilac anemones also. But they are all so lovely and are an immense delight to me. I always rejoice over a new flower. I wish I had time to paint them all, but I have not just now for I am doing a river scene from my studio window. You will say you do not remember a river there. Perhaps, but I will show you the drawing if I have the pleasure of seeing you some time. The spring trees change so quickly, but I am going to put your tulips into this very drawing, where a little girl carries a large bunch of them.

The striped ones are so wonderful, the real old-fashioned ones. They are one of my earliest recollections. I remember walking up a path in my aunt's garden that was two long lines of them, and I was so small that I remember bending them *down to me* to look at their wonderful centres. Again thank you very much for the joy you have given me.—Yours sincerely,
KATE GREENAWAY.

In the latter part of July she paid a visit to Mr. Ruskin and wrote of it :—

KATE GREENAWAY TO MR. PONSONBY

39, FROGNAL, HAMPSTEAD, N.W.,
9th August 1894.

Dear Mr. Ponsonby—I am only just home from Coniston; it has been quite beautiful. I found Mr. Ruskin so much better than I expected, of course not his old self, yet even at times there really seemed no difference—it has been great happiness—and the country there—as you know—is lovely beyond words. I went to see Wordsworth's

186

Latter-Day Art

country and his two houses, Rydal Mount and Dove Cottage—the Cottage is so pretty and they are getting back all the old furniture— (protected by strings from the enthusiastic Americans). I sent you the little plants from the Brantwood Garden. I thought it would be of interest to you to have them—that is the pink and the white. The other is a little bit from our garden, you said you would like to have— I can give you plenty more if it does not live.

Will you please give my love to Lady Maria—I meant to have written to her before this, but I really had *no moments* while I was away, but I shall write to her in a day or two before I go to Cromer, where I think I am going next week. I am looking forward to Bournemouth, it is always such a happy time for me—it is very close and warm here. I hoped I should by now have felt stronger than I do—but I daresay it takes time.—Yours sincerely, KATE GREENAWAY.

On October 16th, she writes to Lady Maria Ponsonby :—

Tell Mr. Ponsonby I HATE Beardsley more than ever. It is the Private View of the Portrait Painters at the New Gallery to-morrow.

21st Oct.

All these days ago and no letter finished—not a moment of time have I had. Some of the Portrait Painters have been slightly up to games. Indeed I'm rather inclined to think a Portrait Exhibition is slightly trying. The different expressions give rather the feeling of what children call making faces. And then there are the different schools. Some you look at through a hazy mist. Others confront you in deadly black and ugliness. I can't somehow help feeling a great deal of Funniness whenever I now visit an exhibition of Pictures.

By November 1st she is again at work and writes to Ruskin :—

I have been drawing a baby six months old this morning. I wished for the back of its head, but I proved so fascinating, it *would* only gaze at me, with a stony stare. The drawing did not prosper—but the baby was a dear.

And on Nov. 29 this child of forty-eight writes of the 'precocious woman of thirteen' (as quaintly alleged) of whom all the world was then talking : [1]—

[1] It will be remembered that although Marie Bashkirtseff was given out to be thirteen the facts in the book prove that she was four years older.

187

Kate Greenaway

I finished the first volume of Marie Bashkirtseff. Have you ever read it? I think her odious—simply—but the book is wonderful in a way, so vivid, and though you—or rather I—hate her you feel she must be clever. You ought to read it if you have never done so. Johnny won't see it is clever because he hates her, but I dislike her but feel she is clever. It is a study of supreme vanity, making yourself the centre of all things. It is queer to be ambitious in that way. You can't feel it a noble ambition—very much the reverse.

She is grown up at thirteen when she ought to be having the most beautiful child's thoughts. I feel it quite dreadful to miss that happy time out of your life. Perhaps one prefers one thing, one another. I hated to be grown-up, and cried when I had my first long dress, but I know many long to be grown-up, but even that longing is childish—but this unfortunate girl was grown-up without knowing it.

Still, her history does affect me, I keep thinking about her. She is so strange—so desperately worldly, and I think so cruel—because she was so vain. I wonder if you have ever read it.

The year 1894, which had begun so sadly with the death of Mrs. Greenaway, had happily in store for Kate the beginning of one of her rare and highly valued intimacies. The acquaintanceship, which soon ripened into friendship and then into warm affection, began with a written request in May for the loan of some of her pictures for an Exhibition in Southwark. The writer was Miss Violet Dickinson, to whom a little later on she was personally introduced by a common friend. From that time forward the two ladies, the old and the young, were much in each other's company at 'private views' and other ceremonies, and the fact that her friend was tall and slim beyond the average and Kate as noticeably short and stout, not only drew attention to their companionship but served as a constant text for the exercise of Kate's humorous invention. Their correspondence by letter was incessant and Miss Greenaway's pencil was generally requisitioned to give an added note of piquancy and fancy to her written communications. Many of these little thumbnail sketches, through Miss Dickinson's kindness, are reproduced in this volume, together with numerous extracts from the letters. One note there is upon which Kate is for ever harping, an underlying fear which is for ever haunting her. As we know she was slow at making friendships, but when they were made they became an

Miss Greenaway's Private Opinions

essential feature of her existence, and she was in constant terror lest they should be lost. '*Don't* begin to find me very dull—don't begin not to want me. Yet you can't help it if you do. I suppose I am so slow and you are so quick '—is but one amongst innumerable examples of the little panics into which she would causelessly fall.

Into one other essential characteristic of hers we obtain some insight in these letters. That Kate held no very definite or orthodox religious opinions, although she had a strong religious instinct, is hinted at in many of her letters to Ruskin and others. But it is only from her letters to Miss Dickinson that we are able to gather anything positive on a subject upon which in conversation her natural reserve restrained her from enlarging.

On this last matter she writes :—' I am such a reserved person. You tell everything to everybody and I can't. There's numbers of things I often long to say to you but I do not dare—and yet you are the one person in the world I'd like to talk about them with.'

To a friend she said one day :—' I am very religious though people may not think it, but it is in my own way,' and the following extracts from letters to Miss Dickinson give us some idea of what that way was :—

March 22, 1896.

You can go into a beautiful new country if you stand under a large apple tree and look up to the blue sky through the white flowers—to go to this scented land is an experience.

I suppose I went to it very young before I could really remember and that is why I have such a wild delight in cowslips and apple-blossom—they always give me the same strange feeling of trying *to remember*, as if I had known them in a former world.

I always feel Wordsworth must have felt that a little too—when he wrote the ' Intimations of Immortality'—I mean the trying to remember.

It's such a beautiful world, especially in the spring. It's a pity it's so sad also. I often reproach the plan of it. It seems as if some less painful and repulsive end could have been found for its poor helpless inhabitants—considering the wonderfulness of it all.—WELL, it isn't the least use troubling.

April 29, 1897.

I think Death is the one thing I can't reconcile with a God. After such wonderful life, it seems such a miserable ending—to go out of life with pain. Why need it be ?

189

Kate Greenaway

July 8, 1896.

You think, I know, that people are well off when they leave this world, but then there's the uncertain other—or nothing—it is a mystery I wish we had known more about.

It feels to me so strange beyond anything I can think, to be able to believe in *any* of the known religions. Yet how beautiful if you but could. Fancy feeling yourself saved—as they say, set apart to have a great reward. For what? Those poor little bits of sacrifice—while many and many an unregenerate one is making such big ones—but isn't to go to heaven?

July 10, 1896.

Did you ever believe at all in religion, I mean did you ever believe it as the Bible gives it? I never did—it's so queer.—*Why*, one tries to be good simply because you must—are so unhappy if you don't.—A conscience is a troublesome thing at times. I woke up at 4 o'clock this morning and I spent the time feeling what a nothing I was, and wishing I was so very different. Then the morning's post brought me a letter from a friend, saying I was so this, so that—it made me really cry, I was so grateful.

Dec. 13, 1896.

I could never believe as long as I can remember—yet I went through all sorts of religious phases of my own—times when I used to write down yes or no in a little book each night as to whether I had done all I thought right in the day or not—oh, and lots of things—but I have never believed—in that religion—though I do in my own. A woman once said to me, 'Any religion that is to be any good to one must be one they make for themselves,'—*and it is so*. She, curiously, was a clergyman's wife.

June 14, 1897.

I wish there was no death. It's so horrible, things having to be killed for us to eat them—it feels so wicked. Yet we have to do it— or die ourselves. These are the sort of things that make you doubt of a future life. There's some people would say animals have no souls— but they have—some sort. . . . . .

Don't you wish you knew if you had got an eternal soul or not? People believe half things in such a funny way, and mix up right and wrong—so that I am so often nearly thinking, *is* there a right and wrong—only I know there is—but I would like it decided once for all what is right and what is wrong.

190

Miss Greenaway as a Humorist

Nov. 3, 1897.

I'm depressed too by the horrid tales about people. You don't know how miserable it makes me—I'm so sorry—it takes all the joy out of things. Goodness is so beautiful and so much best. I hate narrow people who would take all the beauty and gaiety from the world. I love all that, but I hate wickedness. Oh, it is such a pity—and the things people say are horrid. I wish they would not tell me.

In her correspondence with Miss Violet Dickinson, Kate's spirits would sometimes overflow into sketches of a character more broadly comic than the public generally has had any example of. Thus, during the hot July of 1896, she dashes off a sketch of herself enjoying the 'bliss' of a shower from a watering-can, and writes :—

What are you doing in this tropical heat—I'm so hot. I'm crimson when I set out—and purple when I get there—oh, everywhere. Out in the garden—the sun blazes on me. . . .

On the 10th December she accounts for her temporary seclusion by a sketch of herself as a solitary hermit withdrawn from the far-off world ; and a month later, still in the comic mood, she pictures herself in the throes of composition, and writes in answer to her friend's remark upon her verses : 'Dear' (her method of addressing well-loved intimates, omitting their names) :—

KATE GREENAWAY TO MISS VIOLET DICKINSON

Dear.
      Yes it is a fine thing to have a friend who writes lovely poems . . . . . ?

> Across the lonely desert grand,
> Across the yellow ridged sand
> The lurid sunset filled the land
> With desolate despair.

And after a vigorous thumb-nail sketch of the said desert, she adds :—

You can't do as good as that—besides *you* can't make a picter.

The year 1895, which marks Kate's last appearance in the Royal Academy exhibitions, with a 'Baby Boy,' also found her represented at the Liverpool Exhibition, and at the Royal Institute of Painters in Water-Colours by 'Gleaners going Home,' 'Girl and Two Children,' 'Little Girl in Red,' and 'Taking a

191

39 Frognal
Hampstead n W

8th July
1896

Bliss

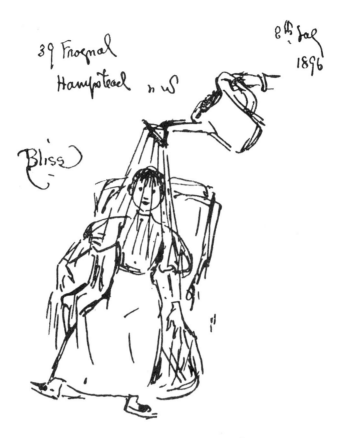

What are you doing in this
tropical Heat — I'm so Hot. I'm
Crimson when I set out — and Purple
when I got there —— oh. everywhere.
out in the Garden — The Sun blazes on me

On a Letter to Miss Violet Dickinson
(showing 'K. G.' in a comic vein).

10. Dec
1896

39, FROGNAL,

HAMPSTEAD, N.W.

Entrance for Hermits Cave.

Solitary Candle

Solitary Cup of tea.

SOLITARY · HERMIT
K.G

Dear — What I shall come to —

the Far H. World.

On a Letter to Miss Violet Dickinson
(showing 'K. G.' in a humorous mood).

25

14. Jan
1897

39, FROGNAL,

HAMPSTEAD, N.W.

Dear. Yes it is a Fine thing to have a
Friend who writes Lonely Poems......
......?.

Across the Lonely Desert. Sand,
Across the Yellow Ridged Sand
The Lurid sunset. Filled the Land,
with desolate despair –

You can't do as good
as that besides you
can't make a
Picture

On a Letter to Miss Violet Dickinson.
(An example of 'K. G.'s' spirit of caricature.)

Letters to Ruskin

Nosegay.' Otherwise the year was uneventful save for her now one-sided correspondence with Ruskin, from which we take the following letters and extracts. They present us with intimate glimpses of her artistic and literary tastes ; her hatred of change and the confusion of life ; her discontent with her work and her determination to do better in the future ; her love of space ; her artistic methods ; her views upon the Impressionist tendency of art ; and last, but not in her eyes less important, extracts from Rover's biography.

KATE GREENAWAY TO RUSKIN

39, FROGNAL,
The New Year, 1895.

. . . . . . I have been to the Venetian Exhibition [1]—but I have not seen it well yet. The crowds of people prevented.

. . . . . . There are some beautiful Ladies' Portraits in such lovely dresses and their hair done into those big rolls all round their faces. I was so impressed by two heads by Giorgione—one a Shepherd with a Flute,[2] so lovely, and Portrait of a Lady Professor of Bologna—the colour is so beautiful (and the way they are painted). I think I will tell you about the beautiful Ladies next time—because I have forgotten entirely the most beautiful Lady's name [3]—though I remember her so well. She is dark and looks at you rather timidly and rather frightened—she has a curious rolled thing round her head, I can't tell what it is made of—little curls of ribbon perhaps and here and there little white bows. She has a background of white flowers, but I will tell you more of her next time.

And Christmas is over and it is nearly the New Year—I fear I am glad Christmas *is* over for I want some lighter days. I don't like getting up in the morning when the moon is shining—and the stars are still about. I see the sun rise as I have my breakfast, pale and cold—but it is very nice to see the daylight come.

I am finishing General Marbot : It is a truly wonderful book, it seems hardly possible people could be so brave—as they are—and most certainly as I could not be—I certainly hope England may never be invaded in my time—too fearful.

How I wish I could have come in to tea with you on New Year's Day. Suppose there was a little tap at your study door—and I came

---

[1] Held at the New Gallery, London.
[2] From the Hampton Court Collection.
[3] Lent by Louisa Lady Ashburton. The 'beautiful lady's name' is unknown.

Kate Greenaway

in carrying a lovely Hot Muffin—would you turn me out, or allow me to sit down by your fire and enjoy myself?

Did I tell you Eddie had come home (from Plauen in Germany) for Christmas—so all my time is taken up in making it a merry time. I had them all to tea and he danced and sang Nursery Rhymes and Looby Loo. Do you know that? it is so pretty.

And then I think you would have liked to have seen my sister's little girl and little boy dance the Barn Dance—I would like to paint it—she is very pretty, and so is the little boy. To-morrow we all go to Olympia—and on Wednesday to Drury Lane—on Thursday I have another tea with more children—Saturday is the sad day he has to go back again. All the little Correggio curls are gone now.

New Year's Day was my Mother's Birthday, so I shall be with no one on that day—except I shall think of the study and you at 5 o'clock, and think I am coming to tea there.

It is shivery—ice everywhere—How much I wish things would not change so much—so soon—so often—I can never understand the *plan* of life at all, it is all so strange—try which way you will to think it out—it all seems of no use—yet you go on trying for this—for that—really for some mysterious end—you don't know.

. . . . . . I hope you will have a very very Happy Year, and have beautiful days, and lots of sunshine—and for myself I will wish that I may see you again before it is ended.

KATE GREENAWAY TO RUSKIN

Feb. 10, 1895.

Did you ever in your life read one of George Meredith's novels? it requires you to be in an angelic frame of mind or else it is that sort of worry—trying to make out what he means—for it isn't encouraging while he describes all his people laughing at a brilliant joke, for you to be *unable* to see the drift of it.

Whatever you do don't read *Lord Ormont and his Aminta*. It all comes of my being sentimental and romantic. The title was so lovely, but don't you be induced by any means to begin it.

But if you do want to read something that is uncommonly nice get *Passages from some Memoirs* by Mrs. Ritchie and read about the children's party at Charles Dickens', about Carlyle and Mrs. Carlyle, about her recollections of her childish days in Paris, her remembrance of Leech, of Charlotte Brontë—it is all so nice, so kind, so clever.

I hear from Mr. Locker-Lampson that there is a real new poet, brand new; he says his name is Davidson and he has written a poem called *The Ballad of a Nun*. That's all I know of it for I have not

Self-Criticism

read it yet. Perhaps I shan't think him a poet. I fear I like them of the sort :—

> When daisies pied and violets blue
> And lady-smocks all silver-white
>
> And all the shepherd swains shall sing
> For thy delight each May morning.

How the beautiful words come into your mind—and then it is spring and you forget it is snowing outside and the wind whirling the wreaths of snow about. It is very Arctic snow, I never saw such lovely little crystals. . . . .

Do you know, I had made up my mind to send you a real valentine —and I invented all, just how it was all to go—then I had a horrid cold and could only think how nice to go to sleep, so the poor valentine never got done. I was very sorry but it could not be helped. And I had also a good deal to do to my Institute drawings, which are very bad. So perhaps it is as well I had the cold, only it was all so nicely ready.

I have got five bad drawings—' Gleaners going Home,' 'A Little Girl in Red,' 'A Girl nursing a Baby,' ' Another Little Girl and a Green Cradle,' and 'A Girl walking with two Little Children.'

The ' Gleaners ' is, I think, the best—I fear you would say *of a bad lot.*

Never mind, I'm going to begin beautiful things directly I can get rid of these—which is next Tuesday—but I always think they are going to be beautiful when I begin, then I generally get to hate them before they are done.

Nov. 11, 1895.

I am still in a state of great perplexity as to what work ●to do and as to what to agree to about books. There is no Almanack this year. Now they want to do it again and I find it hard to decide if I will or not—partly because I do not make up my mind about what I want to do in other ways. But often when I feel like this I wait, and an inspiration comes.

Some beautiful picture or drawing will make me long to do something. The worst of it is, I ought always to do everything the moment it suggests itself, or very likely by the time I go to do it the spirit of it has vanished.

On a Letter to
Ruskin.

I do the technical part of painting so badly, and every one else seems to do it so well. I have no settled way of working—I am always trying this or that. That is why I get on

197

Kate Greenaway

better when I am doing a cottage because I naturally do just what I see and do not think of the way to do it at all.

Does this all bore you or interest you ? I *am* so sorry I can't draw when I am with you and can't do drawings you like much now. One reason is I am never as strong as I was and I can't bear the strain. It is a considerable one to do a large pencil drawing of that sort. It wants to be so fresh and spontaneous—if it is rubbed out at all it is spoiled.

KATE GREENAWAY TO RUSKIN

Nov. 30th, 1895.

You will be grieved to hear that Rover yesterday had a fearful fight with his always enemy, the yellow dog, a truly amiable deer-hound ; why Rover's enemy we can't tell. The fight resulted in a real black eye for Rover, who could not see out of it all yesterday. This morning it is better and he has been standing on his hind legs looking out of the window the last half-hour—liking to look, as he can see again this morning, but also I fear hoping his enemy may pass by and he may renew the fight. The yellow dog has sometimes made overtures of friendship but Rover remains obdurate. I fear he likes an enemy—it offers an agreeable excitement. . . . . . .

The truth of Rover's enmity for the great yellow dog is that one day his tail got caught in the gate, which was a sight not to be resisted by the previously friendly and amiable yellow dog, who at once set teeth in it. Rover was deeply offended at the time, and after brooding awhile over his grievance determined on action. Thus the strained relations of a few days developed into hostilities, thereafter constantly renewed.

Dec. 3.

Some cows have come into the field opposite which have now entirely absorbed Rover's interest. He remains fixed at the dining-room window gazing upon them with a fixed gaze, as much as to say, ' What are these extraordinary large quiet animals, who don't run about and bark ? '

KATE GREENAWAY TO RUSKIN

Dec. 9, 1895.

I am still doing all sorts of drawing—pencil ones with colour—I think them rather pretty. I wish you would like a new sort—a little —I seem to want to put in shade so much more than I used to. I have got to love the making out of form by shade—the softness of it.

198

Her Reading

I love things soft and beautiful—not angular and hard as it is the fashion to like them now. To be an impressionist opens a good wide space for leaving a good deal that is difficult to do *undone*—at least so it seems to me. It is so easy to begin, so difficult to finish.

J am doing Mary like this with a Hoe and a Basket- she looks very Pretty .

A SKETCH OF KATE GREENAWAY'S MODEL, MARY.
On a Letter to Ruskin.

KATE GREENAWAY TO RUSKIN

Dec. 9, 1895.

I have been reading Mrs. Thrale's letters, which have interested me very much. It must have been a mixed pleasure having Johnson

199

Kate Greenaway

for a friend. Yet, how every one liked him though he was so trouble-some ! I must say I should have found it hard work to sit up till four o'clock in the morning, talking and pouring out tea ! Think of the hours ! and they had their dinner at four o'clock in the afternoon. Mrs. Thrale must have been the most good-natured person in the world, indeed I can't help feeling people were not very grateful to her.

KATE GREENAWAY TO RUSKIN

Dec. 16, 1895.

I am reading a horrid book by a man with a horrid face. I once saw the author, and I said, 'Who is that loathsome man ?'—Well, I read no more of his books—that's settled.

CHAPTER XIII

1896-1897

THE LAST OF THE ALMANACKS—OPINIONS ON BOOKS, PICTURES
THE NEW WOMAN, AND ETERNAL MAN—HER DEFENCE OF
RUSKIN.

By way of accentuating the uneventfulness of Miss Greenaway's
quiet life apart from her art, it is perhaps worthy of notice that
the year 1896 found her staying at a hotel for only the second
time in her life, the occasion being a visit to Miss Dorothy
Stanley at Southwold shortly before that lady's marriage to Mr.
Allhusen, M.P.

To Kate the most noteworthy events of this year were her
presence at Lord Leighton's funeral at St. Paul's on February 2nd ;
the purchase of one of her drawings by Lady Dorothy Nevill as
a wedding present for the Princess Maud of Wales ; a single
exhibit, ' Little Bo-Peep,' at the Royal Institute ; and one of her
rare public appearances to give away Mr. Ruskin's gold cross and
chain to the May Queen of the year (by reason of her popularity
among her fellow-pupils) at the May-day celebration at Whitelands College, Chelsea.

He had asked her once before, through Mrs. Severn, but she
had begged hard to be excused :—

50, FROGNAL, HAMPSTEAD, N.W.,
Wednesday.

My dearest Joanie—I'm afraid—and feel I ought not to say yes.
First place, I have been so unwell and get so tired. . . . I'm afraid it
would be exciting to me. Also I can't or ought not to spare the
morning. If it were the afternoon it would make a difference. I don't
like saying *no*, as you and he [Mr. Ruskin] wish it—but if you could

find a nice somebody else, I'd go next year if I were in London. You know I'm not fitted for Public Posts. . . . So do be dear—get some one else to give the cross. . . .

Good-bye, dear Joanie, *don't* think me hateful or anything horrid—and *do do* go to the R.A. and look out for—Your very loving,

KATIE.

Beyond these incidents the interest of the year is confined to her letters. She always had on hand for Ruskin one epistle, to

GOING TO THE POST.
On a Letter to Ruskin.

which she would sit down at any odd moment between meals, exercise, and work, despatching it as soon as the end of the sheet was reached.

As usual these letters are full of references to what she is painting and reading, of her views of life and religion, of her likes and dislikes in art, of her love of flowers, of Rover, and of little touches of self-revelation. Here and there we find a bit of keen observation, and once a half-humorous, half-wistful protest against the comparative homeliness of her appearance.

Love of Street Noises

KATE GREENAWAY TO RUSKIN

Jan. 5, 1896.

I have been reading a curious book called *The Wonderful Visit*.[1]   A man goes out to shoot a strange bird, and shoots instead—an Angel !— Somehow the author does manage to make you feel the angel very beautiful and superior to all about him, but of course it is all unreal, and his idea of heaven doesn't fit in with mine.   I say with mine, and I haven't an idea.   I have often tried to think out what I would like it to be like, and I never can, for there is always something does not fit in.

KATE GREENAWAY TO RUSKIN

Jan. 22, 1896.

Do you like the sound of things in the streets ?   They want to get up a society to suppress the noises—they asked me to belong and seemed to think it very funny when I said I liked them ; what do you think ?

I feel so cheerful when I hear an organ playing nice lively tunes. I love a band.   I like seeing the Salvation Army (though I should, I fear, be angry if I lived near the sound of their preaching) marching along and singing.   I like the sound of the muffin bell, for I seem again a little girl coming home from school in the winter afternoons. I don't like the beggars because I feel too much pain to think of them so destitute, but if I could believe they got pennies enough I could like them.   I like the flower-sellers, and the fruit stalls, and the sound of church bells.

So what could I say ?   I should not like silence always.   It is often when I have had enough silence I go into the cheerful streets and find it a rest.

KATE GREENAWAY TO RUSKIN

39, FROGNAL, 29 *Jan.* 1896.

. . . . . . I am so very sorry Leighton is dead—I did not know him, I never talked to him—yet I am *so sorry*.   He seemed always to me one of the few who cared for real Beauty.   Now it is all something new—something startling, but if it is beautiful does not matter.   All the same there seems some real sorrow that Leighton is dead. . . .

I have got a very interesting book about Mrs. Montague—Mrs. Thrale's Mrs. Montague, I mean.   I seem to have known her slightly so long, but not to have known anything really as to who she was and what she did.   I think she must have been quite delightful.

---

[1] *The Wonderful Visit*, by H. G. Wells (1895).

Kate Greenaway

What a lovely thing a purple crocus is. I told you about a book, the *Midsummer Night's Dream*, illustrated by Anning Bell.[1] He has done little crocuses all over the grass and I think them so pretty. I shall draw some when they come up—but the unkind little sparrows peck them to bits in our garden directly they open. Don't you call that a bad return for giving them bread all their lives?—If I were talking to you, you'd say NO to tease me—I know you would.

But they ARE bad sparrows truly—because they peck the almond blossoms in just the same way. Johnny is so indignant and comes to me and says—' *Look* what *your sparrows* are doing !'—My sparrows?

There was a bad thrush once lived in the garden, a robber thrush, who came to a bad end.

Now if there are no dreadful frosts there will be a great bank of wallflowers by and by. Only once since we have lived here have they succeeded in living well through the winter. Mrs. Docksey sent me such pretty flowers yesterday and a dear little pot to hold them, violets and snowdrops—wasn't it very kind of her ?

[Here comes a little sketch of a fairy flying across the moon.]

That's because I have been looking at the old *Midsummer Night's Dream* with Kenny Meadows' drawings. I DO like them, for they are really fairylike. As a very little child they were my Sunday evenings' amusement whilst my mother and father read. My eldest sister played and sang. I got to know all the plays when I was very little indeed from the pictures. I think the names of the Italian towns got their great charm in my mind from this time, mixed up with so much of the moonlight he puts into them.

The sound of Verona—Padua—Venice—what beautiful sounding names he got for his plays, didn't he ?—but then, he makes that charm over everything. The spring flowers in his hands are nearly as beautiful as themselves, and the girls' names—Viola—Olivia—Perdita.

Oh dear ! Things *are so* beautiful and wonderful, you feel there must be another life where you will see more—hear more—and *know* more. All of it cannot die.

I hope you get out every day for nice walks. Though I do not wish time away I am glad this is February, the first spring month. I wonder what you read now.

KATE GREENAWAY TO RUSKIN

Feb. 18, 1896.

Did you ever read *Peter Ibbetson*, the first book Mr. du Maurier wrote ? I am reading it now. *I think it absolutely beautiful*—it affects

---

[1] Robert Anning Bell, R.W.S.

Du Maurier and Aubrey Beardsley

me so much. I have always liked Mr. du Maurier, but to think there was all *this*, and one didn't know it. I feel as if I had all this time been doing him a great injustice—not to know.

It is such a wonderful thing to have thought of it all—it is so *unworldly*—such a beautiful idea—an exquisite fancy. I long to tell him how much I love it.

Miss Greenaway was also a great admirer of du Maurier as a black-and-white artist, and after his death she wrote to Miss Dickinson :—

All the du Maurier drawings are now at the Fine Art [Society]— I am very sorry to think there will be no more—no more Mrs. Ponsonby de Tomkins. He told me he got so fond of her in the end, he could not let the retribution fall upon her that he intended to finish her up with. I doubt if *Punch* ever gets his like again ; and he was such a nice man.

Feb. 25, 1896.

I wonder if you ever see any illustrations of Aubrey Beardsley's and what do you think of them ? I would like to know. A great many people are now what they call modern. When I state *my* likes and dislikes they tell me I am *not* modern, so I suppose I'm not— advanced. That is why, I suppose, I see some of the new pictures as looking so very funny. You must not like Leighton now, or Millais, and I don't know how much longer I'm to be allowed to like Burne-Jones. Oh dear ! I believe I shall ever think a face should look like a face, and a beautiful arm like a beautiful arm—not that I can do it—the great pity I can't. Why, if I could, they should have *visions*. Sometimes I almost wish I were shut up by myself with nothing to do but to paint—only I'm so dependent on people's affection. I'm not lonely by myself but I want the people I like very much sometimes. I feel I shall not do anything of what I could wish in my life. Isn't it hard sometimes when you have felt the beauty of something in a certain way and have done it so and *no one* you show it to seems to see it at all. But I suppose if it is really a good thing you have done that, after years, some one does feel it, while if it is not worth finding out it goes into oblivion—so Time sifts it all out. Such is not my fate, for I unfortunately can only think of all the beautiful things and have not the skill to do them.

Kate Greenaway

March 2, 1896.

The almond buds are all pink, but I don't want them out till there are some nice little white daisies beneath them.

Do you remember the little poem on the daisy by Jane or Ann Taylor? It is one of the earliest remembrances with me ; my mother used to say it to us so much.

> Little lady, as you pass
> Lightly o'er the tender grass,
> Step about but do not tread
> On my meek and lowly head ;
> For I always seem to say,
> Surely, Winter's gone away.

Now, after saying I remember it, I find I don't, for that is the last verse—and I know part of it goes :—

> For my head is covered flat
> With a white and yellow hat.

Her letters to Miss Dickinson too are full of her garden. Two or three extracts must suffice. In February :—

I've had a deep disappointment to-day. Some one told me of a nice old gardener who wanted a little more work. I thought he would just do for us so I wrote, and when he called, instead of the old man there stood a gorgeous young one in a gorgeous white tie. My heart sank.—He began :—

> ' Path wants gravelling,
> Grass wants seeding,
> Roses want pruning,
> Trees want cutting,
> *Everything* wants rolling,
> Everything wants nailing up.'

A nice idea ! my cherished garden made the exact facsimile of every one in Frognal. I found myself *composing* the *note* that should dismiss him later on. Nothing should induce me to consent to such desecration.

A month later she returns to the subject :—

I can really boast with truth that we have larger and more varied weeds in our garden than you have in yours—in fact, our garden has forgotten that it is a garden and is trying to be a field again.

PORTRAIT OF A LADY.

JOAN PONSONBY, 1891.

BROTHER AND SISTER.

THE BRACKEN GATHERERS.

A SURREY COTTAGE.

THE PINK SASH.

THE PEACOCK GIRL.

VERA EVELYN SAMUEL.

The Opinions of Others

And on April 1 :—

It *is* a Fool's Day—this year snowing so hard—making such a mistake in the time of year—All the poor flowers wondering what's up. How I hate it.

KATE GREENAWAY TO RUSKIN

March 11, 1896.

I do not have much to tell you about dear Rover. He has not been very funny lately. He can't fight—in the muzzle. He tries to but the other dogs don't see it.

Johnny always insists the cause of the fights is that Rover *boasts* of all the superior things he gets here, and the other dogs can't stand it. He says, ' *I* have a mutton chop for *my* dinner'—and what can the other dog say? except that perhaps he partakes of the bone of one, or a paltry dog-biscuit, while Rover revels in beefsteak—beefsteak pie, pork pie, and rabbit.

KATE GREENAWAY TO RUSKIN

March 1896.

How funny it is, the different ways different people feel you ought to work! and people who, you feel, should know. One man said,

'K. G.' WORRIED BY A STRAY PUPPY.
On a Letter to Ruskin.

'Now, what I would like to see is all these things done *life size*! Another comes back as if he had quite a weight on his mind to say he

207

Kate Greenaway

feels he must tell me how much he feels I ought to etch, so that my own original work was kept. Some one else wants me always to do small things ; some one else, landscapes,—so it goes on. The man with the donkey who tried to please everybody is nothing to it !

KATE GREENAWAY TO HON. MRS. SUTTON NELTHORPE

Good Friday, 1896.

I was given quite the wrong sort of body to live in, I am sure. I ought to have been taller, slimmer, and at any rate passably good-looking, so that my soul might have taken flights, my fancy might have expanded. Now, if I make a lovely hat with artistic turns and twists in it, see what I look like ! I see myself then as I see others in the trains and omnibuses with things sticking up over one eye. I say, Ah, there goes me ! I do laugh often, as I look.

In something of the same strain she writes to Miss Violet Dickinson :—

The beautiful Lady looked too lovely for anything yesterday in a pale green bonnet, a purple velvet and sable cloak and a black satin dress. I *do* in a way envy their riches—I could have such beautiful things, you would not know 39, Frognal. You'd come into such a dream of beauty, and the garden too, such a sight would meet your eyes, pots and tubs of lovely flowers all over.

In respect of Miss Greenaway's indifference to fine clothes for herself Mrs. Loftie points out how curious it was ' that with her delicate taste in dressing her subjects she did not know how or did not take the trouble to make the best of herself.'

KATE GREENAWAY TO RUSKIN

July 9, 1896.

I saw two little children in an omnibus yesterday—two little girls. I was so much taken with their faces—they had such small eyes but exactly the shape of some Italian ones. I seemed to know every line as I had seen it in carved Italian faces—it was so beautifully formed, all the eyelid round the eye. . . . I did long to ask their mother to let me draw them. I could have done them with such joy.

Views on Art

July 12, 1896.

I can never define what art really is—in painting, I mean. It isn't realism, it isn't all imagination, it's a queer giving something to nature that is possible for nature to have, but always has not—at least that's my idea. It's what Burne-Jones does when he twists those roses all about his people in the Briar Rose. They don't often grow like that, but they could, and it's a great comfort to like such things, at least I find it so.

KATE GREENAWAY TO RUSKIN

Aug. 13, 1896.

I have not had a nice book this week. I read George Fox, the Quaker, the other day. He was very wonderful, but some things they make a stand for seem hardly worth it, like keeping their hats on. But perhaps that is me in fault, for I don't think I am at all regulated by Forms ; they don't ever feel to me to matter : I don't feel my life gets much shaped by them—but then perhaps it would be better for me if it did !

KATE GREENAWAY TO RUSKIN

Oct. 21, 1896.

The colours are beautiful this year. Here, the Heath looks wonderful, it is all so brilliant—red orange, emerald green, Rossetti's green ; it always makes me think of Rossetti. I see the colour he *tried* for, and how difficult it is ! You can't think what colours to paint it with because it always looks so cold when it is done—not a bit like the real colour. I despair over grass, I can't do it ! I don't know what it is ; I don't know what blue to use—or what yellow. I'm so longing to try more body-colour. It's a curious thing everybody runs it down—yet—all the great water-colour people (the modern ones) have used it—W. Hunt, Walker, Pinwell, Rossetti, Burne-Jones, Herkomer.

KATE GREENAWAY TO RUSKIN

Oct. 28, 1896.

I have not seen any one or been anywhere so there is nothing to tell you about. Yes, I did go out to lunch last Sunday and sat next to an unenthusiastic young architect. I thought this—Am I so dull, or is he dull ? It felt very depressing. I don't mind shy persons if they will only kindle up when you talk to them—often at first I do

Kate Greenaway

not get on with people (especially men), but in a little while generally things take a turn. I suppose I am very shy, really, yet when they are quite the right people I meet I am not so at all. I don't think you thought me so, did you? I know I did not feel so, though before you came I thought so much of your coming it got to be really a pain, and I said I almost wish he was not coming. But then the first moment I saw you, I was glad—so glad.

How different everything is when you are with the right people! When they are wrong they make me so tired. Some people think this so arrogant—I never can see why—I should never mind it at all, or never do mind if people don't find me to their taste, and leave me alone. I think it's far more simple and right, and better so. I don't feel what I think is *best* or *right*, at least of course I *do* think so.

A lady said to me the other day, 'We all do so many things we know are wrong.' Do we? That seems to me a cowardly way to live. Surely we do what *we think* right however mistaken we may be. Why go through those struggles with your conscience? why accept the sacrifice for yourself, the denial of your wishes, and yet think yourself a sinner? No, I can't see it! though I've often tried, because people have, as I said, seemed to think it arrogant—but I have never been able to see it, it don't seem to me to be true. If you did what you thought right, you did right—and there's an end of it; I can't think myself wrong but I can thank what great Power there is that I am led to do what I consider right.

There! there's a dull long talk! What put all that into my head to talk about, to you? Is it rather like Harry and Lucy grown up?

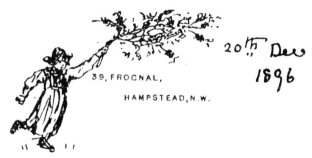

39, FROGNAL,

HAMPSTEAD, N.W.

20ᵗʰ Dec 1896

On a Letter to Miss Violet Dickinson.

The year 1897 saw the last of the Almanacks. The later issues had been so unsuccessful that Routledge & Sons had discontinued their publication. This year, as has been said, another

Work for Mr. Stuart M. Samuel

publisher attempted their revival, but the demand had ceased and
the series was abandoned for good and all.

Mr. Edmund Evans was still the middleman between her
and the public, that is to say, he was the engraver and the
responsible man in the enterprise, and it is impossible to estimate
even approximately by how much her popularity had been en-
hanced by his excellent engraving and his usually excellent
printing. Some idea of the extent of their partnership may be
gathered from the fact that in the twenty years since 1878 there
had issued from the press in book form alone 932,100 copies
of their joint productions. How far this enormous number
might be increased by Christmas cards and independent designs
for magazines it would be useless even to hazard a guess.

This year Miss Greenaway contributed for the last time to the
Royal Institute; she sent 'Girl in Hat and Feathers' and 'Two
Little Girls in a Garden,' but her most important work consisted
of commissions from Mr. Stuart M. Samuel, M.P., to paint a
portrait of his little daughter Vera, and to design 'processions'
for the decoration of his nurseries. Mr. Samuel is also the
possessor, besides many other drawings, of her original designs
for *A Day in a Child's Life.*

KATE GREENAWAY TO Mr. STUART M. SAMUEL

13 *Ap.* 1896.

I cannot tell how much a drawing of your little girl would be. It
depends on the sort of drawing you want. A small water-colour would
be £25—a little girl like a book drawing £10. I can only do certain
kinds of book-plates, nothing heraldic. I do not think I could do a
book-plate to be sure it was a portrait. An ordinary book-plate is £5
or £6. I could only undertake to do a portrait *here*—the little girl
would have to be brought to me.

This was done, and what was considered a successful result
was obtained by January of the following year. The drawing is
reproduced in this volume.

Her personal popularity showed no signs of waning, and she
wrote to Ruskin :—

Every one seems possessed with the desire of writing articles upon
me and sends me long lists of all I am to say. Then America worries
me to give drawings, to give dolls—and I have at last had to give up

211

Kate Greenaway

answering their letters, for the time it wastes is too much to expect wasted.

But though her name was still one to conjure with, there is little doubt that her work was not as acceptable as it had been. Her reign had been a long one and a new generation was knocking at the door. She writes thus of her failing grip upon the public taste :—

KATE GREENAWAY TO LADY MARIA PONSONBY

April 22, 1897.

My mind is in a very perplexed state and I feel very depressed also. I seem not to do things well, and whatever I do falls so flat. It is rather unhappy to feel that you have had your day. Yet if I had just enough money to live on I could be so very happy, painting just what I liked and no thought of profit. It's there comes the bother, but it's rather difficult to make enough money in a few years to last for your life. Yet now every one is so soon tired of things—that is what it comes to.

And on the same date to Ruskin :—

I have been all the morning painting a yellow necklace and touching up a black chair. I *do* take a time—far too much—they would look better if I did them in less. I'm going to do some quite new sorts of paintings. When I have finished this lot, I will please myself. I'm so tired of these and nothing I do pleases any one else now. Every one wants something different so I will please myself now.

Other letters of the year set forth amongst other things how little sympathy she had with the 'Shrieking Sisterhood' and the 'New Woman,' how generous was her appreciation of new and honest artistic endeavour, how she saw through the hollow pretence of what was new and dishonest, and how educative she found her own painting. It will also be seen that she was always on the look-out for a good story with which to amuse the 'Professor.'

KATE GREENAWAY TO RUSKIN

Feb. 2nd, 1897.

People are rather excited over the Woman's Suffrage Bill, but I hope it won't pass next time. I don't want a vote myself and I do not want it at all. Some, of course, might vote well but others would

212

Justice to Women

follow their feelings too much, I am sure—and get up excitements over things best left alone. For my part I do feel the men can do it best and so hope it may remain.

There's nothing but women's everything this year because of the Queen and the festivities, so now there's a chance for them. They always feel they are not done justice to. I must say, I in my experience have not found it so. I have been fairly treated and I have never had any influence to help me. So I can't join in with the things they so often say. And then it is generally the second-rate ones who feel they should be the first if it were not for unfair treatment, and all the while it is want of enough talent. Somehow I have always found, the bigger the man the greater his admiration for talent in others. I suppose his own genius makes him feel the genius in others and rejoice in it. Not one of them can do a picture like a fine Leighton—yet they can't even look at him. I did admire Poynter's speech—and how he went for them.

Christmas Eve
1896

39. FROGNAL,

HAMPSTEAD, N.W.

Dear

I hope you will get the little christmas cards and almanacks by tomorrow. They have been a great disappointment to me, because I did them so badly - and I wanted them to be very nice - when I try to do a thing like that I get nervous and think - and then it is all up

On a Letter to Miss Violet Dickinson.

213

Kate Greenaway

KATE GREENAWAY TO MISS VIOLET DICKINSON

Feb. 11, 1897.

Then there are the strong-minded women, who hold up to my vision the hatefulness and shortcomings of MAN — How they are going to have exhibitions in this Victoria year, and crush MAN beneath their feet by having everything to themselves and showing how much better they can do it—???? Worm as I am, my friend, oh what a worm they would think me if I dared write and say my true views, that having been always fairly and justly treated by those odious men that I would far rather exhibit my things with them and take my true place, which must be lower than so many of theirs. For I fear we can only *hope* to do—what men *can* do. It is sad but I fear it is so. They *have* more ability.

KATE GREENAWAY TO LADY MARIA PONSONBY

Feb. 21, 1897.

My mind is tired out by wretched letters and circulars about various exhibitions—the Victorian and others. I am at special enmity with the Victoria one because they do *go on* so. . . . *Man is such a vile worm.* Women are going to blaze forth at this show, I can tell you—at least that is what they say—not impeded by the *usual fiasco.* Heaven knows what that means, but I suppose it has to do with the guileful doings of *Man.*

Have you ever been to the Exhibition of Lady Artists? You see, *I'm* cross—well, this is what they've done—got the people [*i.e.* the organisers] to say all the women's pictures may be in the women's work part. They agreed at once—no wonder, they must have smiled with joy.

Now *why* can't we just take our places fairly—get just our right amount of credit and no more. Of course we shouldn't get the first places—for the very simple and just reason—that we don't deserve them.

KATE GREENAWAY TO RUSKIN

Feb. 25, 1897.

I am reading a curious book called *The New Republic*, by Mr. Mallock. I don't know yet what it means, but so far it seems so different to its author. Some are, and some are not like their books. You are like your books. I never understand how they can be two

214

On ' The New Republic '

things, yet how often they are. I would rather never see the authors if they are different, for I feel then it isn't what they really *feel* that they write about, and that is not a pleasant feeling at all.

When writing this letter she does not seem to have recognised the identity of Mr. Ruskin with the ' Mr. Herbert ' of *The New Republic.* Had she done so she would hardly, we may suppose, have alluded to the book at all. Within a day or two, however, the thing seems to have dawned upon her, for she wrote on Feb. 28 :—

KATE GREENAWAY TO MISS VIOLET DICKINSON

Feb. 28, 1897.

Did you ever read *The New Republic,* by Mr. Mallock ? It is certainly clever, so much so I feel rather sorry he has written it. I should very much like to know who all the people are meant for—we cannot decide. I suppose Mr. Ruskin is one.[1] Mr. Miller told me they were all people he met at Sir Henry Acland's—I can't remember if his name is spelt Ac or Ack—and that he was furious at Mr. Mallock taking them off in that way. Anyhow it is very amusing and funny, but if the one is Mr. Ruskin he might have done better—but evidently he did not know him well. . . . . . .

KATE GREENAWAY TO RUSKIN

March 3, 1897.

I've got a curious book about the adventures of a young man and a girl on bicycles—it is called *The Wheels of Chance.*[2] It's very funny. The young man is a draper's assistant who is described as weak and vulgar (only in the way he talks) and he turns out so nice. I don't see why he should be supposed to be vulgar because he is a draper's assistant. He could be quite as noble and good being that as having any other trade, as far as I can see. I never can see things that way, and people never seem to me to be vulgar because they don't speak correctly or know quite what is done in a society a little above them.

---

[1] Miss Greenaway raised the point again later on with one of the present writers, and was vastly interested to learn that Ruskin, as she suspected, is presented as ' Mr. Herbert,' Huxley as ' Storks,' Tyndall as ' Stockton,' Jowett as ' Jenkinson,' Kingdon Clifford as ' Saunders,' Carlyle as ' Donald Gordon,' Matthew Arnold as ' Luke,' Pater as ' Rose,' and Hardinge as ' Leslie,' while Lady Dilke is ' Lady Grace ' and Mrs. Singleton ' Mrs. Sinclair.' ' Then who is Lawrence ? ' asked Miss Greenaway. ' Mallock himself.' ' Ah ! ' she replied, ' that settles it ; I don't like him.'

[2] By H. G. Wells.

215

Kate Greenaway

I think it is vulgar to think them so, if they are nice and do and think nice things. But the book has nice feeling, and it would amuse you very much to read it.

KATE GREENAWAY TO RUSKIN

April 15, 1897.

Isn't it a funny thing I can't copy? All the morning I have been blundering over a baby's face from a little study. I can't do it a bit; it is odd. I can't get it a bit like the original. I put it in and take it out, and so it goes on getting worse and worse. And I wish I could do it so much but I never have been able, and it don't matter what it is—it is everything—the most trifling thing. I never do it well except direct from the object or my own mind, but I can't copy a flat thing —it really is curious. . . . .

The gentleman [1] who has his nursery hung round with my drawings has seen those I did for you and is very much taken with them. He wanted me to copy the two big ones, but I told him that was perfectly impossible. So I'm going to do him a procession later on. Also I should not like him to have drawings the same as yours.

KATE GREENAWAY TO RUSKIN

April 22, 1897.

I am very fond of *Nicholas Nickleby.* No one has liked Dickens for so long, but I think I begin to see a little turn coming now. Of course in time it would be sure to come, but it is a certain fate to every one after a time, and then another thing sets in and they take their rank for ever. . . . .

KATE GREENAWAY TO RUSKIN

April 27, 1897.

I went to the R.A. yesterday. Every one has turned portrait painter—Briton Riviere does ladies and their pet animals—Orchardson all portraits—Herkomer also. There is one picture I think beautiful. It is 'Hylas and the Water Nymphs' [2]—the water is covered with water-lilies and the girls' heads above the water suggest larger water-lilies, somehow. They are beautiful, so is Hylas, so is the green water shaded with green trees—it is a beautiful picture—I forget the legend. Then there's one other that impressed me so much—I can't remember the man's name [3] but I should think he's young and new. I think it

---

[1] Mr. Stuart M. Samuel, M.P.
[2] By J. W. Waterhouse, R.A.　　　　　[3] Byam Shaw.

I think the
bonnets must
have been
rather Pretty
sometimes —

Do you
remember the
old illustrations
to Nicholas
Nickleby — the
dreadful Costume
of Miss La Creevy
but Kate Nickleby
looks Pretty in
the large bonnets

Madame Mantelini too

On a Letter to Ruskin.

217   28

Kate Greenaway

is called 'Love's Baubles.' A boy goes along, his hair stuck full of butterflies and carrying a basket of fruits, followed by a train of girls trying to get them ; some apples are dropped which the girls are picking up. The colour LOVELY—strong Rossetti ; it's colour to its highest pitch, and to my mind it is splendid. There's a girl in front smiling—in a green dress lined with purple shot silk ; she has red hair. Her dress is so beautifully painted. The ground is covered with daisies. I shall go on Monday and look again. *There*—it's all true.

KATE GREENAWAY TO MISS VIOLET DICKINSON

29 April 1897.

I am reading George Moore's *Modern Painting* and I feel my cheeks burn. And I long, oh I long—if only I could do it, to write a reply. The answers come surging up while I read—so much of it seems to me a distorted criticism of distorted things. But sometimes he writes well. I am intensely interested in it, though of course I look on Art from an entirely different view. I think it sacrilege to compare Velasquez and Whistler, and when he says the world never repeats itself, we have had a Velasquez now we'll have a funny Whistler. Would the world say that if there was a remote chance even of another ? Wouldn't we all say we'll take the Velasquez, please ?—Not that I don't like Whistler—I do—but it is nonsense putting him at that level. It seems to have aroused feelings in its readers for there are various pencil notes on the margins beginning *shame.*

KATE GREENAWAY TO RUSKIN

May 27, 1897.

I often think, just for the pleasure of thinking, that a little door leads out of the garden wall into a real old flowering garden, full of deep shades and deep colours. Did you always plan out delightful places just close and unexpected, when you were very young ? I did. My bedroom window used to look out over red roofs and chimney-pots, and I made steps up to a lovely garden up there with nasturtiums growing and brilliant flowers so near to the sky. There were some old houses joined ours at the side, and I made a secret door into long lines of old rooms, all so delightful, leading into an old garden. I imagined it so often that I knew its look so well ; it got to be very real. And now I'd like somehow to express all this in painting, especially my love of old gardens with that richness of colour and depth of shade.

British Masters at the Guildhall Art Gallery

KATE GREENAWAY TO MR. PONSONBY

I went the other day to the Guildhall[1]—there are beautiful things there, but not so interesting to me as the last exhibition—that seemed to me the finest collection I had ever seen.

I can't think why, but the Rossettis never seem to go with other pictures, while the Millais' tower above all things. They have the Drummer-boy[2] there, just wonderful, and the early one of the Royalist[3] —but put in the narrow passage, where you can't see it.

KATE GREENAWAY TO RUSKIN

July 14, 1897.

There was a Millais—three Millais'—'The Huguenots,' 'The Gambler's Wife,' and 'The Blind Girl.' Every time I see any of the early Millais' I like them more and more, if possible. 'The Huguenots' is so wonderful, isn't it? Her face! it seems to move and quiver as you look at it—it is a divine picture. I do only wish he had not made the colour in the girl's sleeves yellow, or that yellow. Then the wall and the campanulas and nasturtiums—her hands and his!—

I know you do not always like Tadema, but there is one here I think you would like—both the painting and the subject, but very likely you have seen it. I never have before. It is called 'The Women of Amphissa.' Do you know it? Some women have gone on a pilgrimage and have strayed into an enemy's city and are taken care of and given food by the women of the city. The *food* is so wonderful. There is some honey in the comb, and cucumbers and figs and bread. There are two fair women who are marvels of painting.

Then there's a Holman Hunt—'The Boys Singing on May Morning,'[4]—but the reflections are so exaggerated it cuts it up too much. But well do I love the early one, 'The Two Gentlemen of Verona.' I have often seen this before and I love it. It really is so beautiful to see such pictures.

Then there's a Lewis—such painting, such colour! What a wonderful collection of men they were!

And what will this generation who run them down have to show? For them, *nothing* that I can see at present. There are two Turners,

---

[1] An exhibition of the works of painters who had flourished during Queen Victoria's reign, held at the Guildhall Art Gallery.
[2] 'An Idyll, 1745.'
[3] 'The Proscribed Royalist.'
[4] 'May Morning on Magdalen Tower,' Oxford.

but by the time I got to those I was feeling too tired to stand. I fear I shan't go again for I think it closes to-day.

There, it is all pictures this time, but I feel so much better for seeing them. I always do, if I can see a beautiful thing.

KATE GREENAWAY TO LADY MARIA PONSONBY

July 26, 1897.

An American and his wife came to-day and bought some drawings, and the lady asked me *how much they were a dozen* !

Her American visitors were perhaps scarcely to be blamed ; for Miss Greenaway, alike innocent of the simple strategy of the prudent salesman and incapable of the subtle skill of the accomplished dealer, would make no attempt to 'nurse' her drawings. If she were asked by an intending purchaser what she had for disposal, she would bring out everything she had, partly in order that her client might make the freest choice, partly in a spirit of pure but impolitic self-abnegation. And when her friends remonstrated with her on the imprudence of the proceeding, she would laugh and reply gaily that she evidently was not cut out for a business woman. No wonder that American collector thought that the matter might be approached on a 'wholesale' footing.

KATE GREENAWAY TO RUSKIN

July 28, 1897.

Did I tell you I was now reading a very fascinating book about gardens, only it is conducted on more scientific principles than my gardening and would take much longer. Mine consists in putting something into the ground. When once there it has to see after itself, and can't come up to see after its root, or go to another spot for change of air—perseverance does it ! There's an alstrœmeria that has had quite a desperate struggle for three or four years when it's never grown up—never flowered—But this year there has been a victory, a great bush of lovely orange flowers.

I saw such a great bee in the garden the other day—as large as the Coniston ones that kick so furiously. I thought of the Coniston bees when I saw him, and then—of the Coniston Moor, and the Coniston Lake, and the Coniston Mountains. Ah, well, I shall come and see it again some time—won't you like to see me again, some time ?

220

The New English Art Club

On a Letter to Miss Violet Dickinson.

KATE GREENAWAY TO MISS VIOLET DICKINSON

Nov. 12, 1897.

I've now finished *St. Ives.* I don't like the other man's ending—
—I don't think it is up to Stevenson's usual mark. There are too
many adventures—too many hairbreadth escapes—it wants some spaces
of repose. I don't like all dangers, it becomes painful to me to read.
You no sooner begin to breathe, feeling he is safe, than there he is
again worse than before.

KATE GREENAWAY TO RUSKIN

Nov. 18, 1897.

Oh, I went to the New English Art Club yesterday—*such* productions! I just think it all mere pretence. They are to my mind
mostly all very ugly rough sketches, and they think nothing of leaving
out the head or body of any one if that isn't where they want it——I'd
like you to see some of the *clouds*—solid—absolutely—and to think of
Turner! The place was thronged with students which is sad—but
I believe it won't be for long. I was told the *Times* said the movement began to be popular and so was bad and dangerous. I believe
it will soon all crumble away, for there isn't anything in it except
sketches; none of the good artists would exhibit—the tide will
turn.

Kate Greenaway

39, FROGNAL,

HAMPSTEAD, N.W.

24 November 1897.

On a Letter to Ruskin.

Kate Greenaway to Ruskin

Nov. 24, 1897.

What do you think I have been drawing to-day ? I got so interested it has made me very tired. I am doing a band of little child angels each carrying a lily coming along a hilltop against a green (summer) sunset sky. May-trees are in flower, and they are (one or two of the angels) gathering daisies. The lilies are heavenly lilies, so it doesn't matter their being out at the same time as the May. I have not yet finished the starry sky, but I was constrained to do the angels.

This chapter may fitly be brought to a close by the following handsome defence of Ruskin, inspired by a conversation with Miss Violet Dickinson, and written twelve months before the last letter.

Kate Greenaway to Miss Violet Dickinson

Nov. 2, 1896.

I have been thinking very much about what you said, of the way people talk against him in Venice—I hope you will try a little not to quite believe it all. For believe me it is sure not to be all true, and even if he has been very inaccurate the world owes him so much that one may well and justly (I think) forget his faults.

The world *is* very ungrateful like all nature is, and takes all the good it can get and then flings the giver of it away. That is our way and it is a cruel one. And there's another reason also—a reason that

Defence of Ruskin

once I used not to believe in—but I do now, and that is that so many of the second-rate authors and artists seem to have a most bitter jealousy of the great ones. It is very curious to me but they do. They love to find a fault. Look how delighted they were to think Carlyle was unkind to Mrs. Carlyle, while really I suppose he never was. When Mr. du Maurier died the other day such unfair notices of both his books and drawings!—I feel red-hot angry at lots of the things said about the big ones, and we ought to be so grateful to them instead for what they make the world for us. Nearly always the criticisms are from the lesser man on the great one. How should he know ?—If he did he would be the great one, but he isn't and can't be, and nothing shows more how little and below he is. More than that, he can't reverence and venerate those wonderful souls who shower down so freely for everybody the greatness that is in them. I feel I can say all this to you for you *are* a feeling soul, and I know you'll go with me. Not that I mean for one moment that it is right not to be accurate, and I know in Mr. Ruskin's case he is too ready to believe all he hears, but I think it should be forgiven—that the beautiful things he tells you—and the new life of Art you enter into—compensate.

Never shall I forget what I felt in reading *Fors Clavigera* for the first time, and it was the first book of his I had ever read. I longed for each evening to come that I might lose myself in that new wonderful world.

CHAPTER XIV

1898–1901

BESIDES a visit to Lady Jeune, at whose house Kate again had
the pleasure of meeting the Princess Christian and other royal
ladies, the year 1898 was marked by only one event of any
moment. This was the third exhibition of her pictures at the
Fine Art Society's Gallery, and she approached the ordeal with
considerable misgivings. There was no need for apprehension,
however. Out of one hundred and twenty-seven little pictures
eloquent of her unbounded industry, sixty-six found purchasers,
the total receipts reaching the sum of £1,024 : 16s.[1]

But the results did not satisfy her. After the opening day
she wrote to Miss Dickinson :—

Feb. 22, 1898.

I'm so glad it is over. I hate having to talk to crowds of strangers,
and then it is a very anxious time after working for it so long. At

---

[1] The net profit to Miss Greenaway was £645. The most important pictures sold
were 'Little Girl with Tea Rose' (35 guineas), 'Going to School' (35 guineas), 'Betty'
(35 guineas), 'Girl in Pink and Black—Grey Muff' (60 guineas), 'Little Girl in Scarlet
Coat and Tippet' (35 guineas), 'A Girl in Hat and Feathers' (45 guineas), 'Thoughts
of the Sea' (35 guineas), 'Two Girls in a Garden' (35 guineas), 'Lilies' (35 guineas),
and 'Baby Boy in Blue Coat and Tippet' (35 guineas).

I believe I shall do lots

39, FROGNAL,

HAMPSTEAD, N.W.

Book Plate - after all - I shall like that
see what nice stiff little Tulips I can Put.

and all sorts of Fascinating
Things

On a Letter to Miss Violet Dickinson.

29

Kate Greenaway

the Fine Art they say it will be successful ; that always, if they sell as much as that on the Private View day, that it is all right—but I have very great doubts if it is so, and the large Pencil and Chalk drawings I fear do *not* take at all. The little ones sell, and the dressed-up babies. I've felt depressed about it and I hardly ever feel that unless there is a cause. It was so tiresome—the day people go to buy was such a horrid day of rain and sleet, and now to-day snow. Then there was coming another Exhibition of old mezzo-tints with a private view which they said would be so good for me as so many would be there, but now they have had an offer and sold the whole collection, so that won't come off. They are going to have the Martian drawings [1] and others instead.

Then they had a beautiful sage *Flag* to float outside, but when it came home they had only put one 'e' into my name and it had to go back to be altered.

And three weeks later, in reply to 'kind inquiries' after the exhibition by her friend, she wrote in no better spirits :—

13 March 1898.

No, the drawings are not nearly all sold. If more of the higher-priced ones were gone instead of the others it would not be so bad, but it takes a great number at only a few pounds each to make up anything like enough to pay.

The Fine Art people say the East wind has kept people from going out and they have had so few people in and out in consequence—but I feel far more that my sort of drawing is not the drawing that is liked just now, and also that I am getting to be a thing of the past, though I have not arrived at those venerable years they seem to think fit to endow me with.

Whether or not she had good reason to complain of the fickleness of the picture-buying public, certain it is that those who bought her pictures then have had no reason to repent of their bargains.

In this year Miss Greenaway completed the book-plate she had undertaken to draw in colours for Mr. Stuart M. Samuel's little daughter Vera ; and so conscientious was she that although her price for it was only six pounds, she was occupied upon it on and off for two and a half years ; and when her client sent her a much larger sum than was actually due, she insisted on returning to him the over-payment, while 'feeling it so very kind.' The pains

---

[1] By George du Maurier.

Mr. and Mrs. Stuart M. Samuel

she took were extraordinary—the child, the design, the introduction
of the wreath of roses with the hovering bees (from Mr. Samuel's
own book-emblem), and the lettering, all received the utmost
consideration. The lettering proved too much for her, as on the
occasion when Ruskin so roundly trounced her; so she agreed to
have the words designed for her by a professional letter-draughts-
man for her to copy in her drawing. When it was finished she
took the keenest interest in the reproduction, and she was highly
flattered that Mr. Samuel decided to discard the 'three-colour
process' and adopt the more precious but vastly more expensive
photogravure on copper. In this case each separate impression is
printed from a plate inked *à la poupée*—that is to say, the artist-
printer inks the plate with the various coloured inks carefully
matched to the tones of the drawing; so that, when the plate is
passed through the press only one copy can be obtained from each
printing, and the plate has to be inked again. A few impressions,
therefore—say ten, or thereabouts—cost as much as the original
drawing, but the result justifies the expenditure. The reproduction here given is not from the drawing itself, but is a three-colour
reproduction from the printed impression which has often been
mistaken for the original. The artist was delighted, and wrote—
'How much I should like to do a book like this, but I suppose it
is fearfully expensive. . . . It is really beautifully done.' In this
letter she goes on to revert to her ill-health, and succeeding letters,
in a like strain, led her friends to suspect the true cause of what
she thought was 'influenza.' Thus, on the eve of staying at
Cromer with Mr. and Mrs. Samuel, she writes—on the 15th of
May 1900, after a recurrence of illness—'Please forgive my not
coming. I know you would have been a Vision in the Loveliest
of Colours. I should so much like to come to tea again later on
when I'm not so busy, and see you and some more First Editions.'
And again: 'I hope you are quite well again. I am not yet.
I suppose I've had influenza. I never felt so ill before.' Then
follows a series of letters full of hopes of future meeting, of
acknowledgments of commissions given, and of gratitude for
kindnesses received. The kindnesses, as was usual with her, she
sought to return by the gift of little drawings to her hosts and
their children, for although she loved attentions she never liked
to feel the weight of indebtedness. She used to be a little nervous
in making these presentations. On one occasion, when she made
such a gift to one of the present writers and she was asked to

Kate Greenaway

sign it, she wrote in her flurry 'Kate Spielmann'—and there the quaint signature remains (rather smudged out by her impulsive forefinger) at the present moment.

As in the record of the immediately preceding years, so in that of 1898 we have to depend on letters, written in the main to Ruskin, for any intimate impression of her life and character. They abound in allusions to her hopes, fears, ambitions, enthusiasms, and perplexities, ethical and religious, her preferences in art and literature, her generous appreciation of the gifts of others and her modest estimate of her own.

KATE GREENAWAY TO RUSKIN

Jan. 12, 1898.

I went yesterday afternoon to see the Millais' at the R.A. and I think them more wonderful than ever.

It is splendid the impression of beauty and power—as you first step into the rooms. Do you know well 'The Boyhood of Sir Walter Raleigh'? I think that boy's face is the most beautiful I have ever seen—it makes me cry to look at it. Its expression is so intensely wonderful—so is 'The Stowaway.'—But it is going from one masterpiece to another. Still there are some which do not appeal to me as much as others. The divine 'Ophelia' is there as divine as ever. People are making up to it. I have thought it the most wonderful picture ever since I first saw it.

Then there is the girl's face in 'Yes!'—full of the most beautiful feeling—like the Huguenot girl.—How he painted those children!—Angels of Beauty. He is really a marvel. . . . . .

I should like to have a sort of little packing case made that I could put drawings into and send backwards and forwards for you to see—sometimes—only perhaps you wouldn't like them. If you would it would be rather nice—a very narrow flat box always ready.

I fear the exhibition won't be in the least successful ; there seems to me to be very few pictures sell now—or a person is popular just for a little time. And there's so much fad over art—if you like the new things they say you are modern. I say Art isn't modern : new or old in a way. It is like summer is summer—spicy is spicy, and Art is Art, for as long as the world is—isn't that true ? However, they have woke up to the 'Ophelia' so I forgive them a good deal.

But I can't help feeling boiling over with rage when I read the criticisms in some of the papers—so utterly ignorant ; and then people who don't know are guided by this. I daresay you will say, 'But what do the people who don't know matter ?'—They don't—but it is depressing.

Modern Art

KATE GREENAWAY TO RUSKIN

Jan. 26, 1898.

I wish people would care about what I do more now. This
Millais Exhibition has rather woke them up. They got to think
Leighton was a poor feeble being and Millais nowhere before the
New Art, but I'm rather amused to hear the different talk now.—And
then Poynter and Richmond, to my great joy, have been going for
them in their addresses. For a great many years now I have thought
the 'Ophelia' the greatest picture of modern times and I still think so.
They have unfortunately hung the children being saved from the fire
next to it, which was not a wise choice, as the red of the fire one is,
of course, very trying to those nearest it—but oh, they ARE all
wonderful.[1]

Jan. 27.

I have been to see the Rossettis again to-day for a little change,
for I was too tired for anything. I like the small water-colours more
and more. The colours are so wonderful. I feel I *do* such weak
things and think strong ones, and it is dreadfully tiresome. I do want
to do something nice—beautiful—like I feel—like I see in my mind, and
there I am trammelled by technical shortcomings. I will never begin
a lot of things together again because then you can't do new ideas
or try different ways of work, and I always could only do one thing
at once. I live in the one thing and think about it, and it's like a
real thing or place for the time. Even now, the moment I'm doing a
new drawing the morning rushes by—I'm so happy, so interested, I
only feel the tiredness when I can't go on because it is too late or too
dark.

KATE GREENAWAY TO RUSKIN

Feb. 2, 1898.

I am reading some pretty stories translated from the French of
Madame Darmesteter, but I fancy some of the historical ones are
rendered a great deal more *un*historical, and your sympathy is expected
from a point of view that you can't (or I can't) give, if I think it out.
But I am much more puzzled the longer I live as to what is right and
wrong. I don't mean for myself. The rules I knew as a child are still
good for me—I still think those right. But it's other people's minds
seem to me so strangely mixed up till I feel, why don't people settle

---

[1] She here refers to Millais' 'Rescue,' of which Ruskin had written in 1855 : 'The
only *great* picture exhibited this year ; but this is *very* great. The immortal element is
in it to the full.'

Kate Greenaway

it once for all, and do what they call right and not what they call
wrong ?

It seems to me to be so unjust, often, for there to be two laws
about a thing. I often ask people but I never learn—every one seems
vague and says—'Oh well, if you do right you have your own self-
respect'; but it seems to me more than that. It *is* right to do one
thing—wrong to do another; at least, isn't this true ?

March 29, 1898.

I long to be at work painting May-trees. There are such beauties
on the Heath only they are black instead of grey, or else they twist
about beautifully. May-trees have such sharp curves, don't they,
grow at right angles, in a way, instead of curves. I like it so much.
Do you know them in Hatfield Park ? They are the greyest, oldest
trees I have ever seen.

May-trees don't grow about that way at Witley. The May is all
in the hedges, not growing on the commons in single trees. Yet it
must be very much the same sort of sandy soil that is on the Heath,
and Witley is nearly all uncultivated land.

I always look with envy at the May-tree Burne-Jones painted in
'Merlin and Vivien' :—it is so wonderful.

In the following letter she describes her visit to Lady Jeune
at Arlington Manor, Newbury :—

April 14, 1898.

I feel rather low to leave Lady Jeune, she is so dear and kind. I
can't tell you how kind she is to every one, and Madeline Stanley, the
daughter, is *so beautiful* and so kind and so very unselfish. She played
Lady Teazle and she was a dream of loveliness, and, I thought, acted
it in so refined a manner. I felt considerably out of it all but they
were all very nice people and I did them pictures—I hope gave them
a little pleasure in compensation for their kindness to me. I
went off for two or three little quiet walks by myself on the Common ;
it was a fascination complete—a great joy. It made me wild with
delight to see it all—the yellow of the gorse and the brilliant green
and orange of the mosses, and the deep blue of the sky. Also, I
grieve to say it, and you will be shocked to think it of me, but those
three lovely sirens were rather depressing—one felt so different, one

Miss Madeline Stanley

was of no account. There was Miss Millard ;—black curly hair and
deep, deep grey eyes, and sweet pink cheeks. There was Lady
Dorothy FitzClarence with red-gold hair and eyes like—was it Viola ?
('her eyes are green as glass, and so are mine ') ;—eyes the greenest
(or greyest) of things blue, and bluest of things grey—cheeks the
colour of a pink pale China rose, red lips and creamy complexion.
Then came that beautiful, that dearest siren of them all—Madeline
Stanley—who is so dear one could only rejoice in her altogether.
But think of poor me ! I used to say to Lady Jeune, 'Oh, let
me come away with you, away from these sirens, the air is full of
them.'

No wonder the poor young men thirsted for the stage-manager's
blood, who took the lion's share of the beautiful sirens. They vowed
such vengeance I told them *I* thought it very unfair, but they assured
me their injuries were great.

In another letter on the same occasion she writes, 'I am a
crow amongst beautiful birds.'

KATE GREENAWAY TO LADY MARIA PONSONBY

April 19, 1898.

It was lovely at Newbury—there is a common there just edging
the grounds tenanted by sweet little woolly white lambs—such pictures,
with wide-open anemones and blackthorn bushes. It made me so very
happy to walk about there and look at things.

There was acting going on and the house was filled with young
men and women, so I felt considerably out of it. But they were really
most of them very nice to me, and the three girls were dreams of beauty.
Madeline Stanley is so beautiful and not *modern* ; she is so very dear
and kind—I think her perfection.

KATE GREENAWAY TO RUSKIN

April 20, 1898.

To-morrow is the New Gallery Private View, but there won't be
anything to look at like the Rossettis. How I should like to live
always in a room with two or three Rossettis on the walls. You live
in a great many places at once, don't you, when you have beautiful
pictures hanging on your walls ? You lift up your eyes and you are
away in a new land in a moment.

I should find it hard to choose if I were allowed the choice of
twelve pictures. I would have had one of the Briar Rose pictures,

231

Kate Greenaway

I know : 'The Maidens asleep at the Loom '—a small Rossetti, *I know,* but which I am not quite certain,—perhaps the meeting of Dante and Beatrice in Paradise. (Whenever I write Paradise I think of you. I remember writing it 'Paridise' one day to you, and you were rather cross and wrote back 'I'd write Paradise with an *a* if I were you.' I *did* feel humiliated!)

Then what else! The beautiful Luini Lady with the jasmine wreath and green gauzy veil and the divine smile.[1] It is a great deal to make any one smiling a smile that you can never get tired of.

I'm reading the Diary of Grant Duff ; it is so very interesting and full of such funny pictures. I was rather interested last night, after I had been writing about the twelve pictures, to find he talks of choosing twelve, but his choices are not mine—and I've not chosen my twelve, and besides perhaps my twelve are far away where I shall never see them—I have seen so few.

KATE GREENAWAY TO RUSKIN

May 27, 1898.

I wish I did not have to make any money. I would like to work very hard but in a different way so that I was more free to do what I liked, and it is so difficult now I am no longer at all the fashion. I say fashion, for that is the right word, that is all it is to a great many people.

On a Letter to Ruskin.

KATE GREENAWAY TO RUSKIN

July 6, 1898.

Isn't it curious how one can like good things so much and not do them ? I do love one figure or a number put into a little space with just room for what they are doing. I don't think figures ever look well with large spaces of background. I know how fascinated I was by that one of Rossetti's—the Princess of Sabra drawing the lot. For one thing, my mind runs to ornament or decoration in a way, though it has to be natural forms, like foxgloves or vine-leaves. I can't like a flower or leaf I invent, though I often love those I see done.

---

[1] Apparently, Luini's 'St. Catherine.'

French and 'International' Art

On a Letter to Ruskin.

KATE GREENAWAY TO RUSKIN

July 14, 1898.

I went to see the Guildhall pictures yesterday afternoon, but I can't help it, I like the English ones best. They are splendidly done but—they don't take me. I do like Bastien-Lepage and Millet and Meissonier—I don't think I've got sympathy with French art, it is somehow too artificial. Perhaps I'm very, very wrong but—I can't help it, I feel so. I went one day to the Gallery of International Art. Some things I liked but the greater number I felt wrong and not clever, and some I felt loathsome. That is a strong word but I feel it. Shannon does fine portraits. I think his pictures of girls are perfect, I like them so very much.

Two days later she wrote to Miss Dickinson : 'I went to see the pictures at the International. Some are so funny. I laughed till the tears really came. It is art gone mad.'

233   30

Kate Greenaway

NEWHAVEN COURT, CROMER,
August 26, 1898.

There is a very, very pretty girl sitting opposite doing French. She is occasionally extremely impertinent to me—I tell her *I am going to tell you.* She says she would like to see you, and she likes your face and she sends you her love. This is Miss Maud Locker-Lampson, looking so lovely in a purple and green dress like a wild hyacinth. You would so love all these nice dear children—they are *so* nice—so good-looking. And there is something else you would like—the loveliest tiny grey kitten, such a sweet.

Sept. 1, 1898.

Isn't it a pity more people do not love things ?—The beautiful things of the world are so little to so many ; they go for drives where all they look upon is so lovely and they care not one bit, but long to get home again as quickly as possible.

I can't tell why it is people are always trying to convert me. They seem to look upon me as always such a ready subject, and really there is not a more fixed belief than I possess—I have thought the same way ever since I have had the power to think at all. How is it possible that I should change ? I know I shall not. If there is a God who made all the wonderful things in this world, surely He would require some worship of those also, but I can't help thinking of a power so much greater than all that altogether—a power that the best in us reaches to only.

Sept. 16, 1898.

I'm reading a book that makes me so unhappy—I hate it—I totally disapprove of it, yet I want to read it to the end to know what it is like. I feel all the time how wretched I should be if I had a mind like the man who wrote this book. How curious it is the way people think—the difference of how they think—how curious they are in the narrowness of their—shall I say—vision? And there goes on the wonderful world all the time, with its wonders hidden to, and uncared for by, so many. How is it that I have got to think the caring for Nature and Art of all kinds a *real* religion ? I never can, never shall see it is more religious to sit in a hot church trying to listen to a commonplace sermon than looking at a beautiful sky, or the waves

234

Religion

coming in, and feeling that longing to be good and exultation in the beauty of things.

How dreadful that sordid idea of a God is with the mind getting more and more morbid and frightened. Why was the world made then ? and everything so wonderful and beautiful ?

She recounts how somebody, who had felt it a duty to attempt to convert her, had said, ' " You can't sit on that sofa for five minutes without feeling steeped in sin "; and I said, " I often sit on it, and I don't feel like that ; if I did I should try hard not to do wrong things." And so I would ! '

KATE GREENAWAY TO RUSKIN

Oct. 26, 1898.

How curiously days come back to you, or rather, live for ever in your life—never go out of it, as if the impression was so great it could never go away again. I could tell you so many such. One is so often present I think I must tell that one now. Go and stand in a shady lane—at least, a wide country road—with high hedges, and wide grassy places at the sides. The hedges are all hawthorns blossoming ; in the grass grow great patches of speedwell, stitchwort, and daisies. You look through gates into fields full of buttercups, and the whole of it is filled with sunlight. For I said it was shady only because the hedges were high. Now do you see my little picture, and me a little dark girl in a pink frock and hat, looking about at things a good deal, and thoughts filled up with such wonderful things—everything seeming wonderful, and life to go on for ever just as it was. What a beautiful long time a day was ! Filled with time——

KATE GREENAWAY TO RUSKIN

7 Nov. 1898.

I am reading a strange French Play. I should like to see it acted—*Cyrano de Bergerac.* I feel it would be very taking when played.

It is so strange all the great things are a sacrifice. The thing that appeals supremely seems to me always that. Yet how sad it should be, for to the one it means desolation. It is a strange world this. How queer it all is, isn't it ? living at all—and our motives and things matter, and liking beautiful things, and all the while really not knowing anything about the Vital Part of it—the Before and the After.

235

Kate Greenaway

Oh, so foggy again ! No seeing to paint or draw. I hope it will soon leave off this, but it always is so about Lord Mayor's day. It is nearly always an accompaniment, isn't it ? I saw the people going home the other day with those long papers of the Show. Do you remember them ? How fascinating they used to be to me ! how wonderful they seemed ! Did you like them ? I have only seen Lord Mayor's Show once. I would like to see it again. I hope they will never give it up. I do so wish we had a few more processions, and I'd like to revive all the old May-days, Jacks-in-the-Green, and May-poles—then Morris dancers, all of them. I've seen Morris dancers once only but they looked so nice with their sticks and ribbons.

I wish I had something very nice to send you on this foggy day. I want to go to the Fine Art this afternoon to see Alfred East's drawings. One will have to look at them by gas-light for the fog is so dense.

It really is fatal to me to have to do anything in a hurry, I must have a quiet time. I can do just as much work or more if only I don't feel I've got to make haste—a sort of Dutch temperament—no, it is really nervousness—comes in. Look at dear Rover ! There's a calm life—nothing at all to bother about except to try to get more of the things he likes.

Such, presumably, as two chops instead of the one which, every day of his spoiled life, Kate had grilled for him. And he might eat the cakes and fancy biscuits at tea-time if he chose to commandeer them. The inevitable result of such high living was occasional illness and veterinary attentions.

The following are extracts from undated letters of this year:—

Dear Rover is, I am sorry to say, getting fatter again, after all the trouble we have taken to make him thin. He is evidently meant to be stout. One thing now, he never will go alone. We always have to be with him. Once he would go for long walks by himself. They are quite different, like people, when once you get to know them.

On Heroes and Hero-Worship

I have just heard from Joanie that you spent your day in the drawing-room yesterday—so you would see the Burne-Jones' and the Hunts. How slowly the Hunts have dawned on me—but it is a comfort *they have dawned,* isn't it ? ? ? ? Ah, you say, WHAT a benighted being, what a little Heathen ! to have been so long.

KATE GREENAWAY TO RUSKIN

What a fuss there has been about Sir Herbert Kitchener !—I like it.—He must have felt it was very nice for people to be so glad. I like a great deal made of people who do things.

ROVER IS INDISPOSED AND HAS TO BE BANDAGED.

On a Letter to Ruskin.

In the same strain she had written of another hero to Miss Dickinson the year before :—

I'm very much impressed by Lord Roberts' Indian book. I met him many years ago at a children's party at Lady Jeune's. She told us we were rival attractions and the little Princes and Princesses couldn't make up their minds which of us they wanted to see most.

He *was brave*—so were the others ; they were a brave and noble lot. It seems too wonderful as you read to think how people can be like that, going to certain death—to the suffering of anguish. It feels to me too much to take—too much to accept—but it's beautiful.

In 1899 Kate Greenaway devoted herself seriously to the painting of portraits in oil colours, and her letters of this year are full of the difficulties which beset her and her indomitable determination to master the mysteries of the new medium. Again and again we find her bewailing—' I wish I could paint and not do smooth sticky things '—' I can draw a little but I can't paint '—' Isn't it too bad—too bad—how *much* I can admire and—how *little* I can do.'

In March she said good-bye with a heavy heart to her friends the Tennysons, on Lord Tennyson's departure to take up the Governorship of South Australia. They were destined never to meet again.

237

Kate Greenaway

Jan. 3, 1899.

I'm not doing drawings that at all interest me just now. They are just single figures of children which I always spoil by the backgrounds. I never can put a background into a painting of a single figure, while in a drawing there isn't the least difficulty. Perhaps I don't trouble about the reality in the drawing. I put things just where I want them, not, possibly, as they ought to go. And that seems to me the difficulty of full-length portraits. It is all quite easy with just a head or half length. It is funny the background should be the difficulty. The most modern way is to have a highly done-out background and a figure lost in mist, but I don't see this. So I can't take refuge there.

Miss Greenaway's difficulty with backgrounds is that shared by every artist, more or less. G. F. Watts, R.A., used to quote Rubens, who said that 'the man who can paint a background can paint a portrait.'

Jan. 11, 1899.

What dismal books people do write ! I have just been reading a story by Hardy called *The Woodlanders*, so spoilt by coarseness and unnaturalness. I say spoilt by this, for there are parts of it so beautiful —all the descriptions of the country and the cider-making—it is all so well described you really feel there. The end of the book is simply *Hateful*. I hated to think his mind *could* make it end so. Did you ever read any of his books ? so many people now seem to me to make things unnatural—it is a curious thing to think so, but I'm sure it is that they do—and the natural is so much greater. They like things odd—eccentric.

She never missed an opportunity of seeing Burne-Jones's pictures. Here are two of a hundred instances :—

Jan. 19, 1899.

I am going to-day to see the Burne-Jones drawings at the Burlington Club. His drawings are so beautiful. I do wish you could see the large painting of King Arthur at Avalon. How you would like to have it to look at for a time ! I should like to have it for a week hung opposite to me that I might know it all—every bit.

TWO GIRLS IN A GARDEN.

THE DANCING OF THE FELSPAR FAIRIES.

A BABY IN WHITE.

BOOK-PLATE OF MISS VERA EVELYN SAMUEL.

KATE GREENAWAY BEFORE THE FATES.

THE FABLE OF THE GIRL AND HER MILK PAIL.

THE MUFF (UNFINISHED).

THE STICK FIRE.

Sir E. Burne-Jones's Drawings

How tired one would get of some paintings if one gazed upon them for a week—as tired as one often gets of one's own. I fear it is conceited but there are a *very few* drawings—little ones of my own—that I do not get tired of, though I do of most of them.

Saturday.

I went to see the Burne-Jones drawings yesterday. They are very lovely. There are two or three I would like to have, but indeed there is not one I would not, but there are two or three I would love to possess—a procession with such lovely young girls in it. The studies

On a Letter to Ruskin.

for the pictures are so beautiful—the chalk and pencil drawings. He draws such beautiful faces ; and I like his later drawings often better than his earlier ones. He certainly had not gone off, except perhaps in colour—but that was a phase. He had grown to like colder colour, brown and cold grey, which I did not always like, preferring the beautiful colouring of the ' Chant d'Amour ' and ' Venus Vinctrix.' But then, I like colour so much. Well, the *world is* Coloured, so are people. I see colour higher than things uncoloured for that reason.

KATE GREENAWAY TO RUSKIN

Feb. 21, 1899.

I told you, didn't I, that I was going to try if I could do portraits of children ? I don't at all like it. I don't feel near strong enough for

239

Kate Greenaway

the strain of it. I know what the children are like—quite unaccustomed to sitting still, and then to have to get a real likeness! I prefer the little girls and boys that live in that nice land, that come as you call them, fair or dark, in green ribbons or blue. I like making cowslip fields grow and apple-trees bloom at a moment's notice. This is what it is, you see, to have gone through life with an enchanted land ever beside you—yet how much it has been!

KATE GREENAWAY TO RUSKIN

March 8, 1899.

The summer exhibitions now are never interesting. The poor artists can't afford to paint good pictures. No one will buy them. I think it is very sad and such a pity—the sort of thing that's taken now—cheap, of course, that comes first—then comes the picture if you can call it so (I often don't). The colours are daubed on in great smears and dashes. The drawing has gone—anywhere but to the picture—at a distance it looks like something but close you can't see anything. Now *I hate pictures* that don't look right *close*. Sometimes the colour of them is good, powerful, and strong, but—so was Millais, and with all else, it ought to be added, the more and more do I grow to think Millais wonderful. To me there is no question he is greatest. People quarrel with me because I think him greater than Watts, but, is it conceited to say?—*I know he is.* And Watts himself says so also. Ah! if I could paint like Millais! then, then you'd see a proud person indeed.

KATE GREENAWAY TO RUSKIN

March 17, 1899.

My little model has taken to say such funny things lately. She said yesterday some one had an illness that went in at his head and came out at his feet. She also was talking of a little sister being ill and I said, 'Perhaps she is cutting a tooth.' 'Oh no,' she said, 'she always cuts her teeth with bronchitis.' . . . . . It inspires me so much to see good paintings though I don't think you can ever tell how they are done, or at least I can't. I often think that when I am painting myself no one would guess I did that, or that, the look is all. You may do a thing quite another way from the elaborate theory.

KATE GREENAWAY TO RUSKIN

March 23, 1899.

I make such awful beings in oil—you would be amused, but—I'm going on till I emerge—I'm going to emerge, I'm so interested but SO

240

Attempts at Oil Painting

STUPID. The paint all runs away, and the big brushes! But think of the fine point I've passed my life with! I knew where I was going then. Why, trying to draw with a pencil with *no point* is nothing to it. But, as I said, I'm going to emerge—in the end—triumphant—? ? ? ?— but that appears to be a considerable long way off yet. . . . I should like to paint Spring one day. I see it all. . . . If I could *Paint in Oil,* you see, I could do it,—*don't you see?* or do you smile? You *would* if you saw the Painting in Oil. I sit and laugh at it. My little model says— 'Oh, I don't think it's so bad'—and tells other people I don't get into a mess. Upon which they say, '*That's odd.*' I was rather touched by her assumption of my triumphant progress. You like her for it—don't you? Ah, well, I'm going to do lovely little girls and boys by and by. I *am.*

On the same subject she wrote to Miss Dickinson on April 24 : 'I am more enthralled than ever by the oil paint, which begins to go where I want it instead of where it wants to go itself.'

At the Exhibition of the Home Art Industries at the Albert Hall she has an amusing contretemps.

KATE GREENAWAY TO RUSKIN

30, FROGNAL,
HAMPSTEAD, N.W.

May 9, 1899.

Then the Princess Louise came and I was introduced to her. She is so pretty and looks so young. I actually remembered to curtsey (which I always forget), and I was just congratulating myself on having behaved properly, when all my money rolled out of my purse on to the ground. The Princess laughed and picked it up. Wasn't it nice of her? Something always happens to me.

Kate Greenaway

KATE GREENAWAY TO RUSKIN

May 17, 1899.

I am improving now in my oil-painting. I begin to make the flesh look like flesh and no longer white and chalky. I like doing it so much and if only the models would not talk so much !—But how they talk ! and if you stop them talking they gape and make such ugly faces ! Some one was telling me that Sir Joshua Reynolds, to stop his sitters' talking, had a glass put up so that they could see him working. I think of adopting that plan. You can't think what you are doing while you have to listen. I can't see why they want to talk so and never think. How funny it would be to have a mind that never liked to be alone with its own thoughts—very dreadful I should find it. I get to feel very tired and miserable if I can't have any time to be quiet in.

KATE GREENAWAY TO RUSKIN

May 31, 1899.

You can't think how funny it is—but finding the power of oil-painting now, my curious mind is wishing to see, and seeing, all subjects large ; it seems as if my long-ago and ever-constant wish—to paint a life-size hedge—might now be realised. What a divine thing to do ! A life-sized girl in the front and then the large foxgloves and wild roses, and strawberries on the ground. I should be lost in my picture. I should have to have a stool that moved up and carried me about over my picture. All the same I should not wonder if I *do* do a life-size thing ! Perhaps I have hopes of the capacity of oil paint that won't be realised, but it is nice to get a medium to work in that does what you want more at once. I don't like small oil things half as much as water-colours—but I do lose the *go* of things in water-colours.

KATE GREENAWAY TO RUSKIN

June 7, 1899.

I went to the Tate Gallery the other afternoon, and somehow I didn't like it—much. It is a beautiful Gallery, but somehow tomb-like —and my dearest-loved of English pictures, Millais' 'Ophelia,' doesn't look its best there. Now I feel this picture ought to have a gallery that suits it exactly ! but perhaps some other time I may go and like it ever so much. As it was, I grieve to say, the entrance was what I liked best, going out and coming in. There's the beautiful river and the boats and the opposite shore of wharves and buildings, and I felt how nice it must be at Venice to come out and find the sea—I do like

Resolution

the sea—or a large river to every town. But this view of the Thames fascinated me—like seeing the river from the drawing-room at the Speaker's house. I am almost getting to think that an oil-picture does undergo a change a little while after it is painted—I mean twenty or forty years—and then if it is a real good one settles itself into remaining a wonderful thing for ever. For some of the pictures of forty years ago get a curious look. I'm thinking of Egg, and that time—or are they not quite good enough? For the Leslies remain charming.

KATE GREENAWAY TO RUSKIN

June 22, 1899.

The air is scented with the hay—everywhere—and the wilderness of the garden has fallen before a very hard-working young gardener. I loved it all overgrown, but the gardener told me when he saw it *he could not come again*, he felt so *depressed*. Queer, isn't it, how differently people feel? It is very fresh and flowery at this moment. The rain has brought out the flowers. There are roses, white peonies, purple irises, large herbaceous poppies, lupins, syringa, marigolds, foxgloves, delphiniums, and campanulas, and day lilies, and many others. It is the garden's best moment, and it is summery and not that frightful heat which is too much for me. Do get *Elizabeth and her German Garden*. It [suggests] Alfred Austin's garden books but it is amusing and pretty. . . .

I am depressed often when I can't do this new painting as I like. I take a rush on and think every difficulty is over—when I find myself suddenly plunged deeper than ever in things that won't come right—*but they've got to*—they don't know that, but it is so—I'm not going to be beaten. I can see loveliness surely. My fingers have got to learn to do what my eyes wish—they will have to—so there it is. *I see such* colour and I can't find a paint to make it. In water-colour I

243

Kate Greenaway

could get any colour I could see, but I can't in oils. I get something
pretty like ; then in a day or two some underneath colour has worked
up and horrid colour is the result. However, I'm beginning to find
out many things, so I hope as I go on working I may get to do it all
right.

It poured with rain here yesterday. I hope this may make the
gardener less depressed when he contemplates our weeds. Poor weeds
—fine tall fresh green thistles and docks spreading out their leaves in
lovely curves. I'm sorry for all the things that are not much wanted
on this earth.—And long ago, I loved docks ; we used to play with the
seeds and pretend it was tea. We used to have a tea-shop and weigh
it out and sell it for tea. Perhaps docks do not mean that for any one
else in the world—like the purple mallow and the seeds I used to call
cheeses, sweet little flat green things, do you know ?

Kate Greenaway to Ruskin

July 25, 1899.

Dear Rover's pride has had a fall. There are two swans have
come to live on the White Stone pond, and Rover goes and swims
there on his way home. Johnny said he could see the people round
the pond laughing, and when he got up to it there was Rover swimming about as if the pond belonged to him, while the swans who
thought it belonged to them were fluttering their wings and craning
their necks. Rover still remained unconcerned and imperturbable,
when one of the swans took hold of his tail and pulled it ! This did
vanquish Rover, who left the pond hurriedly amidst the derisive
laughter of the bystanders.

He has some nice friendly swans on the other pond who swim up
and down with him. I suppose he thought all swans were alike.
I am curious to know if he goes in to-day. . . . . . Dear Rover stood
firm and did go in. Johnny saw him quite unconcerned swimming
about with the swans flapping about at the back. Now don't you
think this was much to his credit ? I only hope they won't peck him !

Kate Greenaway to Mrs. Edmund Evans

Dear Mrs. Evans—You don't know how I feel that I don't get
time to write—you must think it horrid—but I have so many things
to do because I can't afford to pay for them being done, and my little
leisure bit of time is taken up writing to Mr. Ruskin every week—for
now he can't go out, or often do things that mean so much to him.
Then I am trying to do children's portraits life-size—in oils ; this

244

Children's Taste

means giving up a lot of time to practising, a year possibly, and making no money. Then I've the house to see to and my dresses and needlework and trying to write my life—as you will, I think, see there is a good deal more than a day's work in each day. I want to come and see you very much but I fear I can't before the autumn— then I shall try. I have wanted rather to go somewhere quite by myself to the sea to try to get on with my book. I might come near you, if not to stay with you. I hope you like Ventnor and that it suits Mr. Evans.

KATE GREENAWAY TO RUSKIN

Sept. 1899.

Do you know, I've had a great deal of pleasure out of oak branches and acorns—what a lovely green they are ! One day walking by the sea, I saw a little bit of lovely emerald green on the sand. When I looked to see what it was there were two *acorns* ! shining and looking so brilliant. I could not have thought a small thing could show so much colour.

I go on liking things more and more, seeing them more and more beautiful. Don't you think it is a great possession to be able to get so much joy out of things that are always there to give it, and do not change ? What a great pity my hands are not clever enough to do what my mind and eyes see, but there it is !

KATE GREENAWAY TO RUSKIN

Nov. 7, 1899.

There are not any very good children's books about just now that I have seen. The rage for copying mine seems over, so I suppose some one will soon step to the front with something new. Children often don't care a bit about the books people think they will, and I think they often like grown-up books—at any rate I did. From the Kenny Meadows pictures to Shakespeare I learnt all the plays when I was very young indeed. It is curious how much pictures can tell you—like the plays without words. I suppose I asked a good deal about them and was told, and read little bits

245

Kate Greenaway

anyhow. I never remember the time when I didn't know what each play was about. They were my Sunday evening's amusement, and another book called *The Illuminated Magazine*[1] that had all sorts of things in it. Some I specially liked, called 'The Recreations of Mr. Zig-Zag the Elder.' Perhaps you know the magazine. And then there were accounts of the old London Churches and old places of interest : the Lollards' Tower, St. John's Gate, St. Bartholomew's Church. No, I believe these were in a book called *The Family Magazine*. I believe one of our three cherished large volumes was that name,—the other two the *Illuminated*. How much prettier those old illustrations are than the modern engraved photograph. I hate the modern book and magazine illustration. But there is a BUT —the illustrations of Hugh Thomson and Anning Bell, also Byam Shaw, are quite beautiful and quite different.

KATE GREENAWAY TO RUSKIN

Nov. 26, 1899.

I am rather liking red and blue just now. I suppose it is the winter makes all faint colours look so pale. I like the strong warm colours of scarlet—it is nice to do. I always like painting fur, which I think is rather curious, for I don't like painting hair and never do it well. Rembrandt painted hair so beautifully—the portrait of Saskia with the fair hair hanging down was so beautifully done ; I did envy that. Then Correggio also—do you remember Cupid's curls ? so lovely ; and some of Sir Joshua's, the Angels' heads—their hair is done so wonderfully. Fair hair is more difficult to paint than dark ; I spoil mine by getting the darks too dark in it, so losing the fair colour of it, though I do think it is easier in oils than in water-colours.

KATE GREENAWAY TO RUSKIN

Dec. 5, 1899.

There is going to be an exhibition for children at the Fine Art— the Private View is on Saturday—but I think it is very likely the children won't appreciate it. I often notice that they don't at all care for what grown-up people think they will. For one thing, they like something that excites their imagination—a very real thing mixed up with a great unreality like Blue Beard. How I used to be thrilled by 'Sister Ann, Sister Ann,' done by the servants in the agonised voice of Blue Beard's wife, and I could hardly breathe when the

---

[1] First volume published in 1843, edited by Douglas Jerrold, and written and illustrated by some of the most brilliant authors and artists of the day.

The Last Letter to Ruskin

On a Letter to Ruskin.

stains would not come off the key.—Those wonderful little books
they used to sell in coloured covers, a penny and a halfpenny each—
they were condensed and dramatic. They are spoilt now by their
profuseness.

I never cared so much for *Jack the Giant-Killer*, or *Jack and
the Beanstalk*, or *Tom Thumb*, as I did for *The Sleeping Beauty
in the Wood*, *Cinderella*, and *Beauty and the Beast*. I did not
like *Puss in Boots* as well either. Of course they were all deeply
fascinating, but the three pretty ones I liked best. It would be
curious to do a book of them from one's remembrance of them in
one's early thoughts. I know my Blue Beard people were not dressed
as Turks then.

Kate Greenaway to Ruskin

Dec. 13, 1899.

It has been so dark lately, I'm quite afraid to do my things. For
a dark day does so much harm—just spoils everything. I'm getting
quite used to oil now, but I still make out things too much, especially
the lines round the eyelids. It is a pity, but I always have that
tendency and this dark weather makes it worse. I hope I may get
out of it in time—but I may never.

Dear Rover has hurt his foot and is quite sulky because Johnny
has gone out this evening. He expects us always to be at home now.
You will say to yourself, why does she write such silly letters to me
just now? and they are. It is my mind has got too much in it—more
than it can hold. Now you will say, 'Oh, I don't think her mind has

247

got anything in it at all.' What do you think it is doing ?—Trying to write a play in the midst of all this bother ! Now I never could think out a *plot* to write a story about, and here, at this most inopportune moment, a play has got into my mind and insists on being written, and goes on and on and develops in a quite curious manner. And there am I with no time to spare and it *will* be written down—isn't that funny ? Of course it won't be good or of any use—only I must do it !

On Saturday, the 20th January 1900, the following entry which says so little, but meant so much to Kate Greenaway, appears in her diary—'Mr. Ruskin died to-day at 2.30 in the afternoon from influenza.'

For him there could be no regret that the 'black archway-gate had swung open to the glittering fields of freedom,' but for those left behind it would be hard to say by how much the world was the poorer. It was not characteristic of her to say much when she felt most deeply.

It was Mr. Stuart Samuel who broke the news to her. 'On Sunday,' she wrote to Mrs. Evans, 'some people came in and said they had seen from the papers he was dead. I didn't believe it, but the next morning I got letters from Brantwood.'

Then on the following day she wrote in her trouble :—

Kate Greenaway to Mr. M. H. Spielmann

22 January 1900.

I'm dreadfully sorry about Mr. Ruskin's death. It was a great shock. I only heard from Mrs. Severn on Saturday morning ; she said then he had influenza, but they did not think of any danger. I've heard again to-day—they only knew there was any fear of it being fatal between 10 and 11 Saturday morning. He died at half-past 2, entirely painlessly all through. I feel it very much, for he was a great friend—and there is no one else like him.

Soon she came round to talk it over and open her heart to this correspondent, who had known Ruskin, too, and loved him well. And it will be observed that up to his death, never in her letters to Ruskin did she write a word about her own ill-health, lest she should distress one for whom she had so affectionate and unselfish a friendship.

Miss Greenaway was now invited by the Royal Commission to contribute as a British artist to the Water-Colour and Black-

'The April Baby's Book of Tunes'

and-White of the Paris Exhibition of 1900, when it was hoped that she would repeat her success of eleven years before. She had written to Ruskin that she was 'too busy to take any trouble over it,' and to a friend to whom she paid the compliment of coming for occasional counsel, she wrote as follows, after due deliberation :—

KATE GREENAWAY TO MR. M. H. SPIELMANN

I have decided not to send to the Paris Exhibition. I have nothing good enough and I don't know who has my things—I can't think of anything I would like to send. I feel pencil drawings look so very pale when they get placed with strong coloured things. Don't you think it better not to send unless you send your best? There was no time to do anything, and I did not want to leave the oil work.

To her question there could be only one answer, and the artist was unrepresented at Paris.

The state of her health was now giving serious anxiety to her friends. She certainly had undertaken and was able to carry to completion the illustrations to *The April Baby's Book of Tunes*, by the author of *Elizabeth and her German Garden*, which was published towards the end of the year, but signs of failing power were only too evident.

The *April Baby* illustrations, which were reproduced by chromo-lithography in place of Mr. Evans's wood-engraving, to which admirers of her work had become accustomed, though charming enough and in harmony with the spirit of the book, are inferior to Mr. Evans's interpretations, and add not much to her reputation. A curious fact connected with them is recorded in the following letter received by us from the delightful and exhilarating author :—

In answer to your letter I can only tell you that I did not, unfortunately, know Miss Kate Greenaway personally, and that while she was illustrating the *April Baby's Book of Tunes* we only occasionally wrote to each other about it. I felt quite sure that her pictures would be charming and did not like to bother her with letters full of my own crude ideas. It was odd that, though she had never seen the babies or their photographs, her pictures were so much like what the babies were at that time that I have often been asked whether she had sketched them from life.

Her letters were exceedingly kind, and one of the April Baby's most

Kate Greenaway

precious possessions is a copy she sent her of *Marigold Garden* with a little pen-and-ink figure on the fly-leaf drawn specially for her. She wrote me that she had been ill for a long time and had not been able to work at my illustrations, and that they had all been crowded into a few weeks at the end of the time given her by the publishers. She apparently thought they had suffered from this, but I think most people will agree that they are as charming as anything she ever did. Naturally I was extremely pleased to have the weaknesses of my story hidden behind such a pretty string of daintiness. So peculiarly simple and kind were her letters that even a stranger like myself who only knew her through them felt, when she died, that there was one sweet nature the less in the world.—Believe me, yours very truly,

THE AUTHOR OF 'ELIZABETH AND HER GERMAN GARDEN.'

That she now rather shrank from undertaking work of this kind we have already seen from the letter written to Mr. M. H. Spielmann, who, as a friend of some years' standing, asked her if she would be disposed to illustrate one of his wife's stories which were appearing in *Little Folks*, and were afterwards published in book form. In the event, the book, which contains brilliant drawings by several leading black-and-white artists of the day, was not lacking in two from the pencil of Kate Greenaway.

At the same time her letters are sadly eloquent of her failing health :—

KATE GREENAWAY TO MRS. M. H. SPIELMANN

11 *Jan.* 1901.

It is so long since I have seen you—so long since I have been. It has not been my fault. I have not been well enough. I seem to have been ill all the year. I had a long illness all the autumn which I am not yet recovered from—and then colds so bad they have been illnesses. . . . . . I have seen no one hardly and done so little work. I'm so sorry when I don't work. For the time so soon goes and I always have so much I want to do, and just now there are so many beautiful pictures to go and see. . . . . . I hope you will believe that though I have not been to see you I have often thought of you and wished to see you.

Ruskin's birthday was on the 8th of February. On the first anniversary of it a year after his death, Kate wrote to Mrs. Severn :—

Kate Greenaway's Illness

39, Frognal, Hampstead, N.W.,
7 *February* 1901.

My dearest Joanie—To-morrow is a sad day again. How I always wish I had done so much, much more. And I should have if life had not been so difficult to me of late years. . . .

If it would get warmer I could get out ; then I should get stronger. As it is I take everything I can. This is the little programme : medicine, 9 times a day ; beef tea, 8 times ; port wine, champagne, brandy and soda, eggs and milk. I'm all day at it. Can I do more ? Am I not a victim ?

My dearest love to you. Your loving   Katie.

A few days later she writes to Mrs. Spielmann :—

. . . I am really, I think, getting much better now, and when I have been away I hope I may return to my usual self. I have never been well enough to go to see you though I have often wished to. Since this time last year there has only been one month (June) without the doctor coming. I have felt it so trying being ill so long.

Yet in spite of her illness it must not be supposed that Kate's desire for industry ever flagged for a moment. She was full of schemes for books—not merely projected schemes, but plans fully matured, first sketches made, and pages fully 'set-out.' There was a book of 'sonnets' of her own—(she called them sonnets, though not all of them were in sonnet form)—plaintive, dreamy, and frequently a little morbid ; and the water-colour drawings to these are occasionally quite or almost complete. The water-colour sketch called 'Dead,' here reproduced, is one of these. Then there was a new *Blake's Songs of Innocence*, to be published at a shilling net, each song with at least one drawing ; this was so fully worked out that for certain of the designs several sketches were made. No fewer than twenty-two sketches were designed for a volume of *Nursery Rhymes* ; there are fourteen to *Baby's Début* ; and twelve and four respectively to Hans Christian Andersen's *Snow Queen* and *What the Moon Saw*. And, finally, *A Book of Girls* was to be illustrated with six of her daintiest pictures. A brave programme, surely, with sketches made, ready to be carried into execution ; but publishers were doubtful, their enterprise declined, and offers were so little generous, that the schemes were not pursued.

Several friends sought to remove the discouragement under

Kate Greenaway

which Kate Greenaway was now labouring, in order to open up new vistas of activity and success in other walks than those she had trodden hitherto : not merely to salve her wounded *amour propre* but to spare her the natural worry incident to the diminution of her earning powers.   For some time she had herself schemed a great dressmaking business in her own name, with herself as designer ; but it never got beyond the talking stage, and that mainly with her sister Fanny—Mrs. Dadd.   Then she had the idea of modelling bas-reliefs in *gesso* for decorative purposes ; but that also came to nothing.   For her heart was in her drawing and painting, and she welcomed cordially a suggestion that the Editor of the *Magazine of Art* should write an article on ' The Later Work of Kate Green-away,' partly in order to draw public attention to her oil-painting, but mainly to bring forward once more her name as an active art-worker, for she was firmly persuaded that she was well-nigh forgotten—' forgotten,' the bitterest word in all the vocabulary to one who has been a public favourite and whose name has rung throughout the world.

Then, in August of 1901, Miss Greenaway was offered the post of editor of a new Magazine for children at a handsome salary, but she refused it, not only because she felt her strength unequal to so exacting an undertaking, but also because she doubted whether she possessed the necessary qualifications.   But sadly enough for the many who loved her the first of these reasons was all too cogent, for only three short months were to pass before ' finis ' was to be written both to work and life.

A fortnight before she had written to Mrs. Stuart Samuel from Cromer :—

I've been very ill—acute muscular rheumatism—horribly painful. I am now, I hope, getting better. It has been so in my mind the wish to write to you. You were so kind, it felt ungrateful to disappear in silence. . . .—Your affectionate   KATE GREENAWAY.

And again, ten days before she passed away : ' I should love a drive when I'm well enough.   I will write and tell you how I get on ; then, if you will, take me one day.   With my love.'

But the end came, at 39, Frognal, on November 6th.

The privacy she wished for in life was observed at her death ; only a few friends attended in the Chapel of the Cremation Society's Cemetery at Woking, on November 12th ; fewer still on the day following, when the casket was quietly interred at Hamp-

Death of Kate Greenaway

stead Cemetery.   But the proofs were overwhelming that she was in a multitude of hearts on that day.

At the news of her passing a chorus of eulogy and regret went up from the press.   Writers and critics, English and American, French and German, vied with one another to do honour to the memory of one who had spent her life in spreading joy and beauty about her without the faintest taint of vulgarity, without the slightest hint of aught but what was pure and delicate, joyous and refined.   Tender and respectful, admiring and grateful, saddened with the note of heartfelt sorrow, these tributes one and all bore witness to the beauty of her life and work.   Of them all none touches a sweeter and a truer chord than the farewell homage of her friend, Mr. Austin Dobson : [1]—

K. G.

Nov : VI : 1901

Farewell, kind heart.   And if there be
In that unshored Immensity
Child-Angels, they will welcome thee.

Clean-souled, clear-eyed, unspoiled, discreet,
Thou gav'st thy gifts to make Life sweet,—
These shall be flowers about thy feet !

For a few years preceding her death Kate Greenaway had occupied herself much with trying to express her feelings in artless and simple verse.

In 1896 we find her writing to Miss Dickinson with her customary pluck and energy :—

Each night when I go to bed I read a little bit of Browning—they are so wonderful—each time I read one I like it better than ever.   That fires me with ambition to try to write something, and I do try, and they won't come good ; isn't it hateful of them to be so poor and weak ?   But I'm going to try more than ever, and I'm going to try other things too if only I can keep well.   I do mean to try and do a little more in my life.   I'm not content, for I have not yet *expressed myself*.   It's such a queer feeling, that longing to express yourself and not finding a means or way—yet it goads you on and won't let you rest.

---

[1] Published by Mr. Austin Dobson in his delightful article on Kate Greenaway in the *Art Journal*, and written by him, on the 29th January 1902, in the Album of Mr. Ernest G. Brown, and here printed by consent of both gentlemen.

Kate Greenaway

The following sonnet, a characteristic and appropriate example, was written when she already felt the coldness of the advancing shadow, and it may be accepted as reflecting her own view of the Great Hereafter :—

> When I am dead, and all of you stand round
> And look upon me, my soul flown away
> Into a new existence—far from the sound
> Of this world's noise, and this world's night and day :
>
> No more the inexplicable soul in this strange mortal body,
> This world and it in severance eternal :
> No more my presence here shall it embody,
> No more shall take its place in time diurnal—
>
> What beauteous land may I be wandering in
> While you stand gazing at what once was I ?
> Why, I may be to gold harps listening
> And plucking flowers of Immortality—
> > Why, Heaven's blue skies may shine above my head
> > While you stand there—and say that I am dead !

In the year following Kate Greenaway's death, a fourth Exhibition of her works was held at the Fine Art Society's Gallery. These were in no sense 'the remaining works of an artist lately deceased,' as auctioneers' catalogues commonly have it, nor yet was it a memorial exhibition. It was, like those of 1891, 1894, and 1898, the result of labour undertaken with the definite purpose of showing what she could accomplish, and of claiming once again the suffrages of the collector. The only difference—a difference that weighed upon every visitor to the Gallery—was that the hand which had produced them was now stiff and the gentle heart by which they were inspired had ceased to beat.

The most important pictures sold were 'Little Girl in Purple,' 'Little Girl in Blue and White,' 'Visitors,' 'Boy with Basket of Apples,' 'Procession of Girls with Roses,' 'Little Girl in Red Pelisse,' 'Procession of Girls with Flowers,' 'The Doorway,' 'Doubts,' 'Girl in Orange Dress (seated),' unfinished, 'Cottage with Children,' 'Girl seated by a Rose Tree,' 'Strawberries,' 'Children passing through the Apple Trees,' 'Susan and Mary and Emily, with their sweet round mouths sing Ha ! ha ! ha,' and 'A Little Girl in Big Hat with Basket of Roses.'

In a table case were also exhibited a selection from the illustrated letters written by Kate to John Ruskin, from which many of the thumb-nail sketches reproduced in this book are taken.

PENCIL AND TINT DRAWING.

In the possession of B. Elkin Mocatta, Esq.

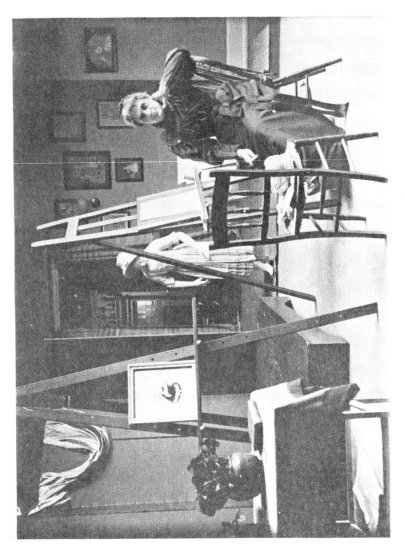

KATE GREENAWAY IN HER STUDIO, 1895.

From a private photograph by Mrs. William Miller.

K.C.
1895

MABEL PONSONBY.

Pencil and Tint.   In the possession of the Hon. Gerald Ponsonby.

K.C
L Nov. 1895

EILEEN PONSONBY.

Pencil and Tint.   In the possession of the Hon. Gerald Ponsonby.

STUDY FROM LIFE.

Illustration ('Ronald's Clock') in 'Littledom Castle' (by Mrs. M. H. Spielmann).
G. Routledge & Sons.

PENCIL STUDY FROM LIFE.

THE PICNIC.

Early Pen-and-Ink Drawing from Kate Greenaway's Sketch-book.

PEN SKETCH IN ONE OF KATE GREENAWAY'S EARLIEST SKETCH-BOOKS.

(*Showing early power of composition.*)

THE KATE GREENAWAY COT

ENDOWED BY FRIENDS AND ADMIRERS · 1903

COMMITTEE

CHAIRMAN. SIR THOMAS WARDLE, J.P.
HON. TREAS. Mʳ ARTHUR L. LIBERTY, J.P.D.L.
HON. SEC. SIR ARTHUR TRENDELL. C.M.G.

LADY DOROTHY NEVILL. LADY MARIA PONSONBY.
LADY VERA HERBERT. HON. LADY FREMANTLE.
LADY JEUNE. Mʳˢ LOCKER-LAMPSON.
MISS MERESIA NEVILL.
SIR WILLIAM AGNEW. Bᵗ. SIR GEORGE BIRDWOOD K.C.I.E. C.S.I.
SIR CASPAR PURDON CLARKE C.I.E. Mʳ WALTER CRANE. A.R.W.S.
Mʳ HAROLD HARTLEY. M.J.S. Mʳ MARION H. SPIELMANN.
Mʳ ASTON WEBB. A.R.A. Mʳ ARTHUR W. À BECKETT. F.J.I.

Kate Greenaway

For the sake of those who have not enjoyed the privilege of seeing any of her original work it should be mentioned that in the Art Library of the Victoria and Albert Museum there are ten of her water-colour drawings, among them illustrations to the *Language of Flowers*, *Little Ann*, and the Almanacks, while in the Picture Gallery at this time of writing hang ' P peeped in it,' an illustration for *A Apple Pie*, one of the illustrations for *A Day in a Child's Life*, and ' Three Girls in White.'

Although such a one as Kate Greenaway is scarcely likely to be forgotten, a movement was quickly set on foot by some of her friends in order to perpetuate her memory in some appropriately practical fashion, and a committee was formed ' for the purpose of promoting a scheme which will secure a fitting memorial to the late Kate Greenaway, who filled so distinctive a place in the Art world, and whose charming treatment of child-life endeared her to every home in the Empire.' The committee consisted of Lady Dorothy Nevill (at whose house the meetings were held), Lady Maria Ponsonby, Lady Victoria Herbert, Lady Fremantle, Lady Jeune (Lady St. Helier), Mrs. Locker-Lampson, Miss Meresia Nevill, Mr. Arthur à Beckett, Sir William Agnew, Sir George Birdwood, Sir Caspar Purdon Clarke, Mr. Walter Crane, Mr. Harold Hartley, Mr. M. H. Spielmann, Sir Arthur Trendell (hon. secretary), Sir Thomas Wardle (chairman), and Sir Aston Webb, with Mr. Arthur L. Liberty as hon. treasurer. The amount of the subscriptions collected—to which Sir Squire Bancroft largely added by his fine reading in St. James's Hall of *The Christmas Carol*—reached £949, which when the expenses were deducted left the sum of £779. It was decided to endow a cot in the Great Ormond Street Hospital for Children—a form of memorial which would assuredly have appealed most strongly to Kate Greenaway herself, supposing it possible that so modest a person would have agreed to or authorised any memorial at all. In due course the purpose of the committee was carried into effect ; and a dedication plate, designed by Mrs. Liberty, is now affixed above a little bed. And when the little ones who lie sick in the hospital ward ask the meaning of the plate upon the wall they are told of one who in spite of much physical weakness and suffering devoted herself whole-heartedly to bringing happiness and delight into the lives of others, particularly of children.

CHAPTER XV

From the early days when Kate Greenaway submitted her crude verses to Mr. W. Marcus Ward and found little encouragement, down to the very end of her life, she spent no inconsiderable portion of her time in fluttering around the base of Parnassus. Competent critics, as we have seen, expressed the opinion that there was poetic fancy and feeling in many of these early attempts. Four thick volumes of neatly written manuscript running to hundreds of pages testify to the industry with which Miss Greenaway followed what she says to her infinite regret proved to be a vain hope. It is not given to every genius to shine in two spheres. These curious volumes as they stand make tantalising reading. A hundred telling themes are gaily launched on a sea of words and all goes well, until we are disturbed by mixed metaphor, faulty rhyme, and defective rhythm, and only here and there do we find a poem which is sustained and carried on successfully to the end.

The fact is, Kate Greenaway—so she told her sister to whom she would read her verses—regarded these efforts only as rough drafts from which she intended some day to select the best and put them into form. She herself considered them defective alike in rhyme, rhythm, and metre, and admitted that they needed rewriting, and she made fair copies into her MS. volumes only in order to preserve her ideas until she could find time to express herself adequately according to the rules of versification. Indeed she did not seem to regard any of them as finished. This should be borne in mind by the reader who would deny these efforts serious consideration, or who would admit them only on the

257   33

Kate Greenaway

ground that no 'Life' of Kate Greenaway would be complete or truly reflective of the artist's work without some reference to an occupation which filled her mind during many years of her career. How far Miss Greenaway might ultimately have gone it is difficult to say ; but we cannot doubt that she possessed some of the qualities of a poet. Hers was a mind full of subtle and beautiful thoughts of a sweet and simple kind, struggling to give them lucid expression.

Let us take for example the following lines in which the anti-climax is really cleverly managed :—

> It is so glorious just to say
> I loved him all at once—one day—
> A winter's day. Then came the spring
> And only deepenèd the thing.
> I think it deepen'd—I'm not sure
> If there was room to love you more.
> Then summer followed—and my love
> Took colour from the skies above.
> Then weeks—and months—and years there came,
> And I, well, loved on—just the same.
> Then, dear, stretch out your hands—and let me lie
> Within them as I slowly die,
> Then stoop your head to mine and give—
> Ah, not a kiss—or I should live.

It must not be forgotten that, like most bright and happy and keenly sensitive natures, Miss Greenaway had many moments of melancholy, almost of morbidness, which she attributed to her being 'a quarter Welsh.' On this element of national sadness she laid the responsibility of her passion for writing love-verses, of a character so yearning and despairing, that she almost found herself, with rôles inverted, playing the Beatrice to some unknown Dante. It pleased and soothed her to work out a poetic problem — to imagine herself appealing to some foolish heartless swain blind to her love and deaf to her appeal—and to feel her way as she developed the character and mind of the love-lorn lady. The case was not her own, and for that reason, no doubt, the experiment was the more alluring. She returned to it again and again, con-stantly from a different point ; and poem after poem is expressive of a passionate desire for a love which never came. Page after page is devoted to apostrophising the imaginary one who is some-where in the world, sometimes perhaps even seeking her—seeking but not finding.

Verse-Writing

First, her heroine takes upon herself the blame for losing him
—'You smiled and I turned me away'; and then declares that
the fault is his for hanging back, for—'man is a fool—such a
fool'—

> Ah, cold, faint-hearted, go—I tell you go!
> Dear God, to think I could have loved you so! . . .
> His eyes were blind that he could not see
> As he turned away to the world from me . . .
> And his soul
> Sought out—a lower soul.
> . . . It may be
> One day God
> Will tell you that you missed
> The Higher Part.
> You grasped the grass
> Who might have held the flower.
> You took a stone
> Who might have won a heart.
> . . . He looks back
> Over the years
> Of the rift and the wrack—

And the lover's soul cries to her soul :—

> Oh, can you forgive me?
> I know to my cost
> The Life that I've missed,
> The Life that I've lost.
> Soul,
> Can you pardon this soul?
>
> God bless you, dear, always and ever,
> God bless you and bless you I say.
> And I know you will pray for the coward,
> The fool who once threw you away.
> Soul, when the stars shine
> Think sometimes of this soul.

Later on, he is not content with forgiveness, but is praying to
be taken back. But it is too late, for

> You rejected—threw the gift away,
> And now bring tears and sorrowful complaint.
> I call you coward, playing at babies' play.
> The woman made no sound, or any plaint,
>
> But took her lot and kept her bitter tears
> In silence all alone and unbefriended—
> Now take her scorn for all the coming years.
> That is her answer, till her life is ended.

259

Kate Greenaway

Then in the verses entitled 'The You that was not You' she makes the discovery that—

> The You I loved was my creation—mine,
> Without a counterpart within yourself.
> I gave you thoughts and soul and heart
> Taken from Love's ideal. . . .

And so the first dream ends and she brings her heroine to a saner mood, with the discovery that all these bitter experiences and disappointments have been sent by God to teach her that she has been pre-ordained to an anchorite's life of Art, for Art's sake. Then half regretful, half resigned, she carries on her character a stage :

> A lonely soul, I am ever alone.
> If love ever comes it is quickly gone—
> Nothing abides and nothing stays.
> I think I have found it, but only to know
> How very soon it is all to go.
> The sunshine is followed by falling snow.
>
> There are sometimes moments when I see
> A sort of divinity in it for me,
> To keep me separate and alone ;
> To hold away and keep my heart
> All for my work, set aside and apart,
> As if I were vowed away to Art.

And then there comes a happier moment when something breaks into her life to compensate and console her for her renunciations :—

> For the world had found a new and lovely voice
> To teach and train me in her secret ways,
> And I saw beauty in all things that are
> And knew that I was blest for all my days.
>
> Above the world now, above its good and ill,
> I ventured on a new and lovely life—
> Sesame ! had been said and I passed in,
> My soul and body no more waged a strife.
>
> Shall I not think you then, oh, best of all ?
> Shall I not call you Friend, and say—'tis He
> Who shook away the chaff and saved the grain
> And gave the whole — God's Heaven —unto me ?

Verse-Writing

The verses here quoted are fair examples of her powers and of her limitations, so far as it is fair to speak of limitations when the verses are avowedly but studies for the finished work, the uncut and unpolished stones. The expression of the ideas is consequently crude, but the ideas are clearly there and have at least become articulate. They are not mock heroics, but the half-spoken utterances of real passion, of the baulked, helpless, disillusioned woman of her creation, who is emerging into a philosophic and sufficiently satisfactory state of mind. And they are representative of by far the larger portion of her literary output.

What Kate Greenaway might have accomplished had she devoted as much time to verses for children as in accumulating poetic material of an introspective nature, may be gathered from the pretty and dainty rhymes with which every one who is familiar with her books is well acquainted. It may be seen, too, from the following lines from 'The Getting Up of the King's Little Daughter'—in which she has many pretty ideas around which she wanders, grasping them fully from time to time. Here is a dainty couplet describing the little princess's bath :—

> Then she rises and fresh water
> Swallows up the King's small daughter ;

and the conclusion—

> For her breakfast there is spread
> Freshest milk and whitest bread,
>   Yellow butter, golden honey,
>   The best there is for love or money.

So, too, in 'Girls in a Garden,' a prettily clothed thought here and there stands out deliciously :—

> The Roses red white fingers take
> And Lilies for their own sweet sake—

is surely a little picture of which no one need to be ashamed. So too—

> By Hollyhocks they measure who
> Is grown the taller of the two ;

and—

> The sky is laughing in white and blue—

reveal to us the true Kate Greenaway of *Under the Window* and *Language of Flowers*, illustrating the sisterhood of her pencil

Kate Greenaway

and her pen. And again there is a touch of infantile delight in the artless little verse—

> Oh, what a silken stocking,
> And what a satin shoe !
> I wish I was a little toe
> To live in there, I do.

Is it too much to say that had Kate Greenaway given as much time and energy to such verses as these as she did to her more ambitious efforts, she might be acclaimed the Babies' laureate as unchallenged on her pinnacle as she is supreme as the Children's Artist ?

From the melancholy of her imaginary heroine, and from the brightness of her joyous self when she appeals to her vast child-constituency, we may turn to the occasional depression which is mirrored in some of her late verses when she considers her own life and achievement. It is not to be supposed for a moment that Kate Greenaway was morbid naturally, but she was easily dejected, particularly when, as we have seen, she fell into despair on realising that the world had forgotten her and passed her by while her imitators were reaping the reward which her own genius and originality had sown. Had she fallen out of fashion merely she would not have complained ; it was the denseness of the public who willingly accepted the counterfeit for the genuine that hurt her. More than once she casts these feelings into rhyme :—

> Deserted, cast away, my work all done,
> Who was a star that shone a little while,
> But fallen now and all its brightness gone—
> A victim of this world's brief fickle smile.
> Poor fool and vain, grieve not for what is lost,
> Nor rend thy heart by counting up the cost.

In spite of the mixed metaphor we must recognise a sincere thought sincerely expressed—no mere idle complaint, but a disappointment honestly and courageously borne. And she proceeds—

> We walk, we talk, we sing our song,
> Our little song upon this earth ;
> How soon we tread the road along,
> And look for death almost from birth.

In point of fact, hopefulness was the note of her character ;

and in spite of all disappointments, she was an optimist to the end.
This note is struck again in the following lines :—

> Take all my things from me—all my gold,
> My houses, and my lands, and all I hold—
>   Even my beauty's grace ;
> Smite down my health, take all my joy,
> Fret all my life with great annoy,
>   If thou wilt still look on my Face,
> If thou wilt still say—This is she
> Who shall be mine, immortally,
>   In Heaven, on Earth,
> In night, in day, in months, in years,
> In joy, in sorrow—smiles and tears—
>   In life—in Death !

Death was a favourite *motif*, but Death regarded as Watts
regarded it—not as a 'skull and cross-bones idea like that of
Holbein,' but as the gentle messenger, remorseless but not
unkind—as the nurse who beckons to the children and puts them
to bed. One set of verses, obviously marked out for revision, is
entitled—

THE ANGEL FRIEND

> God called you—and you left us.
>   Heaven wanted you for its own.
> I guessed you were only waiting
>   Till an Angel fetched you home.
>
> I knew you talked with Angels
>   In the green and leafy wood.
> Some thought you strangely quiet,
>   But I—I understood.
>
> For I saw your eyes looked into
>   The things we could never see,
> And the sound of your voice had the wonder
>   Of the distant sound of the sea.
>
> And all the dumb creatures knew it,
>   And the flowers faded not in your hand.
> You walked this earth as a Spirit
>   Who sojourned in alien land.

Another, equally simple, is illustrated with the sketch for a
water-colour drawing 'Dead,' here reproduced. For each of these
poems, about fifteen in number, Kate Greenaway had made a
drawing more or less complete, with the intention of issuing them

Kate Greenaway

in a volume. The verses for which 'Dead' was designed run as follows :—

LITTLE DEAD GIRL

Hands that no more colour hold
Than the jasmine stars they fold
    In their clasping, still and tender—
Can we doubt, who knew her living,
She was worthy of the giving,
    This gift of Death that God did send her ?

Alas, that we are left to sorrow
Deeply for you on the morrow.
    We stand and envy you the peace
As you lie so, still and blessed,
With your grievings all redressed
    And your soul obtained release.

A final example of her happier mood and we have done :—

THE HAPPY LADY

My Lady, as she goes her ways
By street or garden, gives God praise
    For all His lovely sounds and sights,
    The sunny days, the quiet nights—
The glories of a moonlit sky
With stars all shining silently—
    The rose and red of setting sun,
    And children as they laugh and run,
The flowering fields, the flowering trees,
The strong winds or soft-blowing breeze.
    No evil thing comes ever nigh
    To hurt her sweet tranquillity.

In conclusion, we would draw the reader's attention once more to the verses 'When I am Dead,'[1] which were written on the approach of death, perhaps when, in spite of the confidence based on friendly assurances, her instinct whispered to her that the end was not far off. In these circumstances the lines assume a more pathetic and a tenderer significance, and breathe the pilgrim spirit of Hope and Faith at the very threshold of the Valley of Death.

[1] See p. 254.

CHAPTER XVI

THE ARTIST: A REVIEW AND AN ESTIMATE

In order to judge of Kate Greenaway as an artist, and appraise her true place and position in British art, we must bear in mind not only what she did, but what she was. It must be remembered that she was a pioneer, an inventor, an innovator; and that, although she painted no great pictures and challenged no comparison with those who labour in the more elevated planes of artistry, is sufficient to place her high upon the roll. Just as Blake is most highly valued for his illustration and Cruikshank and Goya for their etched plates, rather than for their pictures, so Kate Greenaway must be judged, not by the dignity of her materials, or by the area of her canvas, but by the originality of her genius, and by the strength and depth of the impression she has stamped on the mind and sentiment of the world. As Mr. Holman Hunt, Millais, and their associates invigorated the art of England by their foundation of the Pre-Raphaelite Brotherhood, so Kate Greenaway introduced a Pre-Raphaelite spirit into the art of the nursery. That is what Dr. Max Nordau, with curious perversion of judgment and lack of appreciation, denounced as 'degeneracy'!—accusing her of creating 'a false and degenerate race of children in art,' while at the worst she was but giving us a Midsummer Day's Dream in Modern England. For him Kate Greenaway, the healthy, sincere, laughter-loving artist, is a 'decadent' such as vexes the soul of a Tolstoi. It is the result, of course, of misapprehension—of a misunderstanding which has revolted few besides him.

The outstanding merit of Kate Greenaway's work is its obvious freedom from affectation, its true and unadulterated

Kate Greenaway

English character. What Dr. Nordau mistook for affectation is simply humour—a quaintness which is not less sincere and honest for being sometimes sufficiently self-conscious to make and enjoy and sustain the fun. Such grace of action, such invariable delicacy and perfect taste of her little pictures, belong only to a mind of the sweetest order—the spontaneity and style, only to an artist of the rarest instinct. Animated by a love of the world's beauty that was almost painful in its intensity, she was not satisfied to render merely what she saw ; she was compelled to colour it with fancy and imagination. She reveals this passion in a letter to Mr. Locker-Lampson :—

KATE GREENAWAY TO F. LOCKER-LAMPSON

22 WELLINGTON ESPLANADE,
LOWESTOFT, Thursday.

Dear Mr. Locker—We are back again in clouds of mist—no more lovely sailing boats. Yesterday afternoon was as fine as we could wish it to be. We went all through the fishing village, and then there comes a common by the sea, covered with gorse. The little fishing houses are so quaint. I was savage, for I had not got my book in my pocket, so shall have to trust to memory to reproduce some of it.

I never saw such children—picturesque in the extreme ; such funny little figures in big hats, the very children I dream of existing here in the flesh ; and lots of clothes hanging out to dry flapped about in the sun and made such backgrounds ! People laugh at me, I am so delighted and pleased with things, and say I see with rose-coloured spectacles. What do you think—is it not a beautiful world ? Sometimes have I got a defective art faculty that few things are ugly to me ? Good-bye, K. GREENAWAY.

The truth is, her poetic emotion and the imagination which so stirred the admiration of Ruskin and the rest, inspired her to express a somewhat fanciful vision of the flowers, and children, and life which she saw around her. She gave us not what she saw, but what she felt, even as she looked. Her subtle and tender observation, one writer has declared, was corrected and modified by her own sense of love and beauty. Her instinctive feeling is, therefore, nobler than her sense of record ; it is big in 'conception' and style, and is immeasurably more delightful than bare appreciation of fact.

It is a touch of tragedy in Kate Greenaway's life, that she to

The Artist

whom the love of children was as the very breath of her life was never herself to be thrilled by that maternal love for the little ones she adored. Still 'her spirit was bright and pure, vivacious and alert,' so that she drew children with the grace of Stothard and the naturalness of Reynolds, investing them with all the purity and brightness that we find in her drawing and her colour. Although her cantata was simple, it was ever notable for its exquisite harmony and perfect instrumentation.

Faults, no doubt, of a technical sort Kate Greenaway shows in many of her drawings, and, as we have seen, mannerisms at times betrayed her. She would exaggerate in her faces the pointed chin that was a charm of her model Gertie's face. She would draw eyes too far apart, as Ford Madox Brown came to do ; yet how exquisitely those eyes were drawn, and how admirably placed within their sockets ! perfect in accuracy of touch, and delightful in their beauty. The knees of her girls are sometimes too low down ; the draperies are often too little studied and lack grace of line ; her babies' feet are at times too large, and are carelessly drawn, or at least are rendered without sufficient appreciation of their form. A score of drawings substantiate every one of these charges — but what of that ? The greatest artists have had their failings, cardinal in academic eyes, for the faults are all of technique. As Boughton exclaimed of his friend George du Maurier—'I respect him for his merits, but I love him for his faults.' In Kate Greenaway's case her faults are forgotten, or at least forgiven, in presence of her refined line and fairy tinting, her profiles and full faces of tender loveliness, and her figures of daintiest grace.

'English picture-books for children,' exclaims Dr. Muther,[1] 'are in these days the most beautiful in the world, and the marvellous fairy-tales and fireside stories of Randolph Caldecott and Kate Greenaway have made their way throughout the whole Continent. How well these English draughtsmen know the secret of combining truths with the most exquisite grace ! How touching are these pretty babies, how angelically innocent these little maidens—frank eyes, blue as the flowers of the periwinkle, gaze at you with no thought of being looked at in return. The naïve astonishment of the little ones, their frightened mien, their earnest look absently fixed on the sky, the first tottering steps of a tiny child and the mobile grace of a school-girl, all are rendered

---

[1] *The History of Modern Painting*, vol. iii. p. 137.

Kate Greenaway

in these prints with the most tender intimacy of feeling. And united
with this there is a delicate and entirely modern sentiment for scenery,
for the fascination of bare autumn landscapes robbed of their foliage,
for sunbeams and the budding fragrance of spring. Everything
is idyllic, poetic, and touched by a congenial breath of tender
melancholy.'

The appreciation of Kate Greenaway's work was universal.
In France its reception was always enthusiastic, and the critics expressed their delight with characteristic felicity. They recognised,
said one,[1] that until Kate Greenaway there had been no author
and artist for the boy citizens whose trousers are always too short,
and for the girl citizens whose hands are always too red. They
knew nothing about her personality, and even doubted whether
her name was not a pseudonym ; but they welcomed in her the
children's artist *par excellence*, who knew that the spirit, the
intelligence, the soul of little ones are unlike those of adults, and
who knew, too, by just how much they differed. At the end
of a glowing tribute M. Arsène Alexandre spoke of her
as having been *naturalisée de Paris*—alluding, of course, not to
herself but to her work,—whereupon an important English newspaper mistranslated the expression ; and so arose the absurd report
circulated after her death, that Kate Greenaway, who had never
quitted the shores of England, had passed the later years of her
life in Paris.

From Paris, declared *La Vie de Paris*, 'the graceful mode of
Greenawisme has gained the provinces, and from wealthy quarters
has penetrated into the suburbs';[2] and the Vienna *Neue Freie Presse*
maintained that 'Kate Greenaway has raised a lasting monument
to herself in the reform of children's dress, for which we have
to thank her.' But the *Figaro* and the *Temps* recognised her
higher achievement. 'Kate Greenaway,' said the former, 'had
une âme exquise. She translated childhood into a divine language
—or perhaps, if you prefer it, she translated the divine mystery
of childhood into a purely and exquisitely child-like tongue.'
'Never,' said the latter, 'has a sweeter soul interpreted infancy

---

[1] The *Journal des Débats*.

[2] So true is it that 'Greenawisme' stands for a phase of art and dress, that in that enter-
taining publication, the *Almanac Hachette* for 1904 (p. 329), under the heading 'L'Histoire
du Costume des Enfants,' the 'Coiffure Greenaway' (*sic*) takes its place in the series of
woodcuts immediately preceding 'la jupe cloche fin du xixᵉ siècle'; and many more
examples might be adduced.

The Artist

and childhood with more felicity, and I know nothing so touching in their naïveté as the child-scenes that illustrate so many of
the artist's books, the very first of which made her celebrated.'
These are but specimens of the scores of tributes that filled the
press of Europe and America at the time of Kate Greenaway's
death, and are sufficient to prove the international appeal she made,
triumphing over the differences of race, fashion, and custom which
usually are an insuperable bar to universal appreciation.

Original as she was in her view of art and in the execution of
her ideas, Kate Greenaway was very impressionable and frequently
suffered herself to be influenced by other artists. But that she was
unconscious of the fact seems unquestionable, and that her own
strong individuality saved her from anything that could be
called imitation must be admitted. The nearest semblance to
that plagiarism which she so heartily abhorred is to be found
in the likeness borne by some of her landscapes to those
of Mrs. Allingham. The circumstance, as already recounted,
that the two ladies were cordial friends and went out sketching
together, the younger student in landscape-drawing watching
her companion's methods, is sufficient explanation of the likeness. Miss Greenaway quickly recognised the peril ; and she
must have realised that her drawings, so produced, lacked much
of the spontaneity, the sparkle, and the mellowness of the work
of Mrs. Allingham. Take, for example, the charming plate called
'A Surrey Cottage.'[1] The landscape is as thoroughly understood
as the picturesque element of the design, with its well-drawn
trees and deftly-rendered grass. The children form a pretty group ;
but they are not a portion of the picture ; they are dropped into
the design and clearly do not fit the setting into which they
are so obviously placed. The artist herself has clearly felt the
defect, and obviated it on other occasions. The love of red
Surrey cottages, green fields, and groups of little children was
common to both artists, and Kate's imitation is more apparent
than real ; her renderings of them are honest and tender, full
of sentiment, and of accurate, vigorous observation. She does
not seem to have studied landscape for its breadth, or sought to
read and transcribe the mighty message of poetry it holds for
every whole-hearted worshipper. Rather did she seek for the
passages of beauty and the pretty scenes which appealed to her,
delighting in the sonnet, as it were, rather than in the epic.

[1] To consult the drawings mentioned see the Index of Illustrations.

Kate Greenaway

Her shortness of sight handicapped her sadly in this branch of art, and prevented her from seeing many facts of nature in a broad way ; for example, while 'The Old Farm House' has great merits of breeziness, truth, and transparency of colour, with a sense of 'out-of-doorness' not often so freshly and easily obtained, the great tree at the back lacks substance, as well as shadow and mystery, for its branches are spread out like a fan, and do not seem, any of them, to grow towards the spectator. There is no such fault in 'The Stick Fire'—a subject curiously recalling Fred Walker ; for here the landscape, although a little empty, is clearly studied from nature and set down with great reticence and intelligence. And what could be prettier than the pose of the two girls, big and little, on the left ? When she leaves realism and touches the landscapes and groups with her own inimitable convention, Miss Greenaway becomes truly herself and can be compared with none other. Glance, for instance, at 'The Bracken Gatherers.' It has the sense of style and 'bigness' which triumphs over any mannerism ; and the heads, especially that of the girl set so well upon her neck, are so full of dignity that they may be considered a serious effort in art.

She was undoubtedly influenced at times by Mrs. Allingham and Fred Walker, as well as by Ford Madox Brown (see 'Brother and Sister,' in which the little girl might almost have come from his pencil). We find traces, too, of Mr. G. D. Leslie, R.A. (in 'Strawberries'—a drawing not here reproduced), of Stothard (as in the masterly sketch for 'The May Dance' with its fine sense of grace and movement, and its excellent spacing), of Downman (as in the portraits belonging to the Hon. Gerald Ponsonby), of Richard Doyle (as in the large drawing of 'The Elf Ring'), and sometimes we recognise echoes of Stacy Marks, of Mason, and of Calvert. But what does it all amount to ? Merely this, that when she wandered beyond the garden of that Greenaway-land which she had called into being, the artist was sometimes moved by the emotions with which she had been thrilled when in past years she gazed with enthusiasm at these men's work. The resemblance was in the main accidental ; for every one of these painters, like herself, is characteristically and peculiarly English in his view of art as in his methods of execution.

There are those who sneer at nationality in art. You can no more speak of English art, laughed Whistler, than you can speak of English mathematics. The analogy is entirely a false one.

TWO AT A STILE.

WAITING.

SPRING TIME.

SWANSDOWN.

'DEAD.'

THE MAY DANCE.

'ALFY' (UNFINISHED).

The Artist

You can say with truth 'English art' as you can say 'German music'; for although art in its language is universal, in its expression it is national, or at least racial; and it is the merit of a nation to express itself frankly in its art in its own natural way, and to despise the affectation of self-presentation in the terms and in the guise of foreign practice not native to itself. It is a matter of sincerity and, moreover, of good sense; for little respect is deserved or received by a man who affects to speak his language with a foreign accent. Kate Greenaway was intensely and unfeignedly English: for that she is beloved in her own country, and for that she is appreciated and respected abroad. Like Hogarth, Reynolds, and Millais, she was the unadulterated product of England, and like them she gave us of her 'English art.'

In the latter part of her career Kate Greenaway modified her manner of water-colour painting, mainly with the view to obtaining novelty of effect and conquering public approval. At the beginning she had tried to make finished pictures, as we see in the moonlight scene of 'The Elf Ring.' Then when she discovered her true *métier*, influenced by the requirements of Mr. Edmund Evans's wood-block printing, to which she adapted herself with consummate ease, she used outline in pen or pencil, with delicate washes in colour: these drawings were made in every case, of course, for publication in books. Their ready independent sale encouraged her to elaborate her little pictures, and her election as Member of the Royal Institute of Painters in Water-Colours confirmed her in the decision to turn her attention to pure water-colour painting. The decreasing demand for book-illustration influenced her somewhat in taking the new work very seriously, encouraged thereto by Ruskin, who, as we have seen, was forever crying out for 'a bit of Nature.' So she painted land-scapes which, in point of technique, lacked some of the accidental grace and freshness and serious depth which should be essential to such work, although they were rich in her own sentimental and tender way of seeing things. Then in figure painting she abandoned her outlines and indulged in the full strong colour which Ruskin always begged from her. That she should have fused this vigour of coloration with her own native faculty for daintiness—as for example in 'Lucy Locket'—must be accounted to her credit.

Later on her colour became more subdued and even silvery. We see it in the little idyll, so pure in drawing and feeling, 'Two at a Stile' (with its curious contrast of exact full face in the girl

271

Kate Greenaway

and exact profile in her swain), and still more in the tender and prettily imagined 'Sisters,' wherein even the red flowers, although they lend warmth to the almost colourless composition, do not tell as a spot, so knowingly is the strength restrained. Indeed, charm and delicacy rather than strength are characteristic of Kate Greenaway's genius. We see them, for example, in the little 'Swansdown' and companion drawings here reproduced full size, and we see them also in the playful 'Calm in a Teacup,' and in 'Mary had a Little Lamb,' which the artist drew as a Christmas card for Professor Ruskin, with their delicate touches of colour and the exquisite pencil outline—so unhesitating and firm nevertheless, that, despite their simplicity, they rarely fail to realise the exact degree of beauty or of character intended.

Her colour indeed was almost invariably happy, exactly suited to the matter in hand. In the early days of her first valentines it was crude enough, and chrome yellow, rose madder, cobalt blue, and raw umber seemed to satisfy her. But soon her eye became extraordinarily sensitive, and whether strong or delicate the scheme of colour was always harmonious. A test drawing is to be found in 'A Baby in White,' wherein the little personage so well fills the page. This is in fact a study in whites—in the dress, the daisies, and the blossoms — of such variety that the artist's judgment and ability are absolutely vindicated. Not that Kate Greenaway always painted her white blossoms, or, for the matter of that, left the white paper to represent them. She became skilled in the use of the knife, and used the artifice consecrated and made legitimate by such masters as Turner and William Hunt, with great dexterity. In 'The Girl and her Milk Pail' —which breathes so pleasantly the memory of Pinwell, and which, well composed and drawn, shows greater regard than usual for the virtue of atmosphere—the blossoms on the branch above the wall are all produced by 'knifing': that is to say, by means of a sharp knife a bit of the paper's surface of the exact shape required is sliced into and turned over when not cut off; and the effect is more vivid and true than any amount of care or paint could otherwise secure.

Except for this, Miss Greenaway used no tricks: she neither 'rubbed,' nor 'scratched,' nor 'washed.' It is perhaps fairer to say that she was too honest than that she lacked resource. She always maintained the legitimacy of the use of body-colour, which some purists profess to abhor; beyond that her work is quite simple

The Artist

and direct, while her technical skill is amply efficacious for all she had to do.

In the matter of models, whether for illustrations or exhibition drawings, she was particular and fastidious. At all times she preferred to draw from the life. Her studies from the nude—made in her youth, with such conscientious accuracy that every form, every fold in the skin, and every undulation of high light and shadow, were rendered with the firmness and with ease that come of practice, knowledge, and skill—had carried her far enough for the model to be reckoned a servant, and not a master. But a realistic drawing is one thing, and a simplified archaistic rendering of a living figure quite another; and we may take it, broadly, that difficulty in figure draughtsmanship increases in direct ratio to the degree of its simplification. With anatomy, we imagine, she was less familiar.

Miss Greenaway selected her models with much care. For her men, as has already been said, her father and brother usually would good-naturedly sit, and the type of old lady she often adopted was based upon Mrs. Greenaway. As for her children, the list of those who were pressed into the service is tolerably long. Some of her models she would secure by visiting schools and selecting likely children, and these again would recommend others. Some were already professional models themselves, or were children brought to her by such. The first of all was the 'water-cress girl' who was employed for her earliest work for the publishers. 'Mary,' who was secured after the publication of *Under the Window*, appears in all the books up to the *Pied Piper*. She belonged to a family of models, and coming to Miss Greenaway when a little girl, remained in her service until she was grown up. And years later another 'Mary' succeeded her. 'Adela' and her sister were the earliest models of whom any record exists, and they were employed for *Under the Window*, for which Miss Greenaway's nephew Eddie also sat. He, indeed, is to be found in the whole series up to and including the *Pied Piper*, that is to say in the *Birthday Book*, *Mother Goose*, *A Day in a Child's Life*, *Little Ann*, *Language of Flowers*, *Marigold Garden*, and *A Apple Pie*. Mary's brother 'Alfred' sat, along with his sister, for the same books as she did; and 'Gertie' is to be recognised mainly in *Little Ann* and the *Language of Flowers*. Gertie became a figure in the Greenaway household; as, from the position of a model merely, she afterwards

273   35

Kate Greenaway

graduated to the rank of housemaid at Frognal, where, when she opened the street door, visitors were surprised and edified to recognise in her a typical 'Kate Greenaway girl,' with reddish hair and pointed chin, as pretty and artless a creature as if she had walked straight out of a Greenaway toy-book. If the reader would see a characteristic portrait of her, he will find one on p. 24 of the *Language of Flowers,* and better still, perhaps, in 'Willy and his Sister' on p. 30 of *Marigold Garden.* Then there were 'Freddie' and his sisters, and Mrs. Webb's children, and 'Isa,' 'Ruby,' the Gilchrists, two sisters, and a little red-haired girl (name forgotten): nearly all of whom were known only by their Christian names, so that their identity must remain unknown to fame. These were the most constant models—these, and the 'little Mary' to whom she frequently alludes in her letters to Ruskin.

That the little ones were a constant tribulation to the artist, whose patience was often put to the severest test, her letters to friends bear frequent witness. For example, to Mr. Locker-Lampson she writes from Pemberton Gardens:—

Kate Greenaway to Frederick Locker-Lampson

You ought to enjoy the beautiful sea and this lovely weather. Do you see those wonderful boats we used to see at Lowestoft? I never saw such magnificent crimson and orange sails, and such splendid curves as they made.

How nice of you having Mr. Caldecott ; you will enjoy his society so much. . . .

I have got a little girl five years old coming to sit this morning—which means a fearfully fidgety morning's work. However, it is the last of the models for my book ; then I can go straight away with the illustrations, which will be a great gain.

And in a lively letter to Mrs. Severn she sends a verbatim report of the bright but discursive dialogue between the 'Chatterbox Mary' and 'Victim' (herself), illustrated with fifteen sketches of Mary's feet in constantly changing postures, driving the artist to distraction and culminating in 'victim—limp—worn—exhausted.'

In the class of drawings which she called 'Processions' Miss Greenaway is entirely original. She could arrange a dozen, or if need be twenty, figures—usually of graceful girls and pretty babes—full of movement and action, in which there is cheerfully worked-out a decorative *motif*, with a rhythmic line running through the composition. In some the work is so delicate as practically to defy satisfactory reproduction ; but sufficient justice can be done to suggest their charm of sentiment and the balance of design. Now and again we have in miniature a reminder of the languorous dignity of Leighton's 'Daphnephoria.' Sometimes the movement is more lively, and we have 'Dances' of all kinds, now quaint and strangely demure, now full of the joy of life. 'The May Dance' is as sober as if it were designed for a panel in a public building ; but in 'The Dancing of the Felspar Fairies' we have a vigorous *abandon* mingled with the conventionality of graceful poses. In most of them, no doubt, the draperies are seldom studied accurately from life ; but it is doubtful whether, if they were more correct in their flow of fold, they would harmonise so well with the character of the figures and general treatment. For throughout, it must be observed, she is a decorative artist. Even in the delightful realism of her flowers, which have rarely been surpassed either in sympathy of understanding or in delicacy and refinement of realisation, she never forgets their decorative value : they are presented to us not for their inherent beauty alone, but for their value upon the paper or upon the decorated page.

For that reason, perhaps, Kate Greenaway was never quite at home as a portraitist : she resented being tied down to a face or figure. No doubt, such drawings as 'The Red Boy' and 'The Little Model' were portraits, but she was free to depart from the truth as much as she chose. The children in the unfinished oil-paintings of 'The Muff' and 'Alfy' were not less portraits, but the motive of these oil pictures (of the size of life) was not likeness merely but practice in what Ruskin called 'the sticky art.' In 'Vera Samuel' an unaccountable width has been given to the head, but without loss of character. There appears more truth in the portrait of 'Frederick Locker-Lampson' with eyelids drooping, an interesting likeness of an interesting man of letters ; the woolliness of effect being mainly due to the translation of stippled water-colour into black-and-white. The head of old 'Thomas Chappell' is one of the artist's masterpieces in portraiture—full of character and insight, and a really brilliant rendering of old age, firmly drawn and elaborately modelled. With the pencil Kate Greenaway was more at home. The rapid unfinished sketch of her brother, 'John Greenaway, Jr.,' is still a likeness although

Kate Greenaway

more than thirty years have passed since it was made; and the two delightfully executed heads of 'Miss Mabel Ponsonby' and 'Miss Eileen Ponsonby,' reinforced with faint colour in the manner of Downman, and with not a little of his delicacy, imply a measure of accomplishment attained by constant practice—the result, perhaps, of South Kensington training. The 'Portrait of a Lady,' in a method somewhat similar, is not entirely successful as a portrait; but it is included here as an example of the new style of work which Miss Greenaway adopted towards the end of her career. Perhaps the most engaging of all is the miniature of 'Joan Ponsonby,' in which we find an artless simplicity, a candour and refreshing naturalness, wholly apart and distinct from the photographically inspired miniature of to-day. The colours are simple and the handling broad for all its precision of drawing, for the artist has resisted the temptation to finish her flowers and other details with the microscopical minuteness which she employed with so much effect on more suitable occasions.

When all Miss Greenaway's work is carefully judged, it will, we think, be seen that it is with the point rather than with the brush that she touches her highest level, whether her manner be precise as in her book-plates, or free as in her sketches. Of her book-plates, the best are unquestionably those of Mr. Locker-Lampson and Lady Victoria Herbert. The latter is formal in treatment and beautifully grouped, yet drawn with a certain hardness typical of what is called the Birmingham School; the former infinitely more sympathetic in touch, the children delightful in pose, the apple-tree drawn with unusual perfection, and the distant city touched in with extraordinary skill. With these, compare the masterly pencil study of a baby toddling forwards— swiftly drawn, loosely handled, instinct with life and character, one of the best things, artistically considered, the artist ever did. Hardly less remarkable is the tiny sketch in a letter to Ruskin of a little bonneted girl holding up her skirt as she walks—a drawing not unworthy of Charles Keene in its vigorous light and shade, and suggestion of the body beneath the clothes (see p. 283). And yet in the text Miss Greenaway laments the badness of the pen! A better pen would have produced a worse sketch. It was a quill that she habitually used, and, in spite of the broad line it com pelled, she made good use of it. In the heading to her letter to Miss Dickinson, dated October 19, 1897, we can positively feel the wind that is scattering the leaves around the old oak. The girl with the

candle, in her letter to Mrs. Locker-Lampson, which reminds us of
Caldecott ; the little 'Violets, Sir ?' which reminds us of Leech ;
the dancing children, one with a tambourine, the other with hand
on hip, who remind us of Stothard ; the group of three dancing
children, which has been compared with the work of Lady Water-
ford ; and the letter to John Ruskin showing the sketch of reaper
and sheaf-binder—are all drawn with the broad-nibbed quill, with

On a Letter to Ruskin.

consummate ease and masterly effect, and they give even more
pleasure to the educated eye than the charming little pencil
sketches such as those in the possession of Lady Pontifex.

The early sketch-books of Kate Greenaway reveal some rather
unexpected phases of her development before she had produced any
work characteristic enough to be recognised as hers by the public.
It is with surprise that we see how well she drew in the very first
stage of her career. As the reader will remember, her first
leanings were towards the comic—as in the humorous sketch of the

lovelorn swain piping to his ridiculous love (p. 279): a drawing

ash trees in the Hedge as a background

and lots of Poppies in the near Corn — I shall do it ———— . Oh. when I can begin some new things ———— I shall feel so joyful. I do like doing one thing only at

From a Letter to Ruskin.

which Phiz might have been willing to acknowledge; or, again,
the little girl and sprite walking arm-in-arm (see p. 75). Then

the romantic moved her, and in the spirit of the great illustrators of the 'sixties she made the rapid pencil sketch (for composition) of a princess in a castle kissing a farewell to some sailor-boy whose ship scuds one way while the sails belly the other ; and, again, a long-hosed gallant gracefully doffing his cap to a ' faire ladye ' at a window (see p. 45). Rough as they are, both are well drawn, especially the latter, but they give no hint whatever of the art which was to spring from them.

Similarly with her pen-sketches. The design, dashed off at

Very early sketch illustrating Kate Greenaway's ambition to be a humorous artist. In the possession of W. Marcus Ward, Esq.

lightning speed, of an eighteenth-century scene at Christmas eve might almost be the work of Phiz or Cruikshank ; and the power of managing many figures on a small sheet of paper is already fully developed. So, too, in a drawing of a totally different class—' The Picnic.' Miss Greenaway had been much impressed, in common with the rest of the fraternity of London artists, by the work of the Scottish artist Mr. William Small, and had attempted to probe into his method of handling, particularly in the technical treatment of form and texture in the coat worn by the central figure. It need hardly be said that these sketches, and others in the manner of Leighton, Mr. Holman Hunt, and so on,

Kate Greenaway

were in no sense copies, or even imitations. They were intended only as studies with a view to analysing each man's style, for the purpose of self-education. That mastered, or at least understood, she turned to her own work, and began to feel her way towards the light.

Once she departed from the heroic and romantic manner of her coloured fairy toy-books and valentines and began the simple sketches from everyday life for 'Poor Nelly'—a serial in *Little Folks* under the anonymous authorship of Mrs. Bonavia Hunt, afterwards republished in volume form—she betrayed a certain weakness in her drawing ; while for a time the garishness of tint which had been demanded of her did not immediately disappear.   But by the time *Under the Window* was reached, five years later (1878), her difficulty of colour was conquered, and she stood alone, with Mr. Walter Crane, in the intelligent combination of healthy children's art and the chastened colour which was being insisted on by William Morris and the so-called Æsthetic Movement.   The reversion in the following year to modern illustration, in the drawings made for Charlotte Yonge's novels, proved once more that the decorative treatment of subjects was her natural rôle.   When she returned to the true Kate Greenaway manner, the change was welcomed by every competent critic.   A German writer expressed himself in terms not less appreciative than those which later came from France and Belgium.   ' It is impossible,' he said, 'to describe in words the wealth of artistic invention, the dignity and loveliness, which characterise this performance.   What a gulf between these delightful works of art of imperishable value, and the trashy caricatures of such stuff as our *Struwelpeter* !   God-speed to Kate Greenaway ! '

Mother Goose was, indeed, an advance on *Under the Window* —which, under the title of *La Lanterne Magique*,[1] the *Revue de Belgique*, in an enthusiastic article, curiously attributed to a male artist, and which the *National Zeitung* extolled as much for its verse as for its bewitching art.   The drawing here is better, and the effect not very seriously injured by the faulty register of many of the copies.   An American journal—the *Literary World*, of Boston—declared that the delicacy and beauty of her faces in outline were as good as Flaxman ; and the curious quality of 'affectionateness' in the drawings, their ingenuousness and prettiness that would have moved the heart of Stothard and touched the soul of Blake, firmly established the young artist in the position to which her former book had raised her.   But not until *A Day in a Child's Life* did Kate Greenaway show her full power as a painter of flowers—by the side of which even her pictures of boys and girls seem to many to yield in interest.   The difficulty, or rather the irksomeness, which she habitually experienced in pure illustration of other people's ideas, in no wise affected her in *Little Ann*, which contains some of the most delightful and

[1] Translated by J. Levoison.   The German version, *Am Fenster*, was translated by Frau Käthe Freiligrath-Kröker.

Kate Greenaway

spring-like drawings she ever did, usually so excellent in composition and fascinating in single figures and in detail that we overlook, if we do not entirely miss, certain little faults of perspective—faults, indeed, which, if noticed at all, only add to the quaintness of the design.

In the *Language of Flowers* and *Marigold Garden* Kate Greenaway rose to her highest point in decision and firmness allied to the perfect drawing of flowers and fruit, although it must be allowed that those who have not seen the original designs can form no accurate judgment from the printed work. The annual *Almanacks*, too, which had been begun in 1883, showed her endless resource and inexhaustible faculty of design; yet it is perhaps to be regretted that so much conscientious effort and executive ability should have been wasted in the almost microscopic rendering of the innumerable illustrations which embellish these tiny books. In *The English Spelling-Book* another change is seen. In several of these beautiful line illustrations there is a freedom in the use of the pencil not hitherto shown, and the drawings of 'Miss Rose and her Aunt,' 'Our Dog Tray,' 'Jane,' and a few others, modest as they are, mark a definite advance in Miss Greenaway's artistic development. She returned to her more formal manner in *A Apple Pie* (1886), as it was more suitable to the large page she had to decorate; and she gives us a greater measure of combined humour and invention than had previously been shown, for the subject fitted her mood of fun and fancy exactly—far better than the same year's *Queen of the Pirate Isle*. On the title-page of the last-mentioned book, however, appears one of the prettiest vignettes she ever drew. Unsuspected power was revealed in *The Pied Piper of Hamelin*. Miss Greenaway was hampered, no doubt, in her attempt to render the pseudo-German medievalism on a large scale. nevertheless, she succeeded in grasping the full significance of the poem, and the spirit maintained throughout and the capacity for dealing with ease with crowds of figures, combine in this volume to constitute a very considerable performance.

A strange contrast with the *Pied Piper* is *Dame Wiggins of Lee*. It is scarcely likely, we think, that readers will endorse with much cordiality the unbounded admiration expressed by John Ruskin for these designs. It must be borne in mind, however, that they are merely rough trial sketches for approval of drawings

The Artist

which were to be made, but that Ruskin, charmed with their spontaneity, declared that they would fit the poem better in their scribbled state than any illustrations more complete.

Miss Greenaway's last book was that admirable volume for children, *The April Baby's Book of Tunes*, by the author of *Elizabeth and her German Garden*, whose humour and love of children were like to Kate Greenaway's own, with an added wit of the most innocent and refreshing kind. The 'babies,' whom the artist had never seen, were sympathetically pictured, and their favourite nursery rhymes were illustrated

Nothing but bad Pens down Here and I dont like going to the studio when its dark I donh like the say Figure — ill get a new Pen

See p. 276.

once more as freshly as if she had dealt with them for the first time.

The survey of her work in the aggregate shows convincingly that even had her technique been on a lower level Kate Greenaway would still have succeeded as the interpreter-in-chief of childhood. Follower though she was in point of time of Mr. Walter Crane and Randolph Caldecott, inspired in some respects no doubt by their example, she nevertheless stands alone in her own sphere. From Lucca della Robbia to Ludwig Richter and Schwind, to Bewick and Thackeray, Cruikshank and Boutet de Monvel, no one has demonstrated more completely the artist's knowledge of and sympathy with infant life, or communicated that knowledge and that sympathy to us. Her pictures delight the little ones for their own sake, and delight us for

283

the sake of the little ones ; and it may be taken as certain
that Kate Greenaway's position in the Art of England is
assured, so long as her drawings speak to us out of their broad
and tender humanity, and carry their message to every little
heart.

On a Letter to Ruskin.

LIST OF BOOKS, ETC.,

ILLUSTRATED WHOLLY OR IN PART BY
KATE GREENAWAY

1871. AUNT LOUISA'S | LONDON TOY BOOKS | DIAMONDS | AND | TOADS. | London. | Frederick Warne & Co. $(10\frac{3}{8} \times 8\frac{7}{8})$

MADAME D'AULNOY'S FAIRY TALES :

c. 1871. (1) THE FAIR ONE | WITH | GOLDEN LOCKS
(2) THE BABES IN THE WOOD
(3) TOM THUMB
(4) BLUE BEARD
(5) PUSS IN BOOTS
(6) THE BLUE BIRD
(7) THE WHITE CAT
(8) HOP O' MY THUMB
(9) RED RIDING HOOD

All published by Gall & Inglis, 6, George Street, Edinburgh.
$(6\frac{11}{16} \times 7\frac{1}{4}$ and $9\frac{3}{4} \times 7\frac{1}{4})$

1874. FAIRY GIFTS ; | or, | A WALLET OF WONDERS : | By Kathleen Knox, | author of 'Father Time's Story Book.' | Illustrations by Kate Greenaway. | Griffith & Farran, | successors to Newbury & Harris, | West Corner of St. Paul's Churchyard, London. | E. P. Dutton & Co., New York. $(6\frac{3}{4} \times 5)$

1876. THE QUIVER OF LOVE : A Collection of Valentines. [By Walter Crane and Kate Greenaway] Marcus Ward & Co.

1878. POOR NELLY ; | By | The Author of 'Tiny Houses,' and 'Two
'Little Folks,' Fourpenny Bits' ; | and | Polly and Joe. | Cassell, Petter,
1877. Galpin & Co., | London, Paris and New York. | [All Rights Reserved.] (*Written by Mrs. Bonavia Hunt*) $(7\frac{3}{16} \times 4\frac{3}{4})$

1878. TOPO : A Tale about English Children in Italy. By G. E. Brunefille. With 44 Pen-and-ink Illustrations by Kate Greenaway. Marcus Ward & Co. (*Written by Lady Colin Campbell*)

1878. UNDER THE WINDOW | PICTURES AND RHYMES | FOR CHILDREN | by | Kate Greenaway | engraved and printed | by | Edmund Evans. | London : | George Routledge & Sons | Broadway, Ludgate Hill. | New York : 416, Broome Street. $(9\frac{1}{4} \times 7\frac{1}{4})$

1879. THE HEIR OF REDCLYFFE | [*By Charlotte M. Yonge*] Illustrated
(Another by Kate Greenaway | London | Macmillan & Co. | 1879 |
edition 1902.) The Right of Translation is Reserved. $(7\frac{1}{2} \times 4\frac{3}{4})$

285

Kate Greenaway

1879. AMATEUR THEATRICALS | By | Walter Herries Pollock | and | Lady Pollock | London : | Macmillan & Co. | 1879. | The Right of Translation and Reproduction is Reserved $(7\frac{1}{8} \times 4\frac{1}{2})$

1879. (Another edition 1902.) HEARTSEASE | or | THE BROTHER'S WIFE | By | Charlotte M. Yonge | Illustrated by Kate Greenaway | London | Macmillan & Co., Limited | New York : The Macmillan Company | 1902 | All rights reserved $(7\frac{7}{8} \times 4\frac{5}{8})$

1879. THE 'LITTLE FOLKS'' | PAINTING BOOK. | A Series of | Outline Engravings for Water-Colour Painting, | By Kate Greenaway, | with descriptive stories and verses by George Weatherly. , Cassell Petter & Galpin : | London, Paris and New York. | (*The book contains* 107 *illustrations,* 88*th thousand.*) $(8\frac{3}{4} \times 6\frac{1}{2})$

1880. KATE GREENAWAY'S | BIRTHDAY BOOK | FOR CHILDREN | with 382 Illustrations, | Drawn by Kate Greenaway, | Printed by Edmund Evans. | Verses by Mrs. Sale Barker. | London : | George Routledge & Sons, | Broadway, Ludgate Hill. | New York : 416, Broome Street. | [All Rights Reserved.] $(3\frac{5}{8} \times 3\frac{1}{2})$

1881. THE LIBRARY. | By | Andrew Lang | with a Chapter on | Modern English Illustrated Books by | Austin Dobson | London | Macmillan & Co. | 1881 | The right of reproduction is reserved.

1881. A DAY IN A CHILD'S LIFE. | Illustrated by | Kate Greenaway. | Music by Myles B. Foster. | (*Organist of the Foundling Hospital.*) | Engraved and Printed by Edmund Evans. | London : | George Routledge & Sons, | Broadway, Ludgate Hill. | New York : 9, Lafayette Place. | [Copyright.] $(9\frac{5}{8} \times 8\frac{1}{8})$

1881. MOTHER GOOSE | or the | Old Nursery Rhymes | Illustrated by | Kate Greenaway | engraved and | printed by | Edmund Evans. | London and New York | George Routledge & Sons. $(6\frac{3}{4} \times 4\frac{3}{4})$

1882. (Printed 1882, published 1883.) LITTLE ANN | AND | OTHER POEMS | By | Jane and Ann Taylor | Illustrated by | Kate Greenaway | printed in colours by Edmund Evans | London : George Routledge & Sons | Broadway, Ludgate Hill | New York : 9, Lafayette Place. | [The Illustrations are Copyright.] $(9 \times 5\frac{1}{8})$

1883. ALMANACK | FOR | 1883 | By | Kate Greenaway | London | George Routledge & Sons | Broadway, Ludgate Hill | New York : 9, Lafayette Place $(3\frac{1}{8} \times 2\frac{7}{8})$

1883-84. (And subsequent editions.) FORS CLAVIGERA | Letters | to the Workmen and Labourers | of Great Britain | By John Ruskin, LL.D., | George Allen, | Orpington and London

1884. ALMANACK | FOR | 1884 | By | Kate Greenaway | Printed by Edmund Evans | London : George Routledge & Sons | Broadway, Ludgate Hill | New York : 9, Lafayette Place | [*Copyright*] $(5\frac{1}{4} \times 3\frac{5}{8})$

1884. Other editions with different title, by F. Warne & Co. A PAINTING | BOOK | by | Kate Greenaway | with Outlines from her various works | for | Girls and Boys | to Paint | London : George Routledge & Sons | Broadway, Ludgate Hill $(9\frac{1}{2} \times 7\frac{1}{8})$

Works Illustrated by Kate Greenaway

1884.   LANGUAGE OF FLOWERS | Illustrated by | Kate Greenaway | Printed in Colours by | Edmund Evans | London : George Routledge & Sons. $(8\frac{13}{16} \times 4\frac{5}{8})$

1884.   THE | ENGLISH SPELLING-BOOK | accompanied by | A Progressive Series | of | Easy and familiar lessons | by | William Mavor, LL.D. | Illustrated by Kate Greenaway | engraved and printed by Edmund Evans. | London | George Routledge & Sons | Broadway, Ludgate Hill | New York : 9, Lafayette Place | 1885. $(7 \times 4\frac{1}{8})$

1885.   ALMANACK | FOR | 1885 | BY | KATE GREENAWAY | London | George Routledge & Sons | Broadway, Ludgate Hill | New York : 9, Lafayette Place $(3\frac{1}{8} \times 2\frac{7}{8})$

1885. (Second edition 1897.)   DAME WIGGINS OF LEE, | AND HER | SEVEN WONDERFUL CATS ; | A humorous tale | written principally by a lady of ninety. | Edited, with additional verses, | By John Ruskin, LL.D., | Honorary Student of Christ Church, | and Honorary Fellow of Corpus Christi College, Oxford. | And with new illustrations | By Kate Greenaway | with twenty-two woodcuts. | George Allen, Sunnyside, Orpington ; | and 156 Charing Cross Road, London. $(7\frac{1}{4} \times 4\frac{1}{2})$

1885.   MARIGOLD GARDEN | Pictures and Rhymes | By | Kate Greenaway | Printed in Colours | By | Edmund Evans | London | George Routledge & Sons | Broadway, Ludgate Hill | New York : 9, Lafayette Place. $(10\frac{3}{4} \times 8\frac{1}{4})$

? 1885.   KATE GREENAWAY'S | ALPHABET. | London | George Routledge & Sons | Broadway, Ludgate Hill | New York : 9, Lafayette Place. $(2\frac{5}{8} \times 2\frac{5}{16})$

? 1885.   KATE GREENAWAY'S ALBUM. With 192 Illustrations within gold borders. Printed in Colours by Edmund Evans. George Routledge & Sons, Broadway, Ludgate Hill. [*Printed but not published.*]

1886.   ALMANACK | FOR | 1886 | By | Kate Greenaway | London | George Routledge & Sons | Broadway, Ludgate Hill | New York : 9, Lafayette Place. $(3\frac{1}{8} \times 2\frac{7}{8})$

1886.   A APPLE PIE | By | Kate Greenaway | Engraved and Printed by Edmund Evans. | London : George Routledge & Sons | Broadway, Ludgate Hill | New York : 9, Lafayette Place $(8\frac{1}{4} \times 10\frac{1}{4})$

1886.   THE QUEEN | OF | THE PIRATE ISLE | By | Bret Harte | Illustrated by Kate Greenaway | Engraved and Printed by Edmund Evans | London : Chatto & Windus | 214, Piccadilly. $(8\frac{1}{2} \times 6\frac{1}{4})$

1887.   ALMANACK | FOR 1887 | By | Kate Greenaway | George Routledge & Sons | The Pictures are Copyright. (3×4)

1887.   QUEEN VICTORIA'S JUBILEE GARLAND. (A booklet made up of illustrations already published.)

Kate Greenaway

1887. RHYMES | FOR THE | YOUNG FOLK | By | William Allingham | with Pictures by | Helen Allingham, Kate Greenaway, | Caroline Paterson, and Harry Furniss | Engraved and Printed by Edmund Evans | Cassell & Company, Limited, | London, Paris, New York and Melbourne. (8 3/16 × 6 1/2)

1888. ORIENT LINE GUIDE | Chapters for Travellers by Sea and by Land | Illustrated. The Third Edition, re-written, with Maps and Plans. | Edited for the Managers of the Line | By | W. J. Loftie, B.A., F.S.A., | Author of ‘A History of London,’ ‘Windsor,’ ‘Authorised | Guide to the Tower,’ etc. etc. | Price 2/6. | London : | Sampson Low, Marston, Searle & Rivington, | Limited, | St. Dunstan’s House, Fetter Lane. | Edward Stanford, 26 and 27 Cockspur Street, S.W. | 1888. | [Entered at Stationers’ Hall.—All Rights Reserved] (8 3/16 × 6 3/8)

1888. KATE GREENAWAY’S | ALMANACK | for | 1888 | George Routledge & Sons (3 5/8 × 2 5/8)

1888. THE PIED PIPER | OF | HAMELIN | by | Robert Browning | with 35 illustrations | by | Kate Greenaway | engraved and printed in colours by Edmund Evans | London | George Routledge & Sons | Broadway, Ludgate Hill | Glasgow, Manchester and New York. (9 3/4 × 8 5/8)

1889. ALMANACK | FOR | 1889 | By | Kate Greenaway | Printed by Edmund Evans | George Routledge & Sons | London, Glasgow, and New York (3 5/8 × 2 5/8)

1889. KATE GREENAWAY’S | BOOK OF GAMES | with Twenty-four Full-page Plates | Engraved and Printed in Colours by Edmund Evans | London | George Routledge & Sons | Broadway, Ludgate Hill | Glasgow, Manchester, and New York. (9 × 7 1/2)

1889. THE ROYAL PROGRESS | OF | KING PEPITO | By | Beatrice F. Cresswell | Illustrated by | Kate Greenaway | engraved and printed by Edmund Evans | London | Society for Promoting Christian Knowledge | Northumberland Avenue, Charing Cross, W.C. ; | 43, Queen Victoria Street, E.C. | Brighton : 135, North Street. | New York : E. and J. B. Young & Co. (8 1/8 × 6)

1890. ALMANACK | FOR | 1890 | By | Kate Greenaway | Engraved and Printed by E. Evans | George Routledge & Sons (3 5/8 × 3)

1891. KATE | GREENAWAY’S | ALMANACK | FOR | 1891 | George Routledge & Sons, Limited (4 × 2 5/8)

1892. KATE GREENAWAY’S | ALMANACK | FOR | 1892 | George Routledge & Sons, Limited (3 5/8 × 2 5/8)

1893. KATE GREENAWAY’S | ALMANACK | FOR 1893 | George Routledge & Sons, Limited (3 5/8 × 2 5/8)

1894. KATE GREENAWAY’S | ALMANACK | FOR 1894 | George Routledge & Sons, Limited (3 5/8 × 2 5/8)

Works Illustrated by Kate Greenaway

1895.   KATE GREENAWAY'S | ALMANACK | FOR | 1895 | George Rout-
         ledge & Sons, Limited   (3⅝ × 2⅝)

1897.   KATE | GREENAWAY'S | ALMANACK | AND DIARY FOR | 1897 |
         J. M. Dent & Co. : | 67 St. James's St., London   (4 1/16 × 3)

1900.   THE | APRIL BABY'S BOOK OF TUNES | with | THE STORY OF
         HOW THEY CAME | TO BE WRITTEN | By the Author of |
         'Elizabeth and her German Garden' | Illustrated by Kate
         Greenaway | London | Macmillan & Co., Limited | New
         York : The Macmillan Company | 1900 | All Rights Reserved.
                                                    (7¼ × 7½)

1882.   THE ILLUSTRATED | CHILDREN'S | BIRTHDAY-BOOK | Edited, and
         in part written | by | F. E. Weatherley. | With Illustrations by |
         Kate Coleman, Kate Greenaway, Robert Barnes, | Mrs. Staples,
         Miss Bennett and others. | London : | W. Mack, 4. Paternoster
         Square.   1882.   (4⅝ × 3½)

         MISCELLANEA :
1868.   *The People's Magazine.*
1873-80. *Little Folks.*   Serial Story of 'Poor Nelly,' etc. etc.   (9½ × 7¼)
1874.   *Cassell's Magazine.*   (10½ × 7)
1881-2. *Little Wide-Awake* (G. Routledge & Sons).   Edited by Mrs. Sale
         Barker.
1882, etc. *Routledge's Christmas Number.*   (10¾ × 8)
         St. Nicholas.
         The Graphic.
         Illustrated London News.
1882, etc. *Routledge's Every Girl's Annual.*   (10 × 6¾)
v.y.   *The Girls' Own Paper.*
              Etc. etc.

Index

Kate Greenaway

292

Index

Kate Greenaway

Index

Kate Greenaway

'Little Girl in Scarlet Coat,' sold, 224
'Little Girl with Doll,' at Royal Academy (1878), 69
'Little Girl with Fan,' at Royal Academy (1880), 85
'Little Girl with Tea Rose,' sold, 224
'Little Girlie,' drawing sold at Chicago, 182
'Little Go-Cart, The,' sold, 183
Little Model, The,' 275
'Little Phyllis,' drawing sold at Chicago, 182
Little Wide-Awake, frontispiece to, 85
Liverpool Exhibition (1895), Kate Greenaway's work at, 192
Locker-Lampson, Frederick, *Under the Window*, 57; beginning of friendship with, 86; association with, 87; portraits of, 89, 275; *London Lyrics*, frontispiece to, 88; tail-piece to, 101; suggestions for names for Kate Greenaway's house at Hampstead, 91; verses for Christmas cards by, 92; criticisms of Kate Greenaway's drawings and verses, 93, 95; on Ruskin, 93; on Burne-Jones, 94; Poems on his children, with illustrations by Kate Greenaway, 96; death of, 96; on Kate Greenaway's imitators, 106; on new studio at Frognal, 144; references to, in Kate Greenaway's letters, 164, 167; introduces Kate Greenaway to Mrs. Allingham, 172; book-plate, 182, 276; visit to, 185
letters to Kate Greenaway, from, 88, 90, 91, 92, 95
letters from Kate Greenaway, to, 86, 89, 91, 92, 94, 96, 266, 274
Locker-Lampson, Mrs., friendship with, 96; letters to Kate Greenaway, 96, 97; member of Memorial Committee, 256
Locker-Lampson, Godfrey, Esq., Kate Greenaway sends drawings to, at Eton, 96; book-plate for, 182
Locker-Lampson, Miss Dorothy, Kate Greenaway corrects drawings by, 96; book-plate for, 182
Locker-Lampson, Miss Maud, 234
Loffelt, M. A. C., on Kate Greenaway's art, 117
Loftie, Rev. W. J., early recollections of Kate Greenaway, 45; on Kate Greenaway's designs for valentine, 48;

'Art at Home' Series, 48; as friend of Kate Greenaway, 167
London Lyrics, frontispiece to, 88; tail-piece to, 101
Lord Ormont and His Aminta, Kate Greenaway on, 196
Lostalot, M. Alfred de, on Kate Greenaway's work, 106
'Love's Baubles' (Byam Shaw), Kate Greenaway on, 218
'Lucy Locket,' sold, 183; daintiness of, 271

Macmillan & Co., illustrations to Miss Yonge's novels for, 77; frontispiece to *Amateur Theatricals*, 78; *St. Nicholas*, 78; *The Library*, 85
Magazine of Art, poem by Mr. Austin Dobson, illustrated by Kate Greenaway, 124; proposed article on 'Later Work of Kate Greenaway,' for, 252
Mallock, Mr., and *The New Republic*, Kate Greenaway on, 214, 215
Mannerisms of Kate Greenaway, 267
Marigold Garden, 58; designs from, in *Painting Book*, 128; publication of, 129; Ruskin on, 133, 151; drawings for, exhibited at Paris (1889), 174; drawing of title-page sold at Chicago, 182; models for, 273; excellence of drawings in, 282
Marks, H. Stacy, R.A., encouragement from, 51; letters to Kate Greenaway from, 80, 81, 84, 104, 121; as friend of Kate Greenaway, 167; on *Pied Piper of Hamelin*, 172; influence of, on Kate Greenaway's work, 270
Martineau, Mrs. Basil, 167
'Mary had a Little Lamb,' 272
Mary, the model, 164, 273
Mason, George, A.R.A., influence of, on Kate Greenaway's work, 270
Mavor's English Spelling Book, 58; Ruskin on, 128; success of, 129; *Athenæum* on, 129; drawings for, used in *Almanacks*, 129; development of style in, 282
'May-Dance, The,' 270, 275
'May Morning on Magdalen Tower' (Mr. Holman Hunt, O.M.), Kate Greenaway on, 219
Mayo, Lady, 167, 180; letters from Kate Greenaway to, 180, 186
Meadows, Kenny, Kate Greenaway on illustrations to *Midsummer Night's Dream* by, 204

296

Index

Kate Greenaway

Ponsonby, Miss Mabel, portrait of, 276
'Poor Nelly,' 280
Portraitist, Kate Greenaway as a, 275
'Portrait of a Lady,' 276
'Portrait of a Little Boy, A,' at Royal Institute (1880), 178
'Portrait of a Little Lad,' at Royal Academy (1890), 178
Portraits in oils, 237
Præterita (by John Ruskin), reference in, to *Mavor*, 129; to *Dame Wiggins*, 130; 145, 151; Kate Greenaway on, 161; last chapter of, 175
Princess Christian, Kate Greenaway's meeting with, 27, 224; introduction to, 100; correspondence with, 100
Princess Louise, meeting with, 241
Princess Maud of Wales, wedding present for, 201
Princess Royal, meeting with, 27
'Processions,' drawings of, 211, 216, 274
Punch, first appearance in, 86; references to Kate Greenaway in 1881, 102; 'Grinaway Christmas Cards,' 102, 103

Queen of the Pirate Isle, The, 58; Ruskin on, 156; publication of, 163; vignette on title-page of, 282
Queen Victoria's Jubilee Garland, publication of, 163
Quiver of Love, illustrations in, 47; publication of, 53

Reading Books (Longman's), Kate Greenaway's refusal to illustrate, 184
Religion, Kate Greenaway's views of, 189, 190, 234, 235
'Rescue, The' (Sir J. E. Millais, P.R.A.), Kate Greenaway on, 229
Richards, Miss Laura E., verses by, 183
Richmond Ritchie, Mrs., letters to and from, 98; friendship with, 100, 167; proposed collaboration with, 100
Roberts, Lord, meeting with, 237
Robinson, Mr. Lionel, on Kate Greenaway as children's artist, 62, 180
'Rock, Moss, and Ivy,' drawing by Kate Greenaway in Sheffield Museum, 134
Rolleston, the Chappells' house at, 10; visits to, 28, 33; fire at, 35
Rossetti, D. G., Kate Greenaway on work of, 229, 231
Routledge, Messrs., work for, 100; *Little Wide-Awake*, frontispiece to, 85;

Every Girl's Annual, 85; *Mother Goose*, 100 *Christmas Number*, frontispiece ('Little Fanny'), 101; *A Day in a Child's Life*, 101; *Almanack*, first (1883), 122; *A Apple Pie*, 155, 156, 160; *Pied Piper of Hamelin*, success of, 171; *Book of Games*, 174; *Almanacks* for, 1892-95, 181
Rover, biography of, 164, 195, 198, 207, 236, 237, 244
Rowfant, Kate Greenaway's visits to, 86, 185
Royal Academy, first exhibit at, 55; 'Little Girl with Doll' (1878), 69; 'Misses' (1879), 78; 'Little Girl with Fan' (1880), 85; 'Portrait of a Little Lad' (1890), 178; 'A Girl's Head' (1891), 179; 'Baby Boy' at (1895), 192
Royal Institute of Painters in Water-Colours, Kate Greenaway elected a Member of, 174, 178, 271; exhibits at (1890), 178; (1891) 'An Old Farm House,' 'A Cottage in Surrey,' 179; (1894) 'A Girl' at, 184; (1895) exhibits at, 192, 197; (1896) 'Little Bo-Peep' at, 201; last exhibits at, in 1897: 'Girl in Hat and Feathers,' 'Two Little Girls in a Garden,' 211
Royal Progress of King Pepito, The, 174
Royal Society of British Artists. *See* Suffolk Street Gallery
Ruskin, John, on Kate Greenaway's work, 5; on *Under the Window*, 63; Lecture on Mrs. Allingham and Kate Greenaway, 65, 114; first meeting with Kate Greenaway, 110; on *Mother Goose* drawings, 105, 116; on Kate Greenaway design on glass, 106; on the 1884 *Almanack*, 127; on *Language of Flowers*, 128; on *Mavor's English Spelling Book*, 128; on *Dame Wiggins of Lee*, 130; portrait of, by Kate Greenaway, 135; suggested collaboration with Kate Greenaway in a book on Botany, 136; on Millais' portraits of 'The Marquess of Lorne' and 'Miss Nina Lehmann' (Lady Campbell), 137; references to Miss Francesca Alexander, 133, 138; on house at Frognal, 142; illness of, 145, 151, 154, 170; *Præterita*, autobiography of, 145, 151, 175; Kate Greenaway on, 161; 'Natural

298

Index

Index

THE END